Financial Freedom for Families

Financial Freedom for Families

Building Wealth Together
(A Step-by-Step Guide to Financial Security and Generational Wealth)

Nicolette Sharma

Mindful Pages

Published in 2025

ISBN: 9789371343398 (PB)
ISBN: 9789371341233 (eBook)

Published by

Mindful Pages
Imprint of Alpha Editions LLC
312 W. 2nd St #1834
Casper, WY 82601, USA

This book was developed using advanced writing tools to support the drafting and ideation process. All content has been thoughtfully curated, refined, and reviewed to ensure quality and relevance.

Content

Introduction The Journey to Family Financial Freedom vii

Chapter 1 Laying the Foundation — Family Money Mindset........xi

Chapter 2 Budgeting as a Family — Managing Money Together..26

Chapter 3 Saving Strategies — Building a Strong Financial Future 51

Chapter 4 Investing as a Family — Growing Wealth Together.....76

Chapter 5 Teaching Kids About Money — Raising Financially Smart Children..101

Chapter 6 Debt Management – Eliminating Financial Burdens ..126

Chapter 7 Planning for Children's Education Without Debt.......151

Chapter 8 Retirement Planning as a Family....................................175

Chapter 9 Insurance and Financial Protection for Families 199

Chapter 10 Creating a Family Wealth Plan — The Roadmap to Financial Independence 224

Conclusion Achieving Financial Freedom Together 247

About the Author 262

Introduction
The Journey to Family Financial Freedom

Financial freedom is not some rarefied prize reserved for the fortunate few—it's a deliberate path, one that any family can embark upon with the right understanding, shared discipline, and a measure of determination. For too long, money has been a source of quiet tension, unresolved conflict, or, in some households, simply an unspoken presence. Yet approached with intention and strategy, it transforms. It becomes a means not just of securing individual wellbeing, but of fostering collective growth. *Financial Freedom for Families: Building Wealth Together* serves as both a practical guide and a deeper reflection on what it means for families to create lasting prosperity—not merely through tactics, but through unity, clarity, and education. At the heart of this journey is a simple yet powerful idea: when a family is financially literate and aligned in purpose, its capacity to generate enduring wealth multiplies.

This transformation begins with literacy—not the kind taught in schools (or rather, too often neglected by them), but financial literacy: the knowledge of how money moves, grows, and works in our lives. It's a skill many adults are left to piece together through trial and error, and for families, the consequences of ignorance can be even more pronounced. Without a clear grasp of basic financial principles, families risk sliding into cycles of debt, missed chances, and unnecessary stress. But when that knowledge is prioritised, something shifts. A financially literate family becomes more agile, better prepared to navigate life's uncertainties and seize the openings that come their way.

And let's be clear—financial literacy isn't just about mastering figures or memorising jargon. At its core, it's about agency. When parents understand how to manage income sensibly, make informed investment decisions, and model wise financial behaviour for their children, they're not simply securing their present; they're laying the foundation for a more secure and expansive future. Families that learn together gain a shared sense of control over their destinies, replacing confusion with clarity and fear with forward motion. In this way, real wealth emerges—not just in pounds or property, but in freedom, time, and peace of mind.

Still, knowledge on its own can only go so far if the mindset remains stuck in survival mode. For many, financial life is lived in reactive terms: the next payday, the next bill, the next unexpected expense. It's a way of living shaped not just by immediate pressures, but often by inherited ideas—beliefs passed down, unexamined, from generation to generation. Escaping this loop isn't about blaming ourselves; it's about stepping back and choosing differently. Moving from reaction to intention. From mere survival to purposeful growth. This shift begins with seeing money not as something to manage just enough to get by, but as a resource to be nurtured and directed with care.

That reframing starts, naturally, with how families see wealth. Rather than treating it as a solitary quest—or worse, a competitive one—families can begin to embrace the idea of wealth-building as a shared endeavour. This isn't about homogenising goals or forcing everyone into lockstep. It's about establishing a common direction, a mutual sense of purpose. When the household begins to act not as separate financial actors, but as a coordinated team, the results can be quietly transformative. Resources are pooled. Goals become shared. Accountability is no longer burdensome—it's empowering.

A family aligned around its financial aspirations doesn't just split expenses; it shares vision. That might mean saving for a first home, funding a child's university education, launching a business, or retiring with grace and dignity. Unity here doesn't demand uniformity. Each member plays their part according to capacity, but all contribute towards the same horizon. In practice, this could take the form of monthly budget check-ins, candid conversations about past financial missteps, or group discussions about future ambitions—spaces where every voice, from parent to teenager, is not just heard but valued.

This collaborative spirit also runs counter to a deep-rooted social norm: the silence around money. In many families, finance is cloaked in secrecy—taboo even. Parents, often with the best of intentions, shield their children from money matters, hoping to spare them stress. But the unintended consequence? Those children grow up lacking the skills and confidence to navigate their own financial lives. By contrast, families that engage in open, age-appropriate discussions—about earning, spending, saving, and investing—equip their children not only with practical tools, but with the confidence to use them. And those skills, once embedded, tend to ripple outward—across decades, across generations.

This book sets out to guide families through just such a transition: from fractured financial habits to unified, long-term prosperity. The journey unfolds chapter by chapter, building upon practical advice while weaving in insights from behavioural science, personal finance, and the nuances of family life. Though financial tools and systems will no doubt continue to evolve, the underlying principles—discipline, communication, shared vision—are remarkably timeless.

We begin at the beginning. Chapter 1 invites readers to examine their existing beliefs about money, some of which may be serving them poorly. It offers tools for cultivating a mindset rooted in growth rather than fear. Not just better habits—but a better foundation. Chapter 2 turns to budgeting, not as a dry spreadsheet exercise, but as a family dialogue. It covers how to track income, weigh needs against wants, and shape spending priorities through collaboration rather than conflict.

Chapter 3 brings savings into focus—both the everyday and the long-term kind. Families are introduced to smart strategies for automating savings, choosing the right accounts, and even involving children in the process in ways that feel natural, not forced. Then comes Chapter 4: investing. Often intimidating, here it is demystified. The essentials are laid out with clarity, and real-life options are presented—from property ownership to junior ISAs—always with an eye to the family context. Because, as any seasoned investor knows, even small, consistent investments, when nurtured patiently, can reshape a family's future.

Chapter 5 shifts the attention squarely onto the next generation. Teaching children about money isn't about passing down a bank account—it's about passing down a mindset. Through everyday tools like allowances, savings jars, chores, and even entrepreneurial experiments, families can instil lessons that far outlast any inheritance. Beyond budgets and piggy banks, children can also learn generosity, delayed gratification, and goal-setting—traits every bit as valuable as compound interest.

Debt, with its quiet weight, is addressed head-on in Chapter 6. Families learn to differentiate between helpful and harmful debt, develop strategies to reduce liabilities, and most importantly, release the shame often tied to financial mistakes. The chapter explores proven methods like snowballing and the avalanche approach, but it doesn't shy away from the psychological toll of indebtedness. Chapter 7 then leads readers into education planning, helping parents navigate the costs of schooling without jeopardising long-term stability.

Retirement, so often deferred to 'later', takes centre stage in Chapter 8. The book argues, persuasively, that planning for later life is not a solo act but a family consideration—especially when thinking multigenerationally. Families are guided through how to integrate retirement savings into a broader wealth strategy, one that offers security without sacrificing freedom.

Next comes Chapter 9, centred on protection—insurance, estate planning, contingency funds. Emergencies don't send calendar invites, but preparation can soften the blow. From life insurance to powers of attorney, the section equips families to protect the progress they've made and the people they love.

Finally, Chapter 10 draws it all together: a full-spectrum wealth plan. Readers are walked through setting measurable goals, diversifying income, conducting regular financial check-ins, and staying adaptable as life throws its inevitable curveballs. Progress is tracked not just in pounds, but in peace of mind.

At every step, this book prioritises empowerment over perfection. Financial freedom is not a fixed number, nor a static achievement. It's a lived experience—marked by confidence, clarity, and choice. It is something families shape day by day, decision by decision.

So, as you step into this process, treat this book not as a lecture, but as a conversation partner. Its chapters are meant to be lived, discussed, challenged, and refined—with your family, not for them. Whether you're newly married, raising young children, or navigating the complexities of a multigenerational household, the path is here. Financial freedom for families is not only possible—it is necessary. And with each honest talk, each mindful habit, each step forward, you're doing more than securing your own wellbeing. You're shaping a legacy. Let's begin.

Chapter 1
Laying the Foundation — Family Money Mindset

Before a budget can be sketched out or a single investment considered, families must first take a deeper and far more personal journey—into their own relationship with money. Not the hard figures or tax codes, but the underlying beliefs, often inherited without question, that quietly shape how each family member thinks about, feels towards, and behaves around finances. These beliefs, though intangible, construct the silent framework within which all financial choices are made. If this framework is shaky, no amount of spreadsheets or strategies will hold. In truth, the mindset a family brings to money is not merely the beginning—it is the cornerstone of enduring financial transformation.

Every individual arrives at adulthood carrying a set of financial stories—scripts, if you will—formed in childhood, absorbed through experience, and usually left unexplored. Perhaps someone was raised in a household where money equalled conflict, where the stress of unpaid bills hung heavy in the air. That experience may seed a lifelong sense of insecurity, even when income later stabilises. Another person might come from a family where money was either abundant or tightly controlled, and equated with self-worth or moral virtue. Some may have grown up in silence around financial matters, where money talk was considered inappropriate or even shameful. These early encounters don't simply fade; they linger in the background, shaping adult behaviour in ways we seldom recognise.

Consider the parent who refuses to check their bank account—not because they're too busy, but because the act triggers an echo of past financial chaos. Or the couple who spar over holiday plans, their arguments really fuelled by clashing money philosophies: one rooted in thrift, the other in a belief that life is for the living. These tensions often stem not from the present moment, but from an older script playing quietly in the background. But here lies an opportunity: these scripts, once seen, can be rewritten. When families bring these hidden assumptions into the light, they can begin making financial decisions with intention, rather than instinct.

This is the first step in nurturing what one might call a wealth-conscious mindset. It is not simply about making more money. Rather, it's a shift in how one views money itself—not as something scarce, fraught with fear, or only for others, but as a resource that can be nurtured, directed, and grown. The scarcity mindset—so common, so corrosive—suggests that there is never enough, that financial wins are always zero-sum, and that safety lies only in clutching tightly to what little one has. That kind of thinking invites impulsivity, hoarding, or paralysing anxiety. In contrast, a mindset of abundance allows for a more expansive view. It sees money as fluid, tied to creativity, resilience, and vision. It doesn't ignore risk—it simply refuses to be paralysed by it.

Families who adopt this broader, more strategic mindset tend to behave differently. They plan rather than react. They save with purpose rather than out of fear. They talk about the future, even when the present feels uncertain. And perhaps most importantly, they share the journey. Financial literacy, in this setting, becomes a living, breathing practice—one passed on not only in words but in everyday actions. Children, for example, learn far more from observing how their parents navigate bills, savings, and generosity than from any classroom lecture. Modelling matters. When parents manage money with discipline and calm, they're handing down something more powerful than cash: they're passing on financial confidence.

But fostering this environment means doing something that's often uncomfortable—talking about money. Not in hushed tones after the children have gone to bed, and not only when something's gone wrong. Money needs to be discussed openly and regularly, if families are to build shared understanding and direction. That doesn't mean every conversation must be perfect. In fact, a bit of imperfection—a few false starts or awkward pauses—can be a sign that real ground is being covered. What matters is that the lines of communication remain open.

Start small. Parents might share with their children how they once made a financial mistake—and what they learnt from it. A missed credit card payment, perhaps, or an impulse purchase that turned into regret. These admissions aren't weaknesses; they're gifts. They show that financial wisdom isn't innate, but acquired. Between partners, setting a monthly time to review finances—even briefly—can do wonders. Not just for staying on track, but for building mutual respect. Over time, these conversations grow into habits, and the family becomes fluent in a financial language that is their own.

Once this culture of openness begins to take root, it becomes far easier to move towards aligned goals. Without shared aims, financial effort can feel scattered—like rowing in different directions. Alignment doesn't require everyone to want the same things, but it does call for agreement on priorities. Perhaps it's clearing debt, saving for a home, or putting aside funds for a child's education. Whatever the vision, making it visible—naming it, mapping it—brings cohesion. Even young children can take part. A family might, for example, agree to forgo eating out for a while in order to build an emergency fund. Involving the children in setting a target, or colouring in a savings chart on the fridge, makes the process tangible.

Such shared projects have a way of doing more than just hitting numbers. They reinforce trust. They teach compromise. They root financial habits in something far deeper than obligation—they become expressions of family identity. And when every expenditure is viewed through the lens of "does this move us closer to our goal?", decisions gain clarity. They may still be difficult, but they are rarely aimless.

Yet, all of this can be undone—quietly, steadily—by unhelpful habits. These bad habits often creep in unnoticed, lodged in the routines of daily life. Overspending when stressed. Avoiding budgeting because it feels too tedious. Putting off big financial decisions until "someday". Most of these behaviours aren't born of ignorance or laziness; they're the residue of emotion. The key is not to judge them, but to observe them. Track them for a month. What are the triggers? What patterns emerge?

Armed with that insight, families can start to swap out damaging routines for better ones. Say a parent tends to scroll shopping apps late at night—perhaps as a release after a tough day. Instituting a 24-hour pause before non-essential purchases might help. Or maybe the family keeps overspending on takeaways. Turning meal planning into a shared Sunday activity—with input from everyone—could address both the spending and the disconnect. What matters most is the spirit behind the change: not punishment, but alignment with long-term goals.

And goals, as life moves on, do shift. That's why none of this is static. Financial behaviour, like any aspect of growth, evolves. The aim is not flawlessness—it's awareness. A family that remains conscious of its values, and returns to those values in moments of uncertainty, will find its way more often than not. Money, after all, is never just about money. It is a mirror, reflecting the hopes, fears, and convictions of those who handle it.

This chapter is not a standalone exercise—it is the ground beneath all that follows. Whether budgeting or investing, saving or planning, every tool and tactic in later chapters will depend on this internal architecture. If that's left unchecked, no system will hold. But if built with care—anchored in self-awareness, open communication, and a shared sense of purpose—it can support a family for generations.

Financial freedom, then, begins long before the numbers make sense. It begins with a shift in vision—a turning inward, a reckoning with past beliefs, and a commitment to new, deliberate habits. Wealth, in this light, becomes more than accumulation. It becomes a kind of wisdom. And that wisdom, once sparked, has the quiet power to change everything.

Understanding Your Money Beliefs

Every financial decision—whether as significant as purchasing a home or as trivial as choosing a brand of cereal—is filtered through an internal lens shaped by deeply rooted beliefs about money. These beliefs are rarely formed through deliberate education or rational evaluation; rather, they are absorbed over time, often without conscious awareness. They are passed down through families, shaped by early experiences, and reinforced by cultural messaging. Before any meaningful financial change can occur, individuals and families alike must take a step back and examine the architecture of their financial thinking. To understand money habits, one must first understand money beliefs.

Our money beliefs begin to form in childhood, long before we earn or manage money ourselves. They are constructed through observations—watching how parents handle bills, how adults speak about wealth and poverty, how financial conflict is managed (or avoided), and how spending or saving is celebrated or criticised. These early impressions coalesce into a set of subconscious assumptions that guide our behaviour long into adulthood. For example, a child who frequently overheard their parents argue about not having enough may internalise a belief that money is a source of stress or danger. That belief may later manifest as anxiety about spending, compulsive saving, or avoidance of financial planning altogether.

Such internal scripts can be surprisingly persistent. A person raised with the message that "money doesn't grow on trees" may grow into an adult who feels guilt when spending, even when financially secure. Another raised in a household where wealth was associated with arrogance or moral compromise may unconsciously sabotage their own earning potential, believing financial success to be incompatible with integrity. These beliefs are not inherently true or false—they are inherited frameworks. But when left unexamined, they can limit financial growth, create conflict within families, and undermine even the most well-crafted financial strategies.

Consider the case of a young couple, Priya and Rohan, who frequently found themselves at odds over how to manage their joint finances. Priya, raised in a modest but financially stable home, had internalised the importance of careful budgeting and long-term saving. Rohan, on the other hand, grew up in a household where money was either plentiful or dangerously scarce, depending on his father's business cycles. For Rohan, money was volatile—something to enjoy while it lasted. Their disagreements were not merely about numbers, but about trust, security, and how each perceived the role of money in their lives. It was only when they began to explore these inherited narratives that they could move from conflict to cooperation.

Understanding your money beliefs requires a willingness to engage in personal introspection. It involves asking hard questions: What messages did I absorb about money growing up? How did my parents or caregivers treat money—was it a source of freedom, fear, secrecy, or pride? What emotions do I associate with spending, saving, or earning? These are not just abstract reflections; they are essential diagnostic tools. Without understanding the psychological roots of your financial behaviours, efforts at change may address the symptoms rather than the cause.

Moreover, these beliefs don't operate in isolation. Within a family, especially one where multiple generations may live under the same roof or be financially interdependent, conflicting money beliefs can create tension and confusion. A teenager taught to be frugal may feel frustrated by a parent who splurges impulsively. A grandparent who survived economic hardship may value security above all, while a younger family member embraces risk in pursuit of entrepreneurial goals. These differences are not inherently problematic, but they require conscious navigation. Understanding one another's money beliefs fosters empathy and opens the door to more collaborative financial planning.

It is also important to recognise the societal forces that influence these beliefs. Cultural background, socioeconomic status, media portrayals of wealth, and peer influence all play significant roles. In some cultures, for instance, financial success is closely tied to family honour or duty, leading individuals to prioritise collective goals over personal ones. In others, individual wealth accumulation may be seen as a measure of self-worth, creating pressure to perform financially even at the expense of well-being. Advertising and social media exacerbate this dynamic by constantly projecting idealised lifestyles, subtly shaping our expectations of what it means to be "financially successful."

Breaking free from unhelpful money beliefs does not require rejecting one's background or culture. It involves discerning which beliefs serve your goals and values—and which do not. This discernment allows you to consciously reshape your financial identity, grounded not in inherited assumptions, but in informed choice. For example, if you were taught to view money as scarce and unpredictable, you might start to reframe that belief by tracking income and expenses in a way that reveals patterns and opportunities, rather than focusing solely on limitations. Or, if you were raised to believe that talking about money is taboo, you might begin by initiating small, non-confrontational conversations with family members about shared goals or financial plans.

For parents, this self-reflection holds even greater importance. Children absorb not only what you teach them explicitly about money, but how you behave with it. If parents speak positively about saving but demonstrate stress or secrecy around finances, children are likely to internalise the behaviour, not the rhetoric. On the other hand, when children see adults engage in thoughtful financial decision-making, discuss money openly and respectfully, and acknowledge both successes and mistakes, they develop a more balanced and empowered relationship with money themselves. This modelling lays the foundation for generational improvement, where each new generation is better equipped to handle the economic realities of their time.

An effective way to start examining your own money beliefs is through journaling or guided reflection. You might begin by writing about your earliest memory related to money, how you felt about it, and what lesson you took from the experience. You could reflect on how money was handled during key transitions in your life—such as moving house, changing schools, holidays, or job changes. These reflections can illuminate recurring themes that influence your current financial decisions. Over time, the goal is to move from unconscious reaction to conscious response—from being driven by past conditioning to making choices that reflect your present values and future aspirations.

Family discussions about money beliefs can also be transformative. While such conversations may feel uncomfortable initially, they are essential for building trust and alignment. A productive dialogue might involve each family member sharing their money story—how they were raised to think about money, what emotions they associate with it, and how their beliefs have changed over time. These stories create a shared emotional vocabulary around finances, allowing the family to identify areas of alignment and friction. For instance, one member's fear of debt might be respected while still allowing for strategic borrowing when necessary, provided there is a shared understanding and plan.

These conversations are not meant to produce instant agreement, but to deepen understanding. By acknowledging the origins of our financial perspectives, we create space for growth. A belief once formed in response to scarcity or instability may have served its purpose, but it can now be revised in light of new circumstances and aspirations. This evolution is not only possible—it is vital for those seeking to build lasting financial health.

Understanding your money beliefs is not a one-time exercise, but a lifelong process of reflection, learning, and adaptation. As life circumstances change—through marriage, parenthood, career shifts, or economic upheavals—so too must our financial thinking. The aim is to develop a mindset that is both grounded and flexible: one that honours past experiences while remaining open to new strategies and perspectives. With this mindset, financial decisions become less about reaction and more about intention.

Ultimately, the beliefs you hold about money shape the financial reality you create. By bringing these beliefs to the surface, examining them with honesty and curiosity, and choosing which to keep and which to release, you reclaim agency over your financial life. More importantly, you create a legacy of conscious, confident financial thinking that can uplift not only your own circumstances but those of your entire family. It is here, in this deep inner work, that the path to lasting financial freedom truly begins.

Building a Wealth-Oriented Mindset

The foundation of financial success is not solely built on knowledge, tools, or even income. Rather, it rests on mindset—how individuals perceive money, its role in their lives, and their capacity to influence their financial outcomes. Central to this is the shift from a scarcity-driven view of money to one rooted in abundance. A wealth-oriented mindset is not defined by how much one has, but by how one thinks. It is this shift in thinking that enables families to build and sustain prosperity, even in the face of economic uncertainty or modest beginnings. Crucially, this mindset is not only cultivated in adults but must be modelled and taught to children, who are forming their financial identities often before they can articulate them.

Scarcity thinking is pervasive and often disguised as pragmatism. It expresses itself in beliefs that there is never enough—that opportunities are limited, wealth is for others, and financial comfort is always just out of reach. This mindset, though frequently reinforced by genuine hardship, ultimately breeds fear, anxiety, and reactive behaviour. Individuals operating from a place of scarcity tend to focus on immediate needs, avoid risk even when strategic, and struggle with long-term planning. They may hoard resources, overvalue security at the cost of growth, or self-sabotage when faced with financial success.

This is not to suggest that scarcity thinking is irrational. It often stems from lived experience—unemployment, debt, unstable housing, or watching one's parents struggle to make ends meet. For many, these experiences shape a protective mindset, where financial decisions are made primarily to avoid loss or prevent vulnerability. However, the problem arises when these protective instincts become default behaviours, even when circumstances have changed. Clinging to a scarcity mindset in times of stability or opportunity limits one's ability to take calculated risks, invest in future growth, or collaborate openly with others.

Shifting to a wealth-oriented mindset requires conscious effort. It begins with acknowledging that money is not just a finite resource, but a tool that can be managed, multiplied, and directed. This shift is not about blind optimism or ignoring real limitations. Rather, it is about cultivating the belief that one has agency in financial matters—that wealth is not a matter of luck or inheritance, but of habits, perspective, and consistent action. It encourages a proactive stance, where setbacks are viewed not as failures but as learning opportunities, and where financial goals are pursued with both discipline and vision.

An example of this can be seen in the experience of a family who, after years of living paycheque to paycheque, decided to approach their finances differently. They began by attending free community finance workshops, tracking their spending, and setting small but meaningful savings goals. Initially, the changes felt uncomfortable. Every expenditure was scrutinised, and progress seemed slow. But over time, the discipline yielded results: an emergency fund, reduced debt, and eventually an investment in a modest property. What changed most significantly was not just their financial position, but their belief in what was possible. They began to think in terms of future potential rather than present limitation—a hallmark of the wealth mindset.

This perspective also reshapes how people relate to opportunity. Those with a scarcity mindset often see success as a zero-sum game: if someone else gains, they must lose. This can breed resentment, comparison, and isolation. In contrast, a wealth-oriented thinker sees success as expansive. They understand that wealth—financial, relational, intellectual—can be created and shared. This attitude fosters collaboration, learning, and generosity, all of which are essential not only for accumulating wealth but for sustaining it within a family and a community.

For parents, modelling this mindset is among the most powerful legacies they can offer their children. Children absorb attitudes toward money long before they comprehend its mechanics. A household where money is always tight, talked about in hushed or panicked tones, or used as a source of control, can instil deep-seated insecurities. Conversely, a home where money is treated as a resource to be managed thoughtfully, discussed openly, and used in alignment with values creates an environment where children can grow into financially confident individuals.

One effective approach is to involve children in age-appropriate financial conversations and decisions. For instance, parents might discuss the budgeting process for a family holiday, explaining the trade-offs and savings goals involved. When children see that financial planning is about choice and strategy—not deprivation—they begin to internalise a sense of control rather than scarcity. This also encourages delayed gratification, a key component of financial maturity. When children are encouraged to save for a toy, manage their own pocket money, or contribute to a family savings goal, they learn that money grows through patience and discipline, not just through earning.

Another dimension of teaching financial confidence is reframing mistakes. Many adults carry shame about past financial decisions—missed payments, poor investments, or periods of financial instability. While it is important to learn from these experiences, it is equally important to discuss them without fear or moral judgement. Sharing these stories with children, framed through the lens of growth and resilience, helps demystify financial failure. It teaches that setbacks are part of life and that recovery is possible through thoughtful action.

Confidence also grows from competence. As children grow older, introducing them to more advanced financial concepts—such as interest, credit, investment, and philanthropy—can further embed a wealth-oriented mindset. For example, opening a savings account with a child and tracking interest earned each month offers a concrete lesson in passive income. Discussing the difference between wants and needs during a shopping trip, or evaluating value for money in a purchase, reinforces critical thinking. The key is not to lecture but to engage, turning everyday moments into teachable opportunities.

Importantly, cultivating a wealth mindset is not about materialism or excessive ambition. It is about equipping individuals and families with the mental framework to make thoughtful, strategic, and values-based financial choices. It allows people to move from reacting to their circumstances to actively shaping their financial future. It also opens the door to generosity—when money is seen as a resource that flows and multiplies, sharing becomes not a loss but a meaningful investment in others.

Within families, this mindset promotes unity and purpose. A family that embraces abundance thinking is more likely to engage in collaborative goal-setting, celebrate each member's contributions, and support one another's ambitions. They are also more resilient in the face of financial challenges, as their mindset enables them to adapt, regroup, and continue progressing. This internal resilience is often what distinguishes families who merely survive financial adversity from those who emerge stronger and more connected.

Building a wealth-oriented mindset is an ongoing process. It requires continuous reflection, dialogue, and adjustment. As life circumstances shift—through job changes, health events, or changing family needs—so too must the mindset evolve. The goal is not to achieve a static state of abundance, but to maintain a posture of openness, agency, and intentionality in all financial matters. Families that commit to this mindset do not simply accumulate money—they build lasting financial health, intergenerational stability, and a legacy of wisdom.

By anchoring financial decisions in a mindset of possibility rather than fear, families create the psychological conditions for long-term success. This does not mean ignoring financial risks or denying hardship, but rather approaching each decision with clarity, confidence, and a sense of direction. Whether a family is just beginning to stabilise their finances or is already building wealth, this mindset is the thread that holds their progress together. It ensures that financial decisions are not only technically sound but emotionally sustainable, fostering a deeper sense of peace and purpose in the process.

Ultimately, wealth begins in the mind. It is a cultivated orientation toward opportunity, growth, and responsibility. When families shift their thinking from limitation to possibility and pass this perspective on to their children, they do more than improve their bank accounts—they transform their entire relationship with money. This transformation becomes a cornerstone of financial freedom, not just for today, but for generations to come.

Money Conversations with Family Members

Money, despite its pervasive influence on our lives, often remains one of the most uncomfortable topics within families. It is paradoxical that something so essential to daily functioning is frequently cloaked in silence, shame, or conflict. Yet, avoiding conversations about money does not eliminate financial stress; it amplifies it. It fosters misunderstanding, breeds resentment, and allows misinformation to take root. Encouraging open and healthy discussions about money within the family is not only a practical necessity—it is an emotional and relational imperative. Such conversations lay the groundwork for cooperation, alignment, and long-term stability, while also modelling transparency and financial maturity for younger generations.

The challenge, however, lies in overcoming the discomfort. Many adults were raised in households where money was not discussed, or if it was, it happened only during moments of crisis. This legacy can result in adults who either perpetuate silence or only talk about money in high-stress circumstances, reinforcing negative emotional associations. Furthermore, when family members operate with unspoken expectations or unarticulated financial boundaries, it can create confusion or conflict over issues such as shared expenses, savings goals, or lifestyle choices. Unaddressed financial stress often finds expression in unrelated arguments, strained relationships, or private worry that corrodes wellbeing.

To shift this dynamic, families must first create a culture in which money is no longer taboo. This does not mean broadcasting every financial detail or imposing rigid rules. Rather, it means establishing an environment where financial topics can be discussed with curiosity, respect, and empathy. This shift begins with intention. Choosing to initiate money conversations proactively—rather than reactively—helps anchor these discussions in stability rather than stress. For instance, scheduling regular family finance meetings, even informally, signals that money is a shared subject, not a secret or a personal burden.

These conversations are most effective when grounded in shared purpose. It is easier to talk about finances when the discussion is framed around mutual goals. A family might begin by discussing their vision for the coming year: perhaps saving for a holiday, reducing household expenses, or contributing to a child's education fund. From this shared goal, the conversation can expand into income, budgeting, roles and responsibilities, and progress tracking. The presence of a unifying objective transforms money from a source of tension into a tool for collective progress.

Open money conversations also provide an opportunity to address financial values and priorities. These may differ substantially between family members, particularly across generations or cultural backgrounds. One person may value frugality and view spending as a risk; another may see spending on experiences as central to a meaningful life. These perspectives are not right or wrong, but they must be acknowledged. When values go unspoken, assumptions fill the void. A teenager might assume their parents are being restrictive for the sake of control, when in reality they are managing a tight budget and trying to prevent debt. Articulating the reasons behind financial decisions fosters understanding and, ultimately, cooperation.

An essential element of healthy money conversations is emotional intelligence. Money is not just a rational subject—it is laden with emotional weight. Fear, shame, pride, guilt, and envy are all common undercurrents in financial dialogue. Approaching these conversations with sensitivity requires active listening, non-judgemental language, and a willingness to see from the other person's perspective. For example, a partner who avoids discussing debt may not be irresponsible but ashamed. A parent reluctant to talk about their retirement savings might be anxious about having too little. These emotional dimensions must be respected if conversations are to be honest and productive.

Children, too, benefit enormously from being included in age-appropriate money conversations. Many parents worry that discussing financial matters with children will burden them. But research and anecdotal evidence suggest that when children are included thoughtfully, they not only gain essential life skills but also develop a sense of trust and inclusion. A ten-year-old who understands why the family is cutting back on takeaways to save for a trip is more likely to feel empowered than deprived. Moreover, involving children in small financial decisions—such as choosing between two affordable family activities or helping to plan a shopping list within a set budget—fosters agency and critical thinking.

These early exposures shape children's attitudes toward money for life. Children who see their parents discuss money calmly and constructively learn that finances are manageable, not mysterious. They internalise the idea that money is not something to fear or fight about, but something to plan for and talk through. This modelling extends to how they eventually manage money in their own relationships and households. In this way, healthy money conversations are not just about immediate decisions—they are about generational financial literacy.

However, not all money conversations are comfortable or harmonious. Differences in income, debt, financial priorities, or levels of financial literacy can lead to friction. In blended families, for instance, conversations about how to split expenses or support children from previous relationships can be particularly sensitive. In multigenerational households, cultural expectations about financial responsibility—such as elder care, inheritance, or familial obligations—may clash with individual goals or capacities. These complexities require deliberate navigation. The key is to approach the conversation with mutual respect, clear boundaries, and, where needed, external support such as a financial counsellor or mediator.

One practical example of this occurred in a family where the adult children noticed their retired parents were struggling financially but were reluctant to accept help. Rather than confronting them with criticism or unsolicited advice, the children initiated a conversation framed around shared planning. They expressed their desire to understand the broader family finances and ensure everyone was prepared for potential medical or housing needs. By shifting the focus from the parents' shortcomings to collective preparedness, the family was able to open up dialogue and create a plan that respected everyone's dignity.

Transparency is also crucial when it comes to financial expectations within the family. Many conflicts arise not from the money itself but from mismatched assumptions. A teenager may assume university expenses will be fully covered by parents; parents may expect their adult children to contribute to household bills without ever stating it outright. Having direct, respectful conversations about what each person can and cannot commit to helps prevent confusion and resentment. These expectations can be revisited over time, as circumstances change.

It is also worth recognising that money conversations should not be limited to times of need or planning. They should include celebration. Families that openly acknowledge financial milestones—such as paying off debt, reaching a savings goal, or starting a new investment—reinforce a positive association with financial collaboration. Celebrating these wins, however small, fosters motivation and helps reinforce the behaviours that made them possible. It also reminds all family members, especially children, that financial progress is a process, made up of many small, deliberate steps.

Technology can be a useful aid in facilitating these discussions. Shared budgeting apps, visual goal trackers, and financial dashboards allow families to see the numbers in real time and make decisions together with clarity. This transparency helps demystify finances and shifts conversations from abstract worries to concrete strategies. For example, a couple using a shared budgeting tool can approach the discussion from a position of shared data rather than subjective feeling. "We've exceeded the grocery budget this month" is easier to address than "You always spend too much on food."

Still, tools alone do not guarantee productive conversations. The most important factors remain emotional honesty, mutual respect, and the willingness to engage. These qualities transform money from a divisive topic into a unifying one. When families engage in regular, open conversations about money, they develop a shared language and rhythm. Over time, the anxiety and discomfort give way to collaboration and empowerment.

Healthy money conversations are a skill—and like any skill, they improve with practice. Families that commit to these discussions, even when they are difficult, cultivate not only better financial outcomes but stronger relationships. They reduce the emotional burden that financial secrecy creates and replace it with trust, accountability, and shared vision. This is particularly important in uncertain economic times, where financial resilience often hinges not just on income or assets, but on the ability to adapt together.

Ultimately, money conversations are about more than budgeting or saving. They are about aligning around what matters most, supporting one another through financial challenges, and celebrating collective progress. They are about demystifying one of the most powerful forces in our lives and using it to strengthen rather than strain the family bond. By embracing these conversations with intention and compassion, families create not just financial clarity, but a culture of openness and mutual respect that enhances every aspect of their shared life.

Aligning Financial Goals as a Family

Financial harmony within a household rarely emerges by chance. It is the outcome of thoughtful communication, mutual respect, and a shared commitment to long-term objectives. Families who align their financial goals are not simply cohabiting individuals managing separate money matters—they are collaborators in a long-term enterprise, working together to build stability, opportunity, and a lasting legacy. Establishing shared priorities and a collective vision for financial success is therefore more than an exercise in planning; it is a cornerstone of familial unity and resilience.

At the heart of this alignment is the recognition that money decisions affect everyone within the household, whether explicitly or indirectly. A decision to take on debt, for example, might impact household spending for months or years. Choosing to invest in education or property shapes not only the present but future options. When these choices are made without consultation or clarity, they often breed confusion, resentment, or mistrust. But when they are anchored in shared goals and discussed openly, they become an opportunity for collaboration and empowerment.

Aligning financial goals as a family begins with developing a clear understanding of what matters most to each member. This may seem like a straightforward process, but in practice, it involves navigating differing perspectives, needs, and timelines. A parent may be focused on saving for retirement, while a teenager may be more concerned about purchasing a car or choosing a university. A couple may agree on the importance of homeownership but disagree on how much debt they are willing to incur to achieve it. Rather than dismissing or overriding individual views, the aim should be to integrate them into a cohesive plan that honours the household's diverse needs while maintaining a unified direction.

Creating this integrated plan starts with intentional conversation. Families benefit from setting aside time—free from distraction or stress—to discuss what financial success looks like to them. This might involve identifying both short-term priorities, such as paying off credit cards or building an emergency fund, and long-term aspirations, such as buying a home, travelling abroad, or funding a child's education. These goals should be discussed not just in abstract terms but within the context of values: why they matter, what they enable, and how they reflect the family's identity.

For example, consider a family where the parents are both self-employed and have variable income. Their children are approaching secondary school, and the family has aspirations of moving to a larger home in a better school district. Simultaneously, they hope to save for a family holiday each year and start setting aside funds for university tuition. Rather than treating these goals as isolated or competing interests, they sit down together to prioritise. They decide that improving their housing situation is the most urgent, but they also commit to modest contributions to a university savings account and a scaled-back, budget-conscious holiday plan. By involving their children in these discussions, they not only increase transparency but also help the children feel invested in the outcome.

This process reveals one of the key benefits of goal alignment: it provides a framework for making trade-offs. No family has unlimited resources. The tension between present enjoyment and future security is a constant balancing act. But when a family has articulated its collective vision, decisions about spending and saving become far less contentious. They are no longer about personal preferences or impulses but about honouring the commitments the family has made together. This shared understanding reduces conflict and increases accountability.

It is equally important to ensure that aligned goals are actionable. A common mistake is to set goals that are vague or aspirational without defining concrete steps for achievement. Saying "we want to be financially secure" is laudable, but what does that mean in measurable terms? Does it involve building six months of living expenses in an emergency fund? Paying off all non-mortgage debt? Saving for retirement at a specific monthly rate? The more clearly defined the goals, the easier it is to track progress and adjust strategies.

Technology can support this process. Families might use a shared budgeting app or financial dashboard to visualise their goals and monitor collective progress. This kind of transparency fosters ongoing communication and helps maintain momentum. When everyone can see how their individual behaviours contribute to the larger picture, it creates a sense of shared ownership and pride. For children, especially, visualising progress—such as seeing a savings thermometer fill up or achieving weekly savings targets—can be highly motivating and reinforce a sense of agency.

Importantly, aligning financial goals also involves acknowledging that goals change. Life is dynamic, and so too must be financial planning. A job change, medical expense, birth of a child, or economic downturn can all necessitate a recalibration. Families that regularly revisit their financial goals—perhaps quarterly or annually—are better equipped to adapt without panic or discord. These check-ins provide a forum not only to assess numbers but also to evaluate whether the goals still reflect the family's evolving priorities.

The process of aligning goals must also account for emotional and psychological factors. Money is not just mathematical—it is deeply emotional. Past experiences, fears, hopes, and even insecurities all influence how individuals relate to money. When one family member avoids talking about finances, it might stem from embarrassment about past mistakes or a fear of judgment. Others may be driven by a need for control or a fear of scarcity. These dynamics must be gently acknowledged if alignment is to be authentic. Emotional safety is essential. Each member must feel that their input is valued, their perspective respected, and that the goal-setting process is collaborative rather than coercive.

This is particularly true in multigenerational households or culturally diverse families, where values around money may diverge significantly. In some cultures, supporting extended family is a financial obligation; in others, independence and self-reliance are prioritised. In some homes, financial discussions are open and analytical; in others, they are private and sensitive. Successful alignment does not require uniformity, but it does require mutual understanding. Where differences arise, they can be acknowledged and negotiated with respect and patience.

Parents have an especially critical role to play in modelling this alignment process for children. When children witness adults working together to set and pursue financial goals, they internalise not only practical lessons but also relational ones: the value of cooperation, the importance of shared purpose, and the discipline of planning. Involving children in family financial goals—such as saving for a group outing, donating to a cause, or reducing household energy use—teaches them that their contributions matter and that financial decisions are a collective responsibility.

Moreover, aligned financial goals extend beyond money. They shape lifestyle choices, time allocation, and even emotional priorities. A family that decides to live below its means to pursue early retirement is also making decisions about career choices, housing, and social engagements. A household focused on charitable giving or community involvement is expressing values that transcend their bank balance. In this sense, financial alignment is not just about what the family wants to buy or save for—it's about who the family wants to be.

In a broader social context, families that function with aligned financial goals are more resilient to external pressures. Consumer culture, economic volatility, and peer comparisons can all undermine financial stability. But a family with a clear internal compass is less likely to be swayed by outside influences. They are anchored in their own vision, capable of navigating distractions or setbacks without losing sight of what truly matters. This internal cohesion becomes a form of financial immunity—a quiet strength that supports not just wealth-building but wellbeing.

Ultimately, aligning financial goals as a family is not a one-time event but an ongoing conversation. It is a practice of revisiting, refining, and reaffirming what the family stands for financially. It requires effort, compromise, and sometimes uncomfortable honesty. But the rewards are profound. A family aligned in purpose experiences less conflict, more clarity, and greater cohesion. They are able to weather challenges together, celebrate milestones together, and build a legacy that reflects shared intention rather than happenstance.

In a world where financial stress remains one of the leading causes of family discord, taking the time to align on goals is both a protective measure and an empowering one. It allows families not only to manage their money but to lead their lives with clarity and intention. By creating a shared vision and working collaboratively toward it, families turn financial planning into a unifying force—one that enhances relationships as much as it does resources. And in doing so, they lay the groundwork for a future that is not only secure, but deeply meaningful.

Breaking Bad Financial Habits

Financial stability is rarely determined by a single decision or event. Rather, it is the cumulative effect of countless small behaviours repeated over time. Habits—those automatic patterns of behaviour that shape our daily lives—are either silent allies or invisible saboteurs on the path to financial wellbeing. While good financial habits lay the foundation for security and growth, poor ones erode that foundation slowly but consistently. Recognising and eliminating these detrimental patterns is therefore not merely advisable; it is essential for any family striving to build a stable and prosperous future.

The difficulty lies not in identifying what is financially responsible—most people have a general idea of what they should be doing. Spend less than you earn. Save consistently. Avoid unnecessary debt. These principles are neither obscure nor new. The challenge is translating this knowledge into behaviour, especially when deeply ingrained habits, emotional triggers, and environmental influences pull in the opposite direction. Bad financial habits are rarely born from ignorance; they stem from a complex interplay of psychology, social norms, and short-term gratification.

Consider the example of habitual overspending. It may appear, on the surface, to be a simple lack of discipline. Yet, for many individuals, it is a coping mechanism. Shopping can provide a temporary sense of control or pleasure in the midst of stress, loneliness, or anxiety. Online purchases, often made with a few clicks and without immediate consequence, disconnect the act of spending from its financial impact. Over time, what begins as an occasional indulgence can become a reflexive behaviour—triggered by emotion and reinforced by ease. Breaking this habit requires more than willpower; it demands a deeper understanding of the underlying emotional need being fulfilled, and the intentional creation of healthier alternatives.

Another common habit is the avoidance of financial oversight. Many people delay checking their account balances, ignore bank notifications, or leave unopened bills in drawers. This form of avoidance is often rooted in fear—the fear of confronting uncomfortable truths about debt, overspending, or insufficient savings. Yet this avoidance only exacerbates the issue, turning manageable problems into crises. Avoidance creates financial blind spots, preventing the timely adjustments that could restore balance. Overcoming it involves building a habit of regular, non-judgemental financial review—treating financial awareness not as a punishment, but as an act of self-respect and stewardship.

One of the more subtle but equally damaging financial habits is lifestyle inflation—the tendency to increase spending in proportion to rising income. While earning more should theoretically lead to greater savings and security, it often leads to a proportional rise in

expenses, effectively cancelling out the benefit. This is particularly common when success is equated with visible markers—larger homes, newer cars, expensive holidays. These choices, while not inherently wrong, can lead to financial vulnerability if not aligned with broader financial goals. To address lifestyle inflation, families must cultivate the habit of intentional spending—asking not just "Can we afford this?" but "Does this align with our values and long-term objectives?"

Credit misuse also deserves scrutiny. Credit cards, when used strategically, can offer rewards, build credit history, and provide short-term liquidity. But when used impulsively or to fund a lifestyle beyond one's means, they become a gateway to chronic debt. The habit of carrying a balance month to month, making only minimum payments, or using credit to cover non-essential spending is a fast track to financial instability. Reforming this pattern involves both structural changes—such as limiting access to credit or automating payments—and behavioural shifts, like delaying purchases and using cash or debit for discretionary expenses.

Procrastination is another silent but pervasive enemy of financial stability. This includes delaying retirement contributions, postponing the creation of a budget, or putting off conversations about insurance or estate planning. These tasks often feel abstract or daunting, yet delay compounds risk. A late start in investing means lost compounding potential. A delay in securing insurance can leave a family exposed to significant loss. Tackling procrastination requires breaking tasks into manageable actions and building consistency through small, repeated efforts. Establishing a recurring financial review, even just once a month, can serve as an anchor to stay engaged and proactive.

To break bad financial habits, the first step is self-awareness. Families must be willing to examine their patterns without shame or defensiveness. This process works best when approached with curiosity rather than judgement. What triggers certain spending behaviours? What beliefs underpin avoidance or inaction? Are there recurring financial decisions that consistently lead to regret? Keeping a financial journal, where each expenditure is briefly noted along with the reason for the purchase, can uncover revealing patterns. Over time, themes begin to emerge—emotional spending, habitual underestimation of costs, or frequent exceptions to planned budgets.

Once these patterns are identified, the next step is to design friction into bad habits and remove friction from good ones. For instance, unsubscribing from promotional emails or removing saved payment information from online retailers creates a pause that allows for reflection before spending. Conversely, automating savings or scheduling regular account reviews reduces resistance to positive behaviours. The structure of our environment plays a significant role in habit formation. Families can support one another by making the desired behaviours easier to adopt and reinforcing them through positive feedback and shared accountability.

Children, too, are active participants in the formation and perpetuation of financial habits. If they observe inconsistent messages—being told to save while watching parents indulge impulsively—they internalise confusion. Conversely, when they see consistent modelling of thoughtful, value-based financial decisions, they learn by osmosis. Involving children in family financial practices—such as helping with grocery budgeting or saving towards a shared family goal—allows them to experience the discipline and reward of intentional money management. Teaching them to reflect on their own small spending choices, and to distinguish between impulse and purpose, fosters lifelong financial mindfulness.

It is also vital to acknowledge that some financial habits are rooted not just in behaviour, but in systems. A family may struggle with saving not because of frivolity, but because their income is insufficient to meet basic needs. In such cases, the focus must expand to include structural adjustments—such as increasing income through skills development, reducing fixed expenses, or accessing community resources. Good habits cannot flourish in an environment of chronic financial strain. Strengthening the underlying system—through planning, advocacy, and support—is a prerequisite for sustainable behavioural change.

Support from others can accelerate progress. Whether through a financial advisor, community education group, or trusted mentor, external accountability provides perspective and encouragement. Some families find it helpful to conduct regular financial check-ins, not only to assess budgets but to reflect on progress and setbacks. This ritual normalises financial discussion, fosters mutual support, and keeps the focus on long-term goals rather than short-term lapses.

Breaking bad financial habits is not a matter of perfection—it is a process of ongoing refinement. It involves recognising that setbacks are part of growth and that each decision presents an opportunity to reinforce a healthier pattern. Families that approach habit change with patience and persistence find that the cumulative impact of small improvements is profound. What begins as a single intentional choice—skipping an unnecessary purchase, reviewing a bank statement, or increasing a savings deposit—can evolve into a lasting behavioural shift.

Over time, these changes do more than stabilise the bank account. They cultivate a sense of financial dignity—a quiet confidence that comes from knowing that money is being managed with purpose and clarity. They reduce anxiety, enhance communication, and open the door to more ambitious financial goals. They demonstrate, both to oneself and to one's children, that financial outcomes are not fixed, but malleable—shaped not by luck or inheritance, but by daily actions and deliberate choices.

Ultimately, the habits we practise shape the financial stories we write. By identifying and eliminating those that no longer serve us, we create space for new patterns—ones that support not only our prosperity but our integrity and peace of mind. A family committed to this practice does not need to be perfect; it needs only to be persistent. In doing so, it lays a foundation strong enough to support not just wealth, but wisdom, resilience, and a more intentional way of living.

Chapter 2
Budgeting as a Family — Managing Money Together

At its core, a budget is far more than just a financial document—it's a deliberate expression of values. It's a statement, really, about what matters to a household and how its resources will be shaped accordingly. But despite this, many families only come to budgeting reactively—usually under pressure, in the wake of debt, or following a financial scare. It's a pity, because this narrow view obscures budgeting's broader potential. Used well, it doesn't merely balance books; it strengthens communication, builds discipline, and lays the foundation for sound financial understanding that can pass from one generation to the next. In managing money together, families don't just keep accounts—they forge a common language for resilience and decision-making.

The process, however, is not merely technical. Far from it. Family budgeting is, at its best, a collaborative venture—part arithmetic, part emotional honesty. It calls for more than tallying receipts and setting limits. There's a need for openness, for negotiating trade-offs, for creating space where even uncomfortable conversations are allowed to breathe. Every family member, regardless of how much they earn—or whether they earn at all—has a role to play in shaping financial outcomes. The aim here isn't to police spending, but to build a shared approach grounded in mutual respect and purpose.

To begin, there's the matter of understanding cash flow—what's coming in, and what's going out. Obvious, perhaps. But in practice, many families operate on assumption rather than precision. Income figures may be roughly estimated, outgoings glossed over or half-remembered. The first step, then, is plain and practical: collect the data. Bank statements, pay slips, utility bills, shopping receipts—bring it all together and form a clear, honest picture of your household's financial ecosystem. From there, the task becomes one of categorising: fixed costs like rent or mortgage, flexible ones such as groceries, and then the discretionary—the treats, the dinners out, the subscriptions that slip under the radar.

With this clearer view, families can start to make informed choices. This is not about frugality for frugality's sake. It's about aligning spending with what truly matters. Suppose, for instance, that the numbers reveal a surprising amount spent on takeaway meals. Rather than cutting this out altogether—often a recipe for resentment—it might be wiser to halve it and redirect the savings to something more meaningful: paying off a debt, building a holiday fund, or adding to a rainy-day reserve. The point isn't to punish pleasure, but to give spending direction.

One of the more challenging, yet essential, aspects of budgeting is drawing the line between needs and wants. Simple in theory, messier in practice—especially in a world that so persistently sells desire as necessity. Needs are the basics: housing, food, healthcare, transport. Everything else, however tempting or pleasant, falls under 'wants'. This isn't about assigning moral weight to spending—it's not "bad" to want—but rather creating a clear lens for prioritisation. A large-screen TV might bring enjoyment, but if it displaces the ability to handle core expenses or prepare for the future, its timing may need a rethink.

Children, particularly, benefit from learning this distinction. And parents can model the thought process behind such decisions. "We've chosen not to renovate the kitchen this year because we're prioritising the emergency fund," a parent might explain. This isn't just instructive; it's empowering. It shows children that spending decisions aren't arbitrary—they're guided by purpose. When a child asks for something new—a game, perhaps—the conversation can become, "Is this a need or a want? And how does it fit into our budget?" Over time, this kind of exchange builds awareness and discourages knee-jerk consumption.

To bring structure to the process, a few time-tested budgeting methods can offer helpful guardrails. One such method is the envelope system—a throwback, perhaps, but still effective. It involves assigning fixed cash amounts to categories like food or entertainment, and once an envelope is empty, that's it—no further spending in that area until the next cycle. In a world increasingly digital, virtual envelopes within budgeting apps can replicate this tactile discipline.

Another popular approach is the 50/30/20 rule. This system proposes dividing after-tax income into 50 percent for needs, 30 for wants, and 20 for savings or debt repayment. It's neat, adaptable, and helps maintain a sense of balance. Not all families will fit neatly into those percentages—some may have heavier obligations in one category—but the principle remains sound. Choose a method that fits, review it regularly, and be prepared to tweak it. A budget, after all, should evolve with your life—not be set in stone.

At the heart of any budget worthy of the name is an emergency fund. Life is nothing if not unpredictable, and even the most carefully crafted plan can be derailed by a sudden medical bill, car repair, or job loss. An emergency fund acts as a buffer—one that prevents short-term crises from turning into long-term debt spirals. Building such a reserve takes time and persistence. Starting small—enough to cover a month of essential costs—and building towards three to six months is a reasonable target. The reassurance this brings is immeasurable. It transforms financial shocks into temporary setbacks rather than existential threats.

Budgeting together also presents a golden opportunity for financial education—especially for children. Rather than keeping money matters behind closed doors, parents might consider involving children in simple, age-appropriate ways. It could be as straightforward as explaining how much is set aside for groceries this month or letting them help compare prices at the supermarket. Older children can manage personal budgets for clothing or school items, learning to juggle limited resources. Some families go further still, creating mock budgets with younger children using play money to instil early financial habits.

And while these lessons do involve numbers, they're not really about maths. They're about values. Children come to appreciate that every spending decision carries a trade-off. They learn patience and prioritisation. Perhaps most significantly, they develop empathy—understanding, even at a young age, that sacrifices made by their parents are often in service of something bigger. This kind of awareness fosters cooperation and can diffuse tension before it begins.

Indeed, one of the most understated benefits of family budgeting is the way it strengthens relational bonds. It creates transparency. So often, financial conflict doesn't stem from the purchases themselves, but from confusion or unmet expectations. A partner may feel blindsided by a sudden expense, or a teenager may chafe against what they see as unfair restrictions. When there's an open, ongoing conversation about the budget—ideally one that happens regularly—these misunderstandings become less likely. Everyone is on the same page, and when problems arise, they're approached as a team.

Of course, there will be slip-ups. Budgets are not infallible. Expenses will crop up unexpectedly. Some months will go over. Mistakes will be made. But perfection isn't the goal—progress is. A budget isn't there to create rigidity. It's there to provide clarity, to guide choices, to help a household respond rather than react. Build in room for irregularities, and revisit the plan often. The more families view budgeting as an adaptive process rather than a rigid obligation, the more durable—and less stressful—it becomes.

In an age where financial pressure is one of the leading sources of domestic strife, budgeting as a family offers a different narrative. It's not about scarcity or restriction—it's about agency. It turns money from a private stressor into a collective endeavour. It fosters values that last: patience, foresight, accountability. And it creates a home environment where each person, young or old, feels empowered to understand and influence their financial world.

When families budget together, they gain far more than cost control. They gain coherence. They develop a financial rhythm, a shared vocabulary, a sense of forward motion. They discover that managing money is not merely a private responsibility—it's a communal discipline. Practised with care, it can become a bedrock for trust, stability, and the kind of success that doesn't just show up on paper, but resonates through daily life.

Creating a Realistic Family Budget

A realistic family budget is not merely a numerical breakdown of income and expenses; it is a living strategy, an evolving reflection of a household's priorities, commitments, and ambitions. More than a financial document, it functions as a behavioural tool—guiding decisions, anticipating challenges, and creating boundaries that empower rather than restrict. For families, budgeting is not about deprivation or strict control; it is about clarity, alignment, and the capacity to make purposeful choices. Yet the effectiveness of any budget hinges on one critical quality: realism.

An unrealistic budget, no matter how detailed, is destined to unravel. It may look good on paper but collapse under the weight of daily life. Families often fall into the trap of crafting budgets based on ideal circumstances—projecting consistent income, underestimating expenses, or omitting infrequent but inevitable costs. The result is frustration, guilt, and ultimately, abandonment of the budgeting process altogether. To create a truly effective budget, families must begin with honesty. They must look not only at their financial statements but also at their habits, needs, and tendencies.

The first step in creating a realistic family budget is to gain an accurate understanding of household income. This includes all sources—salaries, freelance payments, child benefits, pensions, and any other consistent inflows. It is important to use net income (after tax and deductions), as this represents the actual amount available for spending. For families with irregular income—such as those with freelance or seasonal work—budgeting must be based on a conservative estimate, often the lowest monthly average over the past year. This approach cushions against shortfalls and prevents overcommitting to fixed expenses during higher-earning months.

Next comes the process of tracking expenses, a task that many find tedious but which reveals the most critical insights. Without a clear understanding of where money is going, it is impossible to make informed adjustments. Tracking should cover a minimum of three months to capture patterns, irregular costs, and seasonal fluctuations. This includes everything from housing and utilities to transport, groceries, dining out, subscriptions, gifts, and miscellaneous purchases. The aim is not to shame spending, but to illuminate it. Families are often surprised by how much is spent in discretionary categories such as takeaways, digital entertainment, or convenience purchases—areas where minor adjustments can yield significant savings.

One family, for instance, discovered that their monthly streaming and subscription costs exceeded their food budget for the same period. While none of the services seemed extravagant individually, the accumulation of multiple platforms had quietly outpaced essential categories. By identifying this pattern, they were able to cancel unused subscriptions and redirect the funds towards paying off a small loan, reducing financial pressure without compromising their quality of life.

With income and expenditure data in hand, the next step is categorising spending. Categories should reflect the household's actual lifestyle while distinguishing between fixed and variable costs. Fixed costs—such as rent or mortgage payments, insurance premiums, and loan repayments—are non-negotiable and usually consistent. Variable costs, including groceries, fuel, and entertainment, fluctuate and offer greater flexibility for adjustments. It's also helpful to include a "miscellaneous" or "buffer" category to accommodate unplanned but necessary expenses, which are often inevitable and can derail a budget if unaccounted for.

Once spending patterns are categorised, families can begin the process of setting limits for each category. This is where realism must take precedence over idealism. It is tempting to set tight spending limits in an effort to maximise savings, but such rigidity often leads to failure. A budget must reflect actual behaviour while gradually shaping it. For example, if a family currently spends £800 a month on groceries, slashing that amount to £500 without a plan for how to achieve it will likely result in overspending and frustration. A better approach is to reduce the category gradually, finding practical ways to shop more efficiently, reduce waste, or take advantage of bulk buying.

Spending limits should be informed by past behaviour but aligned with future goals. This means asking not just "What did we spend?" but "What do we want to achieve?" For instance, a family saving for a home deposit might aim to reallocate funds from non-essential categories towards their savings goal, while still preserving enough for enjoyment and spontaneity. A budget that feels punitive will not be sustainable. The most effective budgets are those that balance discipline with flexibility, structure with autonomy.

To make budgeting a sustainable household practice, it must be operationalised—embedded into the daily and monthly rhythm of family life. This involves choosing a system or tool that supports consistent engagement. Some families prefer traditional spreadsheets, others favour budgeting apps that sync with bank accounts and offer real-time tracking. The method is less important than the habit. Weekly or fortnightly check-ins allow families to review actual spending against planned limits, address overspending early, and make informed decisions about reallocating funds if necessary.

Budgeting is also a powerful relational tool when it is approached as a shared responsibility. Rather than one partner taking full control or assuming sole responsibility, effective budgeting involves collaboration. This ensures that each person's needs and perspectives are considered and avoids resentment or misunderstanding. For example, a partner who values social outings may feel restricted by a rigid entertainment budget unless given input into its design. Including children, too, can transform budgeting from a household chore into a shared learning experience. Allowing children to see how their activities, clothing, or lunches fit within the family budget fosters financial awareness and a sense of participation.

Budgeting should also account for irregular but predictable expenses—those that do not occur monthly but arise throughout the year. These may include school fees, holiday costs, birthday gifts, car servicing, or annual insurance premiums. A common pitfall in budgeting is treating these costs as surprises, leading to overspending or reliance on credit. The solution is to create a sinking fund—setting aside a small amount each month in anticipation of these expenses. For example, if annual school fees amount to £1,200, allocating £100 per month ensures the funds are available without disrupting other areas of the budget.

A well-designed family budget also includes provision for emergencies. Unexpected costs are a financial certainty, whether in the form of medical bills, home repairs, or job loss. An emergency fund—separate from savings earmarked for goals—acts as a financial shock absorber. Even a modest fund of one to three months' expenses provides peace of mind and prevents crises from becoming catastrophic. Building this fund should be a priority, even if it requires slow, incremental progress. The act of contributing regularly reinforces the habit of paying oneself first, a foundational principle of sound financial management.

Ultimately, the purpose of a family budget is not control for control's sake. It is to create clarity. When each pound is given a purpose, financial decisions become less reactive and more intentional. Families are better able to anticipate challenges, seize opportunities, and align their spending with what truly matters to them. A budget is a mirror that reflects not only financial behaviour but also values, priorities, and aspirations.

Perhaps most importantly, a realistic family budget creates space for hope. It demonstrates that financial security is not dependent solely on income, but on how resources are managed. It shows that even modest earnings can be stretched and directed with skill. It turns abstract goals—such as home ownership, debt freedom, or family holidays—into concrete, attainable milestones. For families facing uncertainty or financial anxiety, a well-constructed budget offers a sense of control and progress.

A budget that is realistic is one that accounts for human nature—for imperfection, change, and the complexity of modern life. It does not require flawless execution or constant sacrifice. It asks only for consistency, honesty, and a willingness to adapt. Families who embrace this process discover that budgeting is not a burden but a liberation—a way to reclaim their financial story and write it with intention, one month at a time. Through discipline and flexibility, insight and action, they build not just a healthier financial foundation, but a stronger and more unified family life.

Needs vs. Wants — Teaching Financial Discipline

One of the most foundational principles in personal finance, particularly in the context of family budgeting, is learning to distinguish between needs and wants. While the concept may appear self-evident at first glance, its practical application is far more complex. The line between a necessity and a discretionary expense is not always sharp or universally agreed upon, and it is further blurred by social influences, emotional motivations, and deeply embedded personal values. Yet, teaching this distinction—both to oneself and across generations—is a critical step in cultivating financial discipline. It empowers families to make intentional choices, preserve long-term stability, and allocate resources in a way that reflects what truly matters.

A "need" can be broadly defined as something essential for survival, functioning, or fulfilment of basic responsibilities. This includes shelter, food, utilities, transport, healthcare, and education. A "want," by contrast, refers to items or services that enhance comfort, convenience, or pleasure but are not strictly necessary. These might range from designer clothing and dining out to streaming subscriptions or the latest gadgets. However, the distinction is not purely binary. It often exists on a spectrum shaped by context and lifestyle. For instance, a car may be a necessity for a suburban family with limited public transport options, but a discretionary luxury for someone living in a city centre with reliable alternatives.

The challenge lies not merely in identifying which items fall into each category, but in fostering the mindset that supports conscious, values-based spending. This requires both awareness and honesty. Families must be willing to examine their expenses critically, asking whether a given purchase serves a fundamental need or simply satisfies a short-term desire. Importantly, this is not about eliminating wants altogether. Rather, it is about ensuring that wants do not consistently take precedence over needs or compromise essential financial goals.

Real-world application of this principle can be seen in countless everyday scenarios. Take, for example, the weekly grocery shop. Purchasing fresh produce and staples such as rice, milk, and bread clearly falls into the category of needs. However, adding premium snacks, imported cheeses, or a bottle of wine edges into the realm of wants. There is nothing inherently wrong with including these items, but doing so should be a deliberate decision made within the constraints of a broader financial plan—not an automatic habit devoid of consideration.

Another scenario might involve back-to-school shopping for children. Basic clothing, school supplies, and uniforms constitute needs. However, insisting on brand-name trainers or the latest fashion trends, while understandable in a social context, reflects discretionary spending. Here, parents face the delicate task of balancing a child's social comfort with the family's financial limits. These are not easy conversations, but they are vital. They present teachable moments—opportunities to involve children in financial reasoning, explain trade-offs, and reinforce the importance of prioritising essentials.

This distinction becomes even more essential during periods of economic strain. When income is reduced due to job loss, illness, or broader economic downturns, the ability to differentiate between needs and wants becomes a tool of survival. Families who have already internalised this discipline are better positioned to make swift, rational adjustments to their spending. They can reduce or pause discretionary expenses without panic, knowing that their core needs remain covered. Those who have not developed this skill often struggle, attempting to maintain previous spending patterns through debt or depletion of savings, thereby compounding their financial vulnerability.

Financial discipline rooted in the needs-versus-wants framework also supports long-term wealth-building. By regularly allocating resources toward needs first—particularly savings, debt repayment, and investment—families create a structure that supports growth.

Discretionary spending, while still present, becomes responsive to what remains after these priorities are met. This approach transforms budgeting from a restrictive practice into a purposeful one. It shifts the conversation from "What can we afford right now?" to "What is the best use of our resources today to serve tomorrow?"

Parents play a crucial role in instilling this mindset in their children. Children observe financial behaviours long before they understand them conceptually. When parents model restraint, thoughtful decision-making, and openness about financial limits, they create a framework of normalcy around prioritising needs. A parent who says, "We're choosing to cook at home more often so we can save for a family trip," is not just explaining a choice—they are demonstrating delayed gratification and aligning present behaviour with future rewards.

There is also value in allowing children to practise distinguishing needs from wants with their own money. For example, a child receiving pocket money may be guided to divide it between savings, essentials, and discretionary spending. If a child spends their allowance on sweets and is then unable to afford a school outing or save for a desired toy, the resulting experience becomes a powerful lesson in budgeting, consequence, and prioritisation. These are skills that compound over time, preparing young people to manage more complex financial responsibilities with maturity and foresight.

Cultural influences can complicate this learning. In a society saturated with advertising and consumerism, the pressure to acquire—often presented as a need for happiness, identity, or belonging—can obscure rational judgement. Marketing strategies are deliberately designed to elevate wants to the status of needs, creating a sense of urgency and inadequacy. The latest phone is presented not just as a tool, but as a symbol of success. A holiday is positioned not as a leisure option, but as a mental health necessity. Families must navigate these narratives carefully, distinguishing between marketing messages and actual requirements.

Social comparison adds another layer of complexity. Families may feel compelled to keep up with peers, even if doing so compromises financial stability. Children may compare their possessions or experiences with those of classmates, prompting questions or feelings of exclusion. Here, open dialogue is essential. Parents can use such moments to reinforce family values and financial goals, explaining that their spending choices are guided by priorities rather than appearances. These conversations are not always comfortable, but they build resilience and confidence—both in children and adults.

To aid in distinguishing needs from wants, some families find it useful to apply a simple evaluative process before making purchases. Questions such as "Is this essential for our wellbeing or obligations?", "Can we meet this need in a simpler way?", or "What will we have to forgo if we make this purchase?" encourage reflection. This pause between impulse and action often reveals whether a desire is fleeting or aligned with genuine priorities.

This discipline also fosters gratitude. When wants are fulfilled occasionally and deliberately, they are more likely to be appreciated. Constant indulgence dulls satisfaction and fuels a sense of entitlement. In contrast, restraint enhances value. A family who plans and saves for a restaurant meal or weekend outing may find the experience more enjoyable and memorable than those for whom such spending is habitual and unexamined.

Understanding needs versus wants is not about moralising spending or aspiring to financial asceticism. It is about clarity. It is about teaching families—especially children—that resources are limited, choices are interconnected, and financial behaviour should reflect considered intention. This clarity is foundational not just for budgeting, but for every aspect of financial life. It informs how families save, invest, borrow, and give. It shapes the household culture around money, influencing communication, conflict resolution, and goal-setting.

When needs are consistently met and wants are pursued mindfully, financial discipline becomes self-reinforcing. Households experience less stress, more control, and greater alignment between their money and their values. Over time, this leads to not just stability but satisfaction—the kind that arises when people live within their means, invest in their future, and make space for meaningful indulgences without sacrificing security.

Ultimately, the ability to distinguish needs from wants is a lifelong skill. It is neither innate nor automatic, but cultivated through reflection, modelling, and intentional practice. Families that embrace this distinction lay the groundwork for financial integrity and intergenerational wisdom. They equip each member with the tools to navigate an increasingly complex financial world with confidence, adaptability, and purpose. Through this lens, financial discipline becomes not merely a matter of arithmetic, but an expression of self-awareness, stewardship, and shared vision.

The Envelope and 50/30/20 Budgeting Methods

Creating a family budget is both an exercise in arithmetic and a statement of values. While the fundamental aim is to ensure that income is distributed in a sustainable and balanced way, the methods by which families approach this task vary widely depending on lifestyle, income stability, and behavioural preferences. Among the many strategies available, the envelope method and the 50/30/20 rule stand out for their simplicity, adaptability, and effectiveness across a range of financial circumstances. Though they differ in execution, both methods aim to instil discipline, reduce impulsive spending, and ensure that financial resources are directed toward the goals that matter most.

The envelope method is perhaps the oldest and most tactile approach to budgeting. Its core idea is disarmingly straightforward: allocate physical cash into designated envelopes, each labelled for a specific category of spending—groceries, transport, entertainment, household essentials, and so on. Once the money in a particular envelope is spent, that category is considered closed for the month. What makes this method so powerful is its visceral nature. Handling cash engages the senses in a way digital transactions do not. The finite amount within each envelope acts as a tangible reminder of limits, creating a natural barrier against overspending.

Although the traditional version involves paper envelopes and cash, the method has been successfully adapted to digital platforms. Families now use apps and banking tools that simulate envelope budgeting through virtual categories, tracking expenditure in real-time. The principle remains the same: pre-allocate money based on anticipated needs, and commit to staying within those boundaries. This method is particularly helpful for families who are trying to regain control after a period of financial chaos, as it imposes structure and creates immediate accountability.

For example, a family struggling with food costs may discover through envelope budgeting that their grocery spending fluctuates dramatically each month due to frequent impulse purchases. By allocating a fixed cash amount for groceries and committing to shop with that envelope only, they begin to plan meals more carefully, stick to shopping lists, and make more strategic choices. Over time, the habit reduces waste, encourages mindful consumption, and frees up funds for other priorities.

However, envelope budgeting is not without its challenges. It requires consistent tracking and can feel restrictive to those unused to such a granular approach. It is also less practical for expenses that are paid online or for irregular costs that don't fit neatly into monthly categories. Still, its discipline-building potential is unmatched, and it can be an excellent method for families working to reset their financial habits or manage a tight budget with clarity.

In contrast, the 50/30/20 budgeting method offers a broader and more flexible framework. Developed by U.S. Senator Elizabeth Warren and her daughter Amelia Warren Tyagi, it proposes a simple division of after-tax income into three categories: 50 percent for needs, 30 percent for wants, and 20 percent for savings and debt repayment. This percentage-based approach is particularly appealing for families who prefer a macro-level overview rather than line-by-line budgeting.

The strength of the 50/30/20 rule lies in its balance. By allocating half of the budget to essentials—such as housing, utilities, groceries, transport, and minimum debt payments—it ensures that the most important obligations are covered. The 30 percent allocated to discretionary spending allows for enjoyment and personal choice, which is often where strict budgets fail. Families need room to engage in leisure activities, celebrate milestones, and make occasional spontaneous purchases. Denying these entirely leads to budgeting fatigue and, eventually, abandonment of the system.

The final 20 percent, directed toward savings and debt repayment, embeds long-term planning into everyday financial behaviour. Whether contributing to an emergency fund, retirement savings, or accelerating loan repayments, this category is what enables families to progress rather than simply maintain. Unlike the envelope method, which primarily addresses short-term cash flow, the 50/30/20 rule integrates immediate needs with future ambitions in a sustainable proportion.

To illustrate, consider a dual-income household with a combined net monthly income of £4,000. Applying the 50/30/20 rule, they would allocate £2,000 to needs, £1,200 to wants, and £800 to savings or debt. Within this framework, they might cover rent, food, and transport with the first portion; enjoy dining out, streaming services, and a modest holiday with the second; and use the third to pay off credit card balances while saving for a home deposit. This proportional system encourages holistic budgeting and is particularly useful for those with a stable income who prefer less administrative oversight.

That said, the 50/30/20 method is not universally applicable without adjustment. Families with high fixed expenses—such as those living in urban centres with elevated housing costs—may find that essential expenses exceed the suggested 50 percent. In such cases, the model should be treated as a guideline rather than a rule. The principles of balance and prioritisation remain valid, even if the exact percentages need recalibration. What matters is maintaining proportionality and ensuring that wants do not routinely override savings, or that future planning is not sacrificed to short-term indulgence.

Both methods can also be combined or used sequentially. Families starting with envelope budgeting to rein in spending may eventually transition to the 50/30/20 rule for broader planning. Conversely, those using the 50/30/20 rule who find themselves frequently overspending in discretionary areas might adopt envelope techniques for those specific categories. This hybrid approach allows for customisation based on changing needs and financial maturity.

When deciding which method to implement, families should consider their behavioural tendencies, technological comfort, and financial objectives. Those who prefer tangible, detailed tracking and benefit from visual cues may find the envelope method more effective. Those who are goal-oriented and comfortable working with percentages may lean towards the 50/30/20 approach. Regardless of the choice, success depends on consistency, honest assessment, and the willingness to adapt.

Importantly, both budgeting strategies serve as tools to open up essential conversations within families. They invite reflection on spending habits, provoke questions about value and priority, and foster mutual understanding. A child included in an envelope exercise might better grasp why the family cannot afford both a cinema trip and a new pair of trainers in the same week. A teenager observing the 50/30/20 rule may begin to understand the trade-offs between lifestyle and savings. These frameworks turn abstract financial literacy into lived experience, deepening awareness and building competency.

Families should also expect these systems to evolve. As incomes change, children grow, and goals shift, so too must the budget. The early years of raising children may prioritise childcare and education costs, while later stages may shift focus to saving for university, paying down a mortgage, or preparing for retirement. Budgets that are reviewed and refined regularly become tools for empowerment rather than constraint. They allow families to respond to life's complexities with foresight rather than reaction.

Moreover, effective budgeting is not about perfection. There will be months when spending exceeds projections, when emergencies disrupt plans, or when discipline falters. These moments are not failures but opportunities for recalibration. A missed savings target or overspent category is a signal—not of personal inadequacy, but of a system that may need adjustment or a habit that requires attention. The strength of the envelope and 50/30/20 methods lies in their capacity to reveal these patterns and provide a structure through which they can be addressed.

Ultimately, budgeting is about stewardship. It is the practice of managing limited resources with intention, foresight, and shared understanding. The envelope and 50/30/20 methods are not ends in themselves but means to create a financial life that is coherent, value-driven, and sustainable. They enable families not just to meet their obligations but to express their aspirations through how they allocate money. Whether saving for a first home, planning a meaningful holiday, or building a buffer against uncertainty, these strategies provide the scaffolding on which financial security and satisfaction can be built.

By embracing either of these budgeting methods—or elements of both—families lay the groundwork for disciplined, informed, and empowered financial decision-making. In doing so, they cultivate not just a healthier relationship with money, but a shared language and rhythm around it—one that strengthens the household today while laying a thoughtful foundation for the years ahead.

Emergency Funds and Unexpected Expenses

No matter how meticulous a budget may be, how disciplined a family is with spending, or how promising the economic climate appears, unexpected expenses will arise. Whether it's an urgent medical bill, a sudden job loss, a major car repair, or a leaking roof in the middle of winter, financial surprises are an inevitability of life. What separates households that weather these events with resilience from those plunged into chaos is the presence—or absence—of an emergency fund.

An emergency fund serves as a financial shock absorber. It is a designated sum of money set aside exclusively for unforeseen expenses that, if unprepared for, could derail a family's financial stability. This fund is not about pessimism or worst-case thinking;

it is a practical, proactive safeguard that allows families to respond to crises without resorting to high-interest debt, dipping into savings earmarked for other goals, or making emotionally driven financial decisions. In essence, it is a buffer between an unexpected event and long-term financial disruption.

For many families, the idea of building an emergency fund can feel daunting, especially when the budget is already stretched thin. The notion of setting aside three to six months' worth of expenses may appear out of reach or unrealistic. However, the key to establishing this fund lies not in achieving the full amount at once, but in committing to the habit of consistent, incremental saving. Starting small is not only acceptable—it is essential. A modest cushion of even a few hundred pounds can provide immediate relief when the boiler fails or when a child requires emergency dental treatment.

Consider the case of a family of four living on a dual-income household where both parents work freelance contracts. Despite being diligent with their monthly budget, they found themselves in a precarious position when one parent lost a client unexpectedly, cutting their income by 40 percent overnight. Because they had taken the time to build a basic emergency fund—covering roughly two months of expenses—they were able to meet their essential bills, maintain their mortgage payments, and buy time to seek alternative work without spiralling into panic. The fund acted not just as financial support, but as emotional ballast during a turbulent period.

The effectiveness of an emergency fund lies not only in its existence but in its accessibility and separation from everyday spending. Ideally, the fund should be housed in a high-interest savings account that is liquid—readily available without penalties, but not so easily accessed that it becomes tempting to use for non-emergencies. The psychological distinction is crucial. The emergency fund must be treated with the same respect as a fire extinguisher: rarely touched, but absolutely vital when needed.

One of the greatest challenges families face in building this fund is competing financial priorities. Saving for education, paying down debt, or investing for the future often take precedence in the household hierarchy. While these are undoubtedly important, an emergency fund should not be viewed as an optional extra, but as the foundation that makes all other financial goals more achievable. Without it, any progress can be undone by a single unplanned expense. In fact, financial planners often advise building a basic emergency reserve before aggressively tackling debt, precisely because emergencies are one of the leading causes of debt accumulation in the first place.

Economic downturns add another layer of urgency to this discussion. The COVID-19 pandemic, for instance, exposed the fragility of many household finances. Families with no cushion were forced to rely on credit, government assistance, or the goodwill of landlords and lenders to survive. While no emergency fund can insulate completely against prolonged unemployment or systemic shocks, it can soften the blow and provide critical breathing room. It allows families to make strategic decisions—such as delaying a major purchase, renegotiating payment terms, or temporarily reducing discretionary spending—rather than reactive ones made under duress.

Teaching children about the role of emergency savings is also an important part of financial education. Just as families plan holidays or birthdays, they can explain that some money is always set aside "just in case"—not because they expect something bad to happen, but because it's wise to be prepared. This normalises the practice of saving for the unknown and helps children understand that life carries uncertainties best met with preparation rather than fear.

Practical implementation of an emergency fund begins with clarity around how much is needed. The conventional benchmark is three to six months of essential expenses—those costs that must be met regardless of income fluctuations. This typically includes rent or mortgage, utilities, groceries, insurance premiums, transport, and minimum debt payments. For families with one primary earner, self-employment, or inconsistent income, a longer runway of six months or more may be advisable. However, it's crucial not to let the target amount intimidate or delay action. Saving even a few hundred pounds provides tangible protection and builds the habit of prioritising resilience.

Setting up automated transfers to a designated emergency account can make the process more manageable. By treating emergency savings as a fixed cost—just like a utility bill—families remove the need for constant decision-making and ensure regular contributions. Even small amounts, transferred weekly or monthly, accumulate over time and send a powerful signal to all family members that financial security is a shared priority.

Emergency funds should be reviewed periodically to ensure they reflect current circumstances. As families grow, take on new financial obligations, or experience income changes, the required buffer may shift. Annual reviews can help assess whether the fund remains adequate or needs adjusting. It's also important to replenish the fund promptly after any withdrawal. While it may be tempting to delay replenishment in favour of other goals, restoring the safety net must remain a priority.

Beyond the technical aspects, an emergency fund provides peace of mind that is difficult to quantify but immensely valuable. It creates a sense of financial control, reducing anxiety and increasing confidence. Families who know they have a buffer are more likely to take thoughtful risks—starting a side business, pursuing further education, or transitioning to a single income temporarily. The psychological comfort of having contingency funds changes how people approach life's uncertainties. It offers the freedom to respond rather than react, to adjust rather than panic.

There is also a moral dimension to emergency preparedness. Families that manage to create and maintain such funds are better positioned to support others during community-wide crises. They may be able to offer assistance to relatives, donate to charitable causes, or volunteer time without jeopardising their own stability. In this way, emergency funds serve not only the household but the broader social fabric, reinforcing the idea that personal responsibility enables collective strength.

Culturally, there is still work to be done in shifting perceptions of emergency funds. Too often, saving for emergencies is viewed as a luxury or an act of fearfulness. In reality, it is a reflection of prudence and self-respect. Encouraging a cultural narrative that celebrates preparedness—not as a sign of pessimism but of empowerment—can help shift attitudes. When families talk openly about the purpose and benefits of emergency funds, they normalise the behaviour and inspire others to follow suit.

Ultimately, the task of building an emergency fund may seem mundane compared to other financial ambitions. It does not carry the allure of high-yield investments or the immediate gratification of paying off a credit card. Yet its value is profound. It is the financial equivalent of laying strong foundations beneath a well-designed house. Without it, even the most architecturally sound structure is vulnerable to collapse under pressure.

An emergency fund represents one of the most powerful expressions of financial discipline and foresight a family can make. It acknowledges that life is unpredictable, that setbacks are inevitable, and that planning for them is a strength, not a weakness. It allows families to navigate turbulent times with composure, preserve their long-term goals, and maintain a sense of dignity when circumstances threaten to destabilise them.

Through consistent effort, open communication, and a clear commitment to safeguarding their financial well-being, families can build emergency funds that do more than serve as lifelines—they become symbols of resilience, responsibility, and readiness. And in a world where uncertainty is the only certainty, such preparation is not just wise—it is indispensable.

Involving Kids in Budgeting

Teaching children how to manage money is not simply about preparing them for adulthood—it is about embedding lifelong habits that foster confidence, responsibility, and intentionality from an early age. Involving children in budgeting offers them a hands-on education that no textbook or classroom lesson can fully replicate. Through real-life engagement, children begin to understand the value of money, the consequences of financial choices, and the rewards of planning and discipline. Far from being too young to grasp these concepts, even primary-aged children can begin to participate in family financial practices in ways that are meaningful, empowering, and developmentally appropriate.

At the heart of this approach is the belief that financial education should not be isolated from daily life. Children absorb the behaviours and attitudes of their caregivers long before they understand monetary systems or economic principles. A child who witnesses a parent stressing over bills or swiping a card without explanation will internalise messages about money that are implicit and emotional. On the other hand, when families intentionally include children in conversations about saving, spending, and budgeting, they transform money from an abstract adult concern into a shared subject of learning and discussion.

One of the most effective ways to teach children about budgeting is to involve them in the practical realities of household financial decisions. This can begin in simple ways, such as discussing the weekly grocery budget and inviting children to help plan meals based on cost considerations. For example, a parent might say, "We have £100 for groceries this week. Let's work together to decide what we need and what we can afford." This not only teaches budgeting but also critical thinking, trade-offs, and the notion that money is finite. Over time, children learn that choices have opportunity costs—that spending more in one area means less available for another.

Another powerful method is to provide children with their own small budgets, often through allowances or designated spending money. While allowances are sometimes seen as a reward for chores, they are far more effective when framed as a tool for learning. A child who receives a fixed weekly sum and is expected to manage it learns firsthand about planning, saving, and delayed gratification. If they spend the entire amount on sweets on Monday, they experience the natural consequence of having no funds for the rest of the week. This kind of real-time feedback is far more impactful than lectures about frugality.

To deepen the learning, parents can help children divide their money into categories—perhaps spending, saving, and giving. While these divisions echo adult budgeting models, they are simplified to suit a child's context. For instance, a child may choose to spend on a toy, save for a larger purchase, and donate a small portion to a cause they care about. These decisions build foundational habits and reinforce the broader values of generosity and forward-thinking. More importantly, they allow children to feel a sense of ownership over their financial decisions, which strengthens self-efficacy and accountability.

The inclusion of children in budgeting is also an opportunity to address the often-hidden emotional aspects of money. Parents can model a healthy relationship with financial planning by speaking openly about how they make choices and how they deal with setbacks. For example, if a family decides to delay a holiday to prioritise home repairs, explaining this rationale to the children helps them see that budgeting is not about deprivation, but about aligning spending with values and needs. It also reassures children that financial limits are normal and navigable, reducing anxiety and promoting emotional resilience.

Real-world applications extend beyond the home. When children accompany parents to the shop, they can be encouraged to compare prices, assess value for money, and make decisions within a set budget. A parent might give a child £5 to choose snacks for a picnic, guiding them to consider quantity, quality, and price. This practice builds numeracy, decision-making, and consumer awareness. Similarly, older children can be involved in planning birthday parties or school events with a fixed budget, learning to prioritise and problem-solve under constraints.

Digital tools can enhance this learning. As children grow older, introducing them to basic budgeting apps or digital piggy banks can mirror adult financial tools and prepare them for managing bank accounts later on. These platforms allow them to track their income and expenses, set savings goals, and visualise their progress. In a world increasingly defined by cashless transactions, such digital fluency is essential. However, it is crucial that digital tools complement—not replace—the values-based, relational learning that happens within the family context.

Parents must also be prepared for mistakes. Children will overspend, forget to track their purchases, or change their minds about what they want to save for. These experiences are not failures—they are integral to the learning process. What matters is the conversation that follows. Rather than criticising or rescuing the child, parents can ask reflective questions: "What would you do differently next time?" or "How did that decision affect your goal?" These dialogues encourage children to think critically about their actions and learn from experience.

Teaching budgeting in this way is not limited to financial literacy; it intersects with broader developmental goals. It nurtures executive function skills such as planning, impulse control, and goal setting. It fosters independence and strengthens self-esteem, as children see the tangible results of their choices. It also deepens family connection. When money is discussed openly and respectfully, it becomes a subject of shared interest rather than tension. Children feel trusted and included, and parents benefit from the increased transparency and collaboration.

The benefits of this early education extend well into adolescence and adulthood. Teenagers who have been gradually exposed to budgeting principles are better prepared to manage part-time job income, navigate peer pressure around spending, and plan for major milestones such as university or travel. They are also more likely to develop healthy attitudes toward credit, debt, and saving. By contrast, young adults who have never engaged with budgeting often struggle to manage financial independence, leading to stress, debt accumulation, and poor decision-making.

Cultural and familial contexts will shape how budgeting is introduced and taught. In some households, money is considered a private matter, while in others, it is openly discussed. Regardless of background, there is always a way to involve children in age-appropriate financial learning. The key is to be intentional. Budgeting should not be a secret world inhabited only by adults. It should be a family practice—visible, accessible, and participatory.

It is also important to challenge outdated narratives that frame budgeting as restrictive or dull. When framed positively, budgeting is about choice, empowerment, and achieving meaningful goals. Families can reinforce this by celebrating financial milestones together, whether it is saving for a holiday, reaching a giving target, or managing to stick within a monthly grocery budget. These moments of success build momentum and reinforce the value of financial discipline.

Involving kids in budgeting does not require perfection or expertise. It requires presence, openness, and a willingness to learn together. It means shifting from a model of silent responsibility to one of shared engagement. When children grow up in households where money is talked about with honesty, handled with care, and aligned with values, they internalise those lessons deeply. They come to see budgeting not as a burden, but as a skill that enables freedom, stability, and generosity.

Ultimately, budgeting is not just about pounds and pence—it is about preparing children to live with intention in a world where money touches nearly every aspect of life. By including them in this essential process, families equip their children with the mindset, tools, and habits needed to thrive, not only financially but holistically. Through real-life practice, thoughtful conversation, and consistent guidance, budgeting becomes not only a mechanism for managing resources but a powerful framework for lifelong learning and empowerment.

Chapter 3
Saving Strategies — Building a Strong Financial Future

Saving money, while perhaps the most elementary of financial principles, is also one of the trickiest to consistently practise. Life, with its steady drumbeat of bills, social pressures, and the ever-present hum of consumerism, makes the act of setting money aside feel, at times, almost rebellious. For families in particular, saving transcends personal discipline. It becomes a collective ethic—a joint strategy, a safeguard, and often, a statement of priorities. Crafting a secure financial future is not about mere good intentions; it hinges on building a system that embeds saving into the rhythm of family life. When done with care, saving evolves beyond a transactional act. It becomes a gesture—towards stability, foresight, and a kind of quiet generosity aimed at those yet to come.

At the heart of any sound saving strategy lies a deceptively simple tenet: pay yourself first. That phrase, often tossed about in personal finance circles, conceals a radical shift in thinking. Instead of saving what's left after expenses (which, let's be honest, often amounts to little or nothing), one sets aside a fixed portion of income *before* anything else is touched. No waiting until the end of the month. No treating saving as optional. It becomes as essential as paying the rent or putting food on the table. This adjustment isn't just practical; it's philosophical. It says, in effect, "Our future matters as much as our present."

There's also a subtle emotional transformation at play here. Saving, approached this way, stops feeling like deprivation. It begins to resemble a reward—an intentional step towards security, or a dream deferred but not forgotten. For families chasing long-term goals—a deposit on a first home, funding a child's university years, an anniversary trip that's been years in the making—this mindset shift is crucial. Saving becomes less about withholding joy and more about designing a future rich with it.

Of course, it's not just *that* you save—it's *where* you save that carries weight. The choice of savings vehicle can significantly shape both the experience and the outcome. High-yield savings accounts, for instance, offer better returns than their standard counterparts, quietly enhancing the growth of your funds without introducing risk. True, interest rates rise and fall with the tide of economic policy, but selecting a solid institution with consistently competitive rates can help your money hold its ground against inflation.

Then there are fixed-term savings accounts—Certificates of Deposit in the U.S., often referred to in the UK as fixed-term deposits. These instruments offer a little more reward in exchange for a little more commitment. Money is locked away for a predetermined period, from six months to several years, with higher interest as the incentive. For families who have earmarked funds for medium-range goals—and who can resist the urge to dip into them on a whim—this structure works well. That said, timing is everything. Penalties for early withdrawal can sting, so these aren't for the "just in case" pot. They are better suited to anticipated costs—a child's tuition, a necessary renovation, or a future celebration.

In recent years, technology has become an invaluable ally in the saving process. Automation, in particular, has changed the game. When savings are transferred automatically from a current account—ideally right after payday—it removes willpower from the equation entirely. And let's be honest: willpower has never been the most reliable financial planner. With automatic savings, you create a sort of financial autopilot. Over time, it's just another routine, like paying the council tax or topping up the gas.

Modern banking apps bolster this automation with a host of clever tools. Some round up your spending to the nearest pound and funnel the difference into a savings account. Others help you name and track specific goals—"New Car", "Emergency Fund", "Barcelona 2026"—providing visual cues and celebratory nudges as progress is made. These digital conveniences do more than organise your finances; they help sustain emotional engagement with long-term goals. Better still, they free you from the mental clutter of trying to remember to save.

But not all savings are created equal, and recognising the distinction between short-term and long-term goals is essential. Short-term savings—covering things like seasonal costs, school uniforms, or that inevitable boiler repair—need to be fluid. They should live in accounts that are easy to access and carry no penalties for spontaneous withdrawals. Long-term savings, on the other hand, are earmarked for more substantial aspirations: the dream home, the retirement fund, the kids' university fees. These require patience, strategic placement, and a tolerance for some reduced access in exchange for better returns.

Getting the balance right between the short and the long of it is a continuous act of evaluation. Family priorities shift. Incomes fluctuate. Life throws curveballs. A young couple might focus on saving for a home and starting a family. Ten years on, they might be more concerned with school fees or elderly care. The ability to reallocate without derailing the entire savings plan—that's what financial maturity looks like.

And while we're on the subject of maturity, there's tremendous value in involving children in the savings conversation. Too often, money is either taboo or taught in abstract, lifeless terms. But when saving is made visible and participatory, it becomes a life lesson far more enduring than any lecture. For younger children, the classic savings jar system—spend, save, give—is still remarkably effective. There's something about watching a jar slowly fill that makes the concept of saving real. It teaches patience, yes, but also agency.

As children grow, those jam jars can evolve into junior bank accounts or digital wallets, complete with their own log-ins and savings targets. Giving them modest amounts of money to manage—paired with clear expectations around saving—can plant the seeds of financial literacy early. Parents might consider offering a pound-for-pound match on savings, or creating small incentives when milestones are met. These conversations and practices shape a child's understanding not only of money, but of values: prudence, planning, and the satisfaction of earned rewards.

Beyond the mechanics, families can benefit from embedding saving into their collective rhythm. Maybe it's a monthly review over

Sunday lunch. Maybe it's a savings challenge—who can go the longest without unnecessary spending? Or perhaps it's as simple as celebrating together when a goal is reached. These shared rituals reinforce the notion that saving is a family affair, not a solitary slog. They also cultivate openness about money—an area that, in many households, is still shrouded in awkwardness or secrecy.

At its core, saving isn't just about financial balance sheets—it's about worldview. It reflects a belief that tomorrow matters, that security is worth more than spontaneity, and that progress is built, often quietly, through small but deliberate acts. This mindset, more than any spreadsheet or app, is what will sustain a family's saving habits through good years and lean ones alike.

For many families, saving is not flashy. It doesn't come with the dopamine hit of a new purchase or the instant glow of a luxury splurge. But it offers something deeper and, arguably, more lasting—peace of mind, a sense of control, and the confidence that comes from knowing the future isn't being left to chance. It turns money into a source of strength, not stress.

As this chapter unfolds, one thing becomes clear: there is no single right way to save. Circumstances differ, preferences evolve. Still, the guiding principles endure—make saving a priority, use the right tools, automate what you can, plan for both the near and the far, and teach the next generation to do the same. With consistency and care, these strategies lay the groundwork not only for financial wellbeing, but for the realisation of a family's shared hopes.

In an age marked by economic volatility and relentless marketing of consumption, the simple act of saving stands as both a practical necessity and a quiet form of resistance. Families that embrace this discipline don't just improve their finances—they claim the right to dream, to plan, and to meet the future with assurance and grace.

The Importance of Paying Yourself First

Among the most enduring and transformative principles in personal finance is the concept of paying yourself first. Despite its simplicity, it remains one of the least consistently practised behaviours, often overshadowed by more immediate financial demands and the cultural imperative to consume. Yet its impact on long-term financial security is profound. Paying yourself first is not about selfishness or indulgence; it is about commitment—to your future stability, to your family's aspirations, and to the kind of financial life you intend to build. It repositions saving from a passive, residual activity to an active, non-negotiable priority.

At its core, paying yourself first means setting aside a portion of your income for savings and investment before you attend to any other expenses. This approach contrasts starkly with the more common method of spending first and saving whatever happens to remain. In practice, that usually amounts to very little, if anything at all. By inverting the process—treating savings as the first 'bill' you pay each month—you create a structure that prioritises your financial goals over spontaneous or habitual consumption.

This shift is not merely logistical; it is psychological. When you save first, you signal to yourself that your long-term wellbeing matters. You acknowledge that your future needs are just as important as your present desires. Over time, this mindset becomes self-reinforcing. As savings grow and compound, they generate a sense of agency and control. You are no longer living at the mercy of unexpected expenses, fluctuating income, or economic downturns. Instead, you are building a buffer, a margin of safety that supports resilience and unlocks new opportunities.

For many families, this practice begins with a small, manageable percentage—perhaps 10 or 15 percent of net income—automatically transferred to a separate savings or investment account upon receipt of wages. The amount is less important than the habit. Regularity is what builds momentum. Once saving becomes a fixed part of the household routine, it is no longer subject to debate or delay. It becomes embedded in the financial culture of the family, much like paying rent or buying groceries. The difference, of course, is that this 'payment' goes towards your future, not someone else's.

Consider a working couple with two young children and an average household income. Like many families, they face ongoing expenses—childcare, transportation, utilities, and the occasional unplanned bill. For years, they operated on a spend-first model, hoping to save from what remained. But something always intervened: a birthday, a car repair, a tempting sale. Savings were erratic at best. After reassessing their priorities, they decided to pay themselves first by automatically diverting £300 each month to a dedicated savings account. They adjusted their spending accordingly—not drastically, but consciously. Within a year, they had accumulated a significant emergency fund. Within two, they were on track for a house deposit. What changed was not their income but their intent.

This example illustrates a key truth: paying yourself first is less about capacity and more about consistency. Most people don't save because they believe they can't afford to. But when saving is treated as essential, rather than optional, it becomes an expected part of cash flow. People adapt. They find efficiencies. They re-evaluate discretionary spending. The act of prioritising savings invites a broader examination of values and consumption patterns. It encourages families to ask, "What matters most to us?" and to allocate resources in alignment with the answers.

One of the major advantages of paying yourself first is that it protects against the very human tendency to inflate lifestyle with income. Known as lifestyle creep, this phenomenon describes how expenses naturally rise to match increased earnings, often without deliberate choice. A salary increase, rather than resulting in higher savings, leads to upgraded holidays, more frequent dining out, or subscription accumulation. While enjoyment is not inherently problematic, when it displaces savings, it compromises future freedom. Paying yourself first imposes a pause. It ensures that new income translates into enhanced financial security before it is absorbed by new spending.

Another benefit lies in the compounding effect of early and consistent saving. Even modest contributions, when made regularly and allowed to grow, produce disproportionately large results over time. A family that sets aside £200 a month starting in their 30s, invested with a reasonable return, could accumulate tens of thousands of pounds by the time their children reach university age or they themselves near retirement. This growth is not merely a result of the amount saved, but of time and habit—the two elements most easily secured by paying yourself first.

Technological tools make this process more accessible than ever. Automated transfers, standing orders, and app-based financial platforms allow families to set up and maintain this habit with minimal effort. The key is to make saving invisible—to remove the element of choice and temptation. When money is automatically redirected to a separate account on payday, there is no need for deliberation. It is simply part of the financial rhythm. Many families find success by using accounts that are slightly less accessible—ones that require a login or waiting period—thus reducing the likelihood of casual withdrawals.

Teaching this principle to children and teenagers is equally important. When children observe that savings are not an afterthought but a first priority, they internalise a powerful lesson. They learn that money is not just for spending, but for building. This can be reinforced through allowance systems, where children are encouraged—or required—to save a portion before spending the rest. As they witness their savings accumulate, they develop a tangible sense of progress and self-discipline. These early experiences shape their financial habits for decades to come.

Of course, paying yourself first does not mean ignoring pressing obligations or existing debt. In fact, it works in tandem with other financial responsibilities. A well-structured budget will allocate funds toward essential expenses, minimum debt repayments, and savings simultaneously. In some cases, particularly where high-interest debt is concerned, families may choose to balance savings with aggressive debt repayment. Even then, maintaining a small savings habit ensures continuity and keeps the behaviour intact, even as financial priorities shift.

This principle is especially vital for those with irregular income, such as freelancers, seasonal workers, or entrepreneurs. For these households, income predictability is limited, but the need for savings is amplified. Paying yourself first in this context may mean saving a higher percentage of income during peak months or setting aside income from each project before covering other costs. The discipline to do so is what prevents future cash flow problems and enables long-term planning, even in the face of volatility.

Critics of the pay-yourself-first model often argue that for low-income families, saving before spending is unrealistic. While it is true that structural inequalities and high living costs present genuine challenges, the principle remains relevant at all income levels. Even setting aside £10 per week creates momentum, a habit, and a cushion. It signals that financial security is worth prioritising, even in constrained circumstances. Over time, small amounts add up, and the habit becomes scalable as income grows.

Moreover, this practice creates emotional benefits that extend beyond finances. It instils a sense of control in a world where money can often feel unpredictable. It reduces stress by building buffers. It encourages goal-setting and forward thinking. It shifts the household narrative from scarcity and reaction to intention and preparation. And it fosters a culture of self-respect—one that acknowledges that your future deserves as much care and attention as your present.

In family life, where competing demands are constant and financial pressures unrelenting, it is easy to defer saving for another time. But time, once lost, cannot be reclaimed. The earlier and more consistently families adopt the practice of paying themselves first, the more resilient they become—not just to financial shocks, but to the psychological wear and tear of living from one paycheque to the next.

Paying yourself first is not a trick or a trend. It is a timeless principle grounded in behavioural finance and common sense. It works not because it is flashy, but because it is dependable. It leverages routine to produce extraordinary outcomes over time. For families who seek not just to survive but to build, it is an indispensable starting point. Through this one act—simple, repeatable, and profoundly impactful—families lay the first stone in the foundation of their financial future. And from that foundation, everything else becomes more possible.

Best Savings Accounts for Families

For families striving to build financial stability, choosing the right place to keep their savings is not a trivial decision. The type of savings account selected can dramatically affect how quickly funds grow, how easily they are accessed, and how disciplined the family remains in pursuit of their goals. As with all financial tools, the best savings account is not a one-size-fits-all solution; it is a matter of matching needs, timelines, and financial habits to the features and benefits offered by different account types. Whether saving for an emergency fund, a child's education, a home deposit, or a long-anticipated holiday, understanding how to maximise savings through appropriate accounts is essential.

At the top of the list for many families seeking to earn more from their deposits are high-yield savings accounts. These accounts offer interest rates significantly above the national average, allowing money to grow passively over time. Often found at online banks or credit unions, high-yield accounts tend to outperform traditional current or standard savings accounts offered by high street banks. The reason is simple: online institutions have lower overhead costs and can pass those savings on to consumers in the form of higher returns.

A family with £10,000 sitting in a conventional savings account earning 0.5% interest annually would accrue just £50 in interest over the course of a year. In contrast, a high-yield account offering 3.5% would yield £350 in the same period—a difference that compounds significantly over time. The impact becomes more pronounced with larger balances or longer saving horizons. This makes high-yield accounts an ideal place to store emergency funds or short-term savings goals that require liquidity but still benefit from interest accrual.

It is important, however, to assess more than just the advertised interest rate. Families should examine whether the rate is variable or fixed, what minimum balances are required, whether fees are charged for withdrawals or inactivity, and how frequently interest is compounded. Daily compounding, for instance, allows for faster growth than monthly or annual interest structures. Also, while online-only banks often offer the best rates, families should consider ease of access, mobile app functionality, and customer support reliability when choosing a provider.

For medium-term goals or savings that do not require immediate access, fixed-rate savings products like Certificates of Deposit (CDs)—or fixed-term savings accounts, as they're more commonly known in the UK—can be a valuable addition to the family financial toolkit. These accounts lock in a fixed interest rate for a predetermined period, ranging from a few months to several years. In exchange for this commitment, they typically offer higher returns than regular savings accounts. For families who have earmarked a portion of their savings for a specific future use—such as school fees due in two years or a home renovation planned for next summer—fixed-term savings accounts provide a disciplined way to grow money while avoiding the temptation to dip into the funds prematurely.

The main trade-off with such accounts is liquidity. Early withdrawals usually incur penalties, which means they should not be used for emergency funds or flexible spending needs. However, they work exceptionally well when paired with more accessible accounts. For example, a family might keep three months' worth of essential expenses in a high-yield account for emergencies while placing additional savings in staggered fixed-term products with varying maturity dates. This strategy, often referred to as a savings ladder, provides both growth and access over time.

Another valuable option for families looking to maximise savings is the use of Individual Savings Accounts (ISAs), particularly cash ISAs and Junior ISAs in the UK context. A cash ISA allows individuals to earn interest on their savings without paying income tax on the returns, making it especially beneficial for higher-rate taxpayers or those with larger savings balances. Although interest rates on ISAs have not always matched those of the best high-yield accounts, the tax advantages can make them more profitable in real terms. For families saving toward long-term objectives, such as higher education or a property purchase, ISAs offer a compelling blend of growth and tax efficiency.

Junior ISAs, on the other hand, are designed to help parents and guardians save for their children's future. Contributions are capped annually, but the interest earned is tax-free, and the funds are locked until the child turns eighteen. This structure makes Junior ISAs an ideal vehicle for building a university fund or providing a financial head start in adulthood. The restricted access also aligns with many families' intentions—ensuring that the money remains untouched until it is genuinely needed. Importantly, Junior ISAs serve an educational purpose as well, giving children a sense of financial continuity and purpose as they approach financial independence.

Technology has further expanded the options available to families through innovative fintech solutions that combine the best features of traditional savings accounts with digital convenience. Many apps now offer goal-based savings features, allowing users to allocate money into virtual "buckets" or "pots" for specific purposes within a single account. For instance, a family might create one pot for a holiday, another for Christmas expenses, and a third for emergency repairs. This mental and visual separation of funds supports better decision-making, as it reduces the likelihood of overspending from a shared pool and clarifies the progress made toward each goal.

Some platforms also offer round-up features, where purchases made using a linked debit card are rounded up to the nearest pound and the spare change is automatically saved. Though seemingly minor, these micro-savings accumulate steadily, particularly when combined with regular contributions. For families who struggle to find spare funds at the end of each month, these small, automatic increments can create momentum without imposing noticeable strain on the budget.

Choosing the right combination of accounts often depends on a family's stage of life and financial priorities. A young couple with no children might focus on building an emergency fund and saving for a home, prioritising high-yield and fixed-term savings A family with school-aged children may place greater emphasis on ISAs and Junior ISAs, aiming to support education costs or future transitions. Meanwhile, a multi-generational household supporting both young dependents and ageing parents may need a more diversified approach—balancing accessibility, growth, and tax efficiency in a cohesive strategy.

It is also worth noting that the best savings accounts do not operate in isolation. They are part of a broader financial system that includes budgeting, debt management, and investing. The account alone does not determine success; it is how consistently and intentionally it is used. An excellent savings product with a high return is of little value if contributions are irregular or if funds are frequently withdrawn for non-essential spending. Therefore, the discipline of saving—automating deposits, reviewing goals, and monitoring growth—is as important as the technical features of the account itself.

Regular financial reviews can help ensure that savings accounts continue to meet the family's needs. Interest rates change, new products enter the market, and personal circumstances evolve. A savings account that was ideal two years ago may no longer be competitive or aligned with current goals. Many families benefit from conducting an annual audit of their savings—reviewing balances, interest rates, maturity dates, and liquidity needs—to make adjustments as necessary. This proactive approach ensures that their money continues to work efficiently and supports evolving priorities.

Finally, choosing a savings account is not just a financial decision; it is also a behavioural one. The right account supports the family's habits, reinforces its values, and reduces barriers to saving. Whether the goal is to create security, fund aspirations, or teach children about financial stewardship, the right accounts make those goals more achievable. They provide a framework within which discipline is easier to maintain, progress is visible, and savings become an integrated part of daily life.

In a financial landscape increasingly defined by complexity and consumer pressure, families who approach saving with clarity, intention, and the right tools position themselves not just for short-term stability, but for enduring strength. The accounts they choose are not merely repositories for money—they are instruments of empowerment, helping households transform earnings into opportunity, and intention into impact. With the right strategy and ongoing engagement, every pound saved becomes a building block in a future shaped by foresight and resilience.

Automating Savings for Success

Saving money is one of the most universally recommended personal finance habits, yet for many individuals and families, it remains a persistent challenge. Despite the best of intentions, saving often becomes an afterthought—a practice relegated to whatever funds might remain at the end of the month, which are frequently negligible or quickly diverted by unplanned expenses. The modern financial landscape, however, offers a powerful solution to this dilemma: automation. By leveraging technology to remove the friction of manual saving, families can create a system that not only simplifies the process but dramatically increases the likelihood of long-term financial success.

At the heart of automation is a behavioural insight that has been widely validated by economists and psychologists alike: when good behaviours are made easy and consistent, they are more likely to endure. Automating savings transforms it from a decision that must be actively made into a routine that happens by default. Rather than relying on willpower, discipline, or the presence of surplus funds, automation ensures that saving occurs regardless of changing moods or shifting priorities. It reconfigures the household's financial habits from reactive to proactive, instilling a rhythm of preparation rather than one of recovery.

One of the simplest and most effective methods for automating savings is the establishment of a standing order or scheduled transfer from a current account to a designated savings account. By timing this transfer to occur immediately after income is received—whether weekly, fortnightly, or monthly—families replicate the discipline of paying a bill, except in this case, the recipient is their future self. This small act, repeated consistently, creates a foundation of financial resilience that strengthens over time.

For example, consider a couple who receive their salaries on the 28th of each month. By setting up an automatic transfer of £300 to their savings account on the 29th, they guarantee that a portion of their income is set aside before other spending begins. They are not left to wrestle with whether they can afford to save after paying their bills or indulging in discretionary purchases. Instead, saving becomes a fixed feature of their cash flow—predictable, sustainable, and largely invisible.

The power of invisibility should not be underestimated. When savings are automatically deducted and housed in a separate account—especially one that is not linked to a debit card or easily accessible—families are less tempted to dip into these funds for non-essentials. Out of sight truly does mean out of mind, and this mental separation reinforces the perception that the money is unavailable for casual use. Over time, this reinforces the behaviour loop of saving, reward, and increased confidence.

Technology has significantly expanded the tools available for automating savings beyond traditional standing orders. Fintech platforms and digital banking apps now offer highly customisable solutions that cater to diverse family needs and preferences. Many apps allow users to create virtual "pots" or "buckets" within a single account, each designated for a different goal—emergency funds, holidays, school expenses, or home improvements. These sub-accounts enable families to visualise their goals and track progress in real time, making the act of saving more tangible and emotionally satisfying.

Round-up features are another innovation that has gained popularity, particularly among younger savers. These features round up each transaction to the nearest pound and automatically deposit the spare change into a savings account. While the amounts are small, they add up quickly, especially when paired with regular contributions. A parent purchasing weekly groceries might not notice the extra 75 pence being set aside, but over several months, that spare change can accumulate into a meaningful fund for

Christmas gifts or school supplies. This form of "stealth saving" is particularly effective for individuals who find it difficult to commit to larger, scheduled contributions.

Other platforms take automation a step further by using algorithms to analyse income and spending patterns, then determining safe amounts to move into savings without compromising bill payments or day-to-day expenses. These tools, often powered by artificial intelligence, remove the guesswork from saving and adapt dynamically to changes in financial behaviour. For families with fluctuating income—such as freelancers, shift workers, or those in seasonal employment—this kind of adaptive automation can provide a welcome buffer against the unpredictability of earnings.

Despite the advantages of automation, some families may hesitate to embrace it fully due to fears of overcommitting or concerns about losing control. These concerns are valid and underscore the importance of starting with modest amounts and adjusting gradually. Automation should feel empowering, not restrictive. If the amount transferred is too aggressive, it may lead to frequent withdrawals, which can undermine the habit and create frustration. A better approach is to begin with an amount that feels manageable—even £25 a week—and increase it over time as confidence and capacity grow.

Communication is also key when automation involves shared accounts or joint financial goals. Partners should discuss their expectations, review their automated systems regularly, and agree on how savings will be used. For instance, one parent may want to save aggressively for a child's future education, while the other may prioritise building a buffer for unforeseen medical costs. Aligning these priorities ensures that the automation supports shared values and avoids potential conflict. Regular financial check-ins—perhaps monthly or quarterly—allow families to assess whether their savings strategies are working and make adjustments as needed.

Children, too, can benefit from the concept of automated saving. While they may not have formal accounts initially, parents can simulate automation through consistent allowance structures that require a portion of money to be set aside before spending. As children grow older and acquire bank accounts, they can be encouraged to set up their own standing orders into youth savings accounts. This early exposure to automated systems builds familiarity and normalises the behaviour, reducing the likelihood that saving will be viewed as burdensome in adulthood.

Employers can also play a role in supporting automated savings. Some companies offer payroll deductions for savings accounts, retirement contributions, or savings schemes such as Help to Save in the UK. Where available, these programmes are invaluable tools for low- and moderate-income families, as they combine automation with employer incentives or government matches. Families should explore whether such options are offered by their employers and take full advantage of any schemes that align with their financial goals.

The cumulative effect of automating savings is difficult to overstate. Over weeks, months, and years, what begins as a small transfer grows into a substantial reserve. This financial buffer provides not only practical support in times of need but also psychological assurance. Families who have a solid savings foundation report lower levels of financial anxiety, greater confidence in decision-making, and more optimism about the future. They are also better positioned to respond to unexpected opportunities—such as educational courses, home improvements, or entrepreneurial ventures—because they are not shackled by immediate financial limitations.

Moreover, automation enables families to focus their energy on higher-order financial decisions. When savings are taken care of, they can devote more attention to debt reduction, investment planning, and wealth building. It shifts the financial narrative from survival to strategy. In this sense, automation is not just a tool—it is a catalyst for upward mobility and long-term prosperity.

Yet it must be remembered that automation, for all its benefits, is only as effective as the intentions behind it. Setting up automatic transfers without a clear goal can lead to disengagement or a lack of motivation. Families should revisit their financial objectives regularly and use their savings systems in service of those aims.

Whether it's securing a child's future, achieving homeownership, travelling together, or simply sleeping more peacefully at night, automated savings are a means to those ends—not an end in themselves.

As digital tools become more sophisticated and accessible, the opportunity to make saving seamless and habitual has never been greater. Families that embrace these tools, while staying grounded in their values and goals, will find that saving becomes less of a struggle and more of a strength. It becomes an integrated, almost invisible part of life—quietly working in the background, laying the groundwork for resilience, flexibility, and freedom.

In a world where demands on time and attention are constant, automation offers a rare reprieve. It enables families to make wise choices once and let those choices carry forward, reinforcing good habits without requiring daily effort. In doing so, it transforms saving from a chore into a lifestyle—one that builds security not through sudden leaps, but through steady, consistent steps that compound into meaningful progress. For any family serious about their financial future, automation is not just helpful; it is indispensable.

Short-Term vs. Long-Term Savings

Effective financial planning requires more than the discipline to save—it demands clarity about *why* we are saving. Families juggle a multitude of financial priorities, many of which unfold on very different timelines. A holiday next summer, a child's birthday in two months, a home deposit five years from now, or a retirement that may still be decades away—each of these goals calls for a distinct strategy. To manage these varied demands, it is essential to distinguish between short-term and long-term savings and to structure financial habits around both horizons.

Short-term savings refer to money set aside for expenses expected within the next one to three years. These may include planned costs such as school uniforms, medical treatments, home repairs, car maintenance, or special occasions. While not emergencies per se, they are foreseeable events that will require funding. Long-term savings, by contrast, are funds reserved for future goals with a more distant horizon—typically five years or more. This category includes saving for higher education, purchasing a property, starting a business, or building a retirement fund.

Understanding the distinction is not merely semantic—it has practical implications for where money is held, how it is accessed, and what kind of risks and returns are acceptable. Short-term savings must prioritise liquidity and stability. Because these funds are needed within a predictable time frame, they should be stored in low-risk, easily accessible accounts, such as high-yield savings accounts or short-term fixed-rate deposits. The emphasis here is not on maximising returns but on capital preservation and ready access.

Consider a family planning a summer holiday a year from now. If they estimate the cost at £2,000, they might divide that amount into monthly savings targets and store it in a separate, labelled savings account. This approach allows them to track progress while insulating the money from everyday spending. If, instead, they were to invest that amount in a volatile market-based product in the hope of a better return, they could risk falling short if the market dips when the funds are needed. With short-term goals, predictability matters more than performance.

For long-term savings, however, a different approach is warranted. When the timeline stretches to five, ten, or twenty years, the opportunity to pursue higher returns becomes more viable and often necessary to outpace inflation and build meaningful wealth. Here, families might explore tax-efficient investment accounts such as Stocks and Shares ISAs, long-term fixed-rate products, or retirement-specific accounts like pensions or SIPPs. The longer time horizon allows for greater risk tolerance and the potential to recover from market fluctuations, making investment a prudent strategy for these objectives.

Take, for example, a couple with a newborn child who wishes to save for university fees eighteen years down the line. Placing money solely in a low-interest savings account might preserve the capital but offers limited growth. By allocating part of the savings to a diversified investment portfolio, they can leverage compounding returns and potentially accumulate a much larger sum by the time their child begins higher education. Of course, such an approach requires careful planning, regular reviews, and a willingness to accept interim volatility in pursuit of longer-term growth.

The challenge many families face is managing both types of savings concurrently. Short-term needs often feel more pressing, and it is easy for long-term goals to be postponed or underfunded. A well-structured financial plan addresses this by treating both categories as essential and integrating them into the monthly budget. Automating transfers into separate accounts for short- and long-term goals ensures that neither is neglected. Over time, this dual-track strategy builds not just financial capacity but flexibility—the ability to address current needs without compromising the future.

One useful analogy is that of a train journey with multiple stops. Short-term savings are the local stops—frequent, necessary, and close together. Long-term savings are the destination—the reason for the trip itself. If the traveller only focuses on the next stop, they may lose sight of where they're ultimately heading. But if they ignore the nearby stations, they might miss opportunities or encounter avoidable setbacks. The key is to plan for both, acknowledging their different functions and adjusting strategies accordingly.

Real-world examples illustrate how this balance plays out in everyday life. A family might be saving for a new car in the next twelve months while also contributing to a pension. The car fund requires a low-risk, liquid account to ensure funds are available when the time comes to buy. The pension, on the other hand, benefits from long-term investment, possibly through an employer scheme that offers matching contributions. By differentiating the strategies for these goals, the family ensures that immediate plans are met without compromising future financial security.

The psychological dimension of short- and long-term savings should not be overlooked. Short-term goals provide motivation and gratification. Achieving them reinforces the value of saving and encourages continued discipline. Long-term goals, while less immediately rewarding, offer a sense of purpose and vision. Together, they form a virtuous cycle: short-term wins build momentum for sustained long-term behaviour, and long-term aspirations give meaning to the sacrifices made in the present.

Families can also use these distinctions to involve children in financial learning. Short-term goals like saving for a toy, school trip, or birthday celebration provide an opportunity to teach budgeting, delayed gratification, and the satisfaction of reaching a goal. Long-term savings—perhaps for university or their first car—introduce the concept of planning ahead and show how regular effort yields significant rewards over time. By modelling this dual approach, parents equip their children with tools and habits that will serve them well into adulthood.

Importantly, both types of savings contribute to financial resilience. Short-term savings help absorb unexpected costs without derailing the household budget. They reduce reliance on credit cards, overdrafts, or high-interest loans in times of need. Long-term savings provide security against more systemic risks—like income loss in retirement, inflation, or the inability to support a child's education. Together, they form a protective buffer that guards against the financial uncertainties of life.

Some families find it helpful to visualise their savings goals using charts, apps, or physical tools like savings jars and goal boards. This visual reinforcement clarifies the purpose of each fund and maintains engagement. For example, a family might have a digital tracker showing progress toward a holiday, alongside a long-term investment dashboard showing projected retirement growth. Seeing both in parallel reminds them of the broader context and the importance of balance.

The practice of reviewing savings strategies regularly is equally critical. Life changes—such as a new baby, job transition, illness, or inheritance—can shift priorities and alter timelines. Annual or biannual reviews allow families to recalibrate their contributions, adjust for inflation, and reaffirm their goals. These check-ins also help surface any imbalances, such as over-saving for a long-term goal while neglecting a short-term need, or vice versa.

Ultimately, the distinction between short-term and long-term savings is not merely academic—it is deeply practical. It informs how families allocate their resources, how they navigate trade-offs, and how they construct a life that honours both present needs and future dreams. When these categories are clearly defined and thoughtfully managed, saving becomes not just a financial act but a strategic one. It becomes a framework for living with purpose, planning with clarity, and responding to life's challenges with preparedness rather than panic.

For families seeking to build stability and prosperity, mastering the balance between short- and long-term savings is indispensable. It requires intention, communication, and ongoing attention—but the rewards are substantial. Not just in terms of money accumulated, but in peace of mind earned, opportunities created, and values reinforced. In the end, it is this thoughtful balance that transforms saving from a vague aspiration into a powerful, life-shaping habit.

Teaching Kids the Power of Saving

Helping children understand the value of money is one of the most enduring gifts a parent or caregiver can offer. It is a foundational skill that not only equips them to navigate future financial responsibilities but also shapes their attitudes towards discipline, patience, and long-term thinking. At the heart of this education is the concept of saving—delaying gratification today to achieve something meaningful tomorrow. Teaching children the power of saving doesn't require complicated financial systems or formal instruction. What it does require is consistency, modelling, and hands-on experience that links intention to outcome in tangible, age-appropriate ways.

Children's early impressions of money are formed not through lectures but through observation. They watch the adults in their lives—how they speak about money, how they make spending decisions, and how they react to financial stress. A parent who regularly sets aside money for goals, who discusses financial priorities openly, and who models contentment in moderation is already laying the groundwork for a child's financial literacy. But to move from observation to understanding, children also need direct involvement. This is where practical tools such as savings jars, structured allowances, and goal-setting come into play.

The use of savings jars is a remarkably effective entry point for younger children. Physical, visible, and interactive, jars make the abstract concept of saving concrete. A child can see the coins accumulating over time, feel the weight increasing, and experience the satisfaction of watching their efforts build toward something purposeful. Typically, three jars are used, each labelled for a different function—saving, spending, and giving. Some families add a fourth jar for investing or larger future goals, depending on the child's age and comprehension. The act of dividing pocket money into these categories helps children internalise the idea that money is not a singular entity but a resource with multiple uses and responsibilities.

For example, a six-year-old who receives a weekly allowance of £2 might be guided to place £1 in the saving jar, 50 pence in the giving jar, and 50 pence in the spending jar. Over time, the child will learn that the money in the spending jar can be used immediately for small items like sweets or toys, while the savings jar is intended for something larger—a board game, a trip to the zoo, or even a contribution to a family purchase. The giving jar might go to a charity of their choice or be used to buy a gift for a sibling. This early experience introduces key financial principles: prioritisation, allocation, and the satisfaction of achieving a self-defined goal.

As children grow older, the system evolves. Physical jars may give way to spreadsheets, mobile apps, or junior bank accounts, but the structure remains. Introducing a formal allowance at this stage becomes particularly valuable. An allowance provides a predictable, controlled opportunity for children to practise financial decision-making in a safe environment. It shifts the focus from asking for money to managing it. When tied to expectations—such as completing household responsibilities or meeting school targets—

an allowance also reinforces the relationship between effort and reward, a core tenet of financial success.

The amount given is less important than the structure and consistency. A ten-year-old receiving £5 a week can be encouraged to plan how much will be saved, spent, or donated. Regular conversations about how those decisions unfold—why a certain purchase felt worth it or how saving for a new game took effort—turn each week's allowance into a micro-lesson in budgeting, trade-offs, and intentionality. Parents can guide rather than dictate these choices, allowing children to make small mistakes, reflect on them, and adjust. A child who spends their entire allowance on a novelty item and then has to wait two weeks to afford a desired book will experience a memorable lesson in opportunity cost—far more effectively than through a parental lecture.

Goal-setting adds another critical layer to the learning process. When children save toward something meaningful to them, they build not only discipline but emotional investment. The process of defining a goal, breaking it into smaller savings milestones, and tracking progress activates a sense of ownership and delayed gratification. The goal might be as simple as a new set of art supplies or as significant as contributing to a class trip. What matters is that it belongs to the child and requires effort over time.

Parents can support this by helping children create visual trackers—charts or graphs on the fridge that show how close they are to reaching their goal. Digital tools can also help, with apps designed for young savers that gamify the experience and allow real-time monitoring. Progress updates become moments of encouragement and reflection, reinforcing the value of perseverance. Celebrating milestones along the way—such as reaching the halfway mark—adds motivation and joy to the process, keeping the child engaged and inspired.

Importantly, teaching the power of saving does not mean eliminating all spontaneity or restricting enjoyment. Children, like adults, benefit from the ability to spend occasionally on fun and non-essential items. Allowing them to do so within the framework of a spending category teaches them to enjoy money responsibly. It also prevents saving from becoming associated with deprivation or moral rigidity. A balanced approach helps children see money as a tool—one that can be used wisely, enjoyed thoughtfully, and managed with care.

Real-world experiences further reinforce the lessons learned at home. Taking children to the bank to deposit money into their account, or showing them how interest accumulates over time, introduces them to broader financial systems. Discussing family financial decisions—like planning for a holiday, budgeting for birthdays, or postponing a purchase—provides context for how saving operates at the household level. Children begin to see that adults, too, make trade-offs and must plan ahead to afford what they value. These conversations, when handled with transparency and age-appropriate language, foster financial empathy and shared understanding.

It is also helpful to involve children in minor family budgeting tasks. They might help compare prices at the supermarket, assist in tracking a small household expense, or participate in deciding how to allocate a family entertainment budget. These activities link saving to everyday life and show that financial decisions are a regular, shared responsibility. As children mature, parents can introduce more complex topics such as income, taxes, or investment basics—building a scaffolded financial education that evolves alongside the child's development.

The ultimate goal is not simply to produce children who know how to save money but to nurture individuals who value foresight, understand scarcity, and are empowered to make thoughtful financial choices. Saving, after all, is about more than money—it is about setting goals, exercising patience, and creating a sense of control over one's future. It is about recognising that immediate desires can be weighed against longer-term benefits, and that self-discipline leads not to limitation but to expanded freedom.

In the context of a family, this education is best delivered through consistency and modelling. Children must see that the adults in their lives practise what they teach—that saving is not just encouraged but exemplified. When they observe their parents budgeting, delaying purchases, or celebrating a savings milestone, they absorb those values. When conversations about money are open, frequent, and positive, children learn to approach finances with confidence rather than fear or secrecy.

Ultimately, teaching kids the power of saving is not about rigid formulas or perfection. It is about creating an environment where saving feels natural, purposeful, and rewarding. It is about offering experiences that allow children to connect effort with outcome, to make mistakes in a safe context, and to grow into financial habits that support their wellbeing for years to come.

By starting early, engaging consistently, and building on their evolving understanding, families can raise children who not only save but thrive—children who grow into adults capable of navigating a complex financial world with clarity, integrity, and intentionality. In doing so, they give their children not just a skill, but a lifelong advantage.

Chapter 4
Investing as a Family — Growing Wealth Together

For many families, the word *investing* tends to stir equal parts curiosity and caution. Saving feels familiar, almost cosy—something we're taught to do from an early age. Investing, though? That can seem distant, a bit esoteric, maybe even risky. But here's the truth: when you take a broader view of financial wellbeing, investing isn't just for the affluent or the financially fluent—it's a cornerstone of sustainable prosperity. More than simply accumulating money, investing is about making time your ally, harnessing compound returns, and putting your hard-earned cash to work. It's the bridge that turns consistent saving into enduring wealth, potentially spanning generations.

Why does investing matter so much? Because inflation, relentless and invisible, chips away at the value of money over time. Leave your savings in a low-interest account for ten or twenty years and you'll discover that the pound you protected so carefully has quietly diminished in purchasing power. Investing, however, provides a means not merely to protect value but to increase it. Whether through equities, property, or other income-producing avenues, investing shifts a family's role in the financial system—from passive savers to active stakeholders in wealth creation.

A common misconception persists: that investing demands vast sums, intricate knowledge, or perfect timing. Not so. In fact, getting started can be surprisingly straightforward—and even enlightening. Take the stock market. Once considered the domain of the initiated few, it's now more accessible than ever. User-friendly platforms, zero-commission trades, and fractional shares mean that families can invest modest amounts into global businesses, diversified index funds, or exchange-traded funds (ETFs) with relative ease. These tools open a window into the broader economy, allowing families to earn returns not only from price appreciation but also through dividends.

The mechanics of stock market investing needn't be overwhelming. Families can approach it as a shared learning experience—exploring together what it means to own equity in a company, how dividends are paid, or why spreading risk across sectors (diversification) matters. ETFs and index funds are an excellent starting point. Take, for example, an ETF tracking the FTSE 100. With one simple product, you're investing in a broad slice of the UK's leading businesses—mitigating the potential blow if one or two underperform. That kind of diversification offers peace of mind, especially for those just stepping onto the investment path.

Property, too, holds strong appeal—particularly for those thinking across decades rather than years. Owning real estate, whether it's a family home, a rental flat, or a stake in a property trust, delivers not just potential capital gains but often a reliable stream of income. It's tangible. It's familiar. And with prudent planning, it can be transformative. Consider a family purchasing a modest second property in a town on the cusp of revitalisation. If managed carefully, rental income covers costs, the property appreciates, and before long, it becomes a financial lever—funding a university degree, seeding a business venture, or bolstering retirement. And when children are looped into managing the asset—tracking income, inspecting repairs, learning the ins and outs of tenant relations—they're gaining something no textbook can offer: practical fluency in real-world finance.

Of course, the investment landscape stretches far beyond shares and bricks-and-mortar. Families can explore other avenues that align with their values, energy, and appetite for risk. Dividend stocks, which provide regular income from company profits, are a favourite among those looking to reinvest and accelerate growth. For the more entrepreneurial, launching a side business—perhaps something that draws on family expertise or creativity—can generate additional income and even become a legacy project. Then there are less traditional but still viable options like peer-to-peer lending or digital product royalties. What binds these choices is a shared principle: cultivate income-producing assets that don't demand constant oversight. This is the essence of passive income—and over time, it brings not just financial cushioning but real freedom of choice.

One strategy that deserves far more attention is investing on behalf of children. Start early enough, and the magic of compound interest does most of the heavy lifting. Through Junior ISAs, custodial accounts, or similar vehicles, parents can begin building wealth for their children in a structured, tax-efficient way. The key is consistency—even modest, regular contributions can grow handsomely across 15 or 20 years. And more than the financial boost, this act carries emotional resonance: it says to a child, *your future matters enough for us to plant these seeds today.*

Having clear goals sharpens investment decisions. Each family's vision will differ—perhaps early retirement, debt-free education, a sabbatical abroad, or leaving behind a charitable legacy. These aspirations should anchor the investment approach. Shorter-term goals typically warrant conservative strategies, while longer timelines permit calculated risks. Articulating these aims aloud, aligning on priorities, and revisiting them periodically turns investing into a collective journey. It ceases to be a solitary task delegated to one financially savvy member and instead becomes a shared project, deepening trust and understanding within the household.

Just as importantly, involving children in investment conversations builds lasting financial literacy. When a parent explains why they've chosen to invest in a particular fund, or what a return-on-investment really means, they demystify a process often seen as off-limits. Kids begin to grasp that investing isn't wizardry—it's planning, patience, and paying attention. They begin to internalise a way of thinking that views money not as a static resource to be spent or hoarded, but as a tool that can be grown, shared, and stewarded.

Some families formalise this learning by establishing regular investment check-ins. Maybe it's once a month, maybe quarterly—whatever fits. These meetings might include reviewing a portfolio's performance, discussing headlines from the financial pages, or debating a new opportunity. Over time, they become rituals that foster reflection, strategic thinking, and a sense of ownership—qualities as valuable as any return on capital.

That said, investing is not without risk. Markets can—and do—wobble. Property values sometimes slip. Not every side hustle will flourish. But these aren't reasons to avoid investing; they're reminders to be measured, to spread risk, and to remain focused on the long arc. Families who invest with clarity, restraint, and long-term thinking are more likely to weather volatility and emerge not only intact, but wiser for the experience.

And we mustn't forget: not all returns are financial. When a child learns to track the performance of their investment account, that's a gain in confidence. When a rental property pays for a long-overdue holiday, that's a return in shared joy. When knowledge and know-how are passed from one generation to the next, the value lies beyond the balance sheet. These are dividends of a different kind—human, relational, lasting.

In essence, family investing is about far more than multiplying money. It's about exercising agency. It's about claiming the power to shape your future rather than surrendering to circumstance. It's about showing children that wealth isn't something you stumble upon—it's something you cultivate, with patience, vision, and grit. And it's about building a base from which each generation can reach a little further, dream a little bigger, and stand a little steadier.

In the following pages, we'll unpack the practical tools available to families of every income level—from beginner-friendly investment accounts to the ins and outs of property acquisition, passive income strategies, and beyond. Whether you're just beginning or fine-tuning an existing approach, these ideas are designed to help your family not only preserve wealth—but grow it. Not only to hope for the future—but to shape it.

Why Investing is Key to Long-Term Wealth

The foundation of long-term financial security is not built solely on saving; it is built on investing. While saving money ensures liquidity and short-term stability, investing enables wealth to grow, adapt, and endure. This distinction is not semantic—it is structural. Saving protects, but investing propels. For families aiming to achieve not only comfort in the present but prosperity in the future, understanding the essential role of investing is vital.

At the heart of this imperative is inflation. Though it often goes unnoticed in everyday transactions, inflation steadily diminishes the purchasing power of money. A pound today will not buy the same amount of goods or services ten years from now. When money is left idle in accounts offering minimal interest—often below the rate of inflation—it effectively loses value over time. What seems like a prudent act of caution can inadvertently become a slow erosion of financial potential.

To illustrate this, consider a family that saves £10,000 in a standard savings account earning 0.5% interest annually, while inflation averages 3%. After ten years, the account balance may show a modest increase, but the actual value of that money—the real goods and services it can purchase—has declined. The family has technically saved, but they have not preserved value. Investing, by contrast, offers the possibility of beating inflation through returns that not only maintain but increase purchasing power over time.

The most compelling reason to invest is the power of compounding—interest earned on interest, or gains that generate further gains. This mathematical phenomenon, described by Albert Einstein as the "eighth wonder of the world," accelerates growth significantly over long periods. A modest investment, if made early and left untouched, can outpace larger, later contributions thanks to this exponential effect. For example, investing £200 a month from age thirty to sixty at an average annual return of 7% yields nearly £240,000. If the same investment begins at forty, the final figure drops by almost half, even with the same monthly contribution.

This compounding effect underscores why time in the market is more powerful than timing the market. Attempting to predict when to buy or sell assets based on short-term fluctuations is a strategy fraught with risk and typically favours professionals with access to advanced tools and data. For families, the more reliable path is long-term, consistent investment—riding out volatility in exchange for steady, upward momentum over time. Markets will dip and recover, often unpredictably, but historically they trend upward. The key is to remain engaged through the ups and downs, allowing growth to unfold across decades rather than weeks or months.

Beyond protecting against inflation and leveraging compounding, investing also builds passive income—regular earnings from assets that do not require continuous effort. This income can come from dividends paid on stocks, interest from bonds, or rent from property. For families, passive income offers a critical advantage: it introduces an additional stream of cash flow that supports everyday expenses, emergency buffers, or future savings goals without being tied to a traditional salary. Over time, this income can supplement or even replace employment income, providing greater flexibility and financial independence.

Take, for instance, a couple who, over fifteen years, invest in a diversified portfolio of dividend-paying shares. With consistent reinvestment, their portfolio grows both in capital and in income generation. By the time they reach their late forties, the dividends alone contribute several thousand pounds annually—effectively a part-time income stream with no ongoing labour. This supplemental income not only enhances their lifestyle but also reduces their dependency on work-related income, freeing them to make different life choices: reducing working hours, starting a business, or retiring earlier than expected.

Property investment offers another route to passive income, though it comes with a different risk and management profile. A well-chosen rental property can provide steady monthly income while also appreciating in value. For families with the means to acquire and maintain real estate, it becomes a dual-purpose asset: a source of regular income and long-term capital gain. While property management entails more hands-on effort than equities, it also provides tangible value and a hedge against market volatility, making it an attractive component in a diversified wealth strategy.

The accessibility of investing today marks a significant cultural shift. Historically, investing was perceived as the preserve of the affluent or the financially savvy—a world dominated by brokers, jargon, and gatekeepers. Now, with the rise of digital platforms, fractional shares, and no-commission trading, families of all income levels can begin investing with small amounts. A parent can set up an investment account from a smartphone, allocate £50 to a global index fund, and monitor its progress with a few taps. These changes democratise access and reduce the barriers that once prevented everyday families from building long-term wealth.

However, accessibility does not eliminate the need for education. Families must still make informed decisions—choosing between asset classes, balancing risk, and setting realistic expectations. It is essential to understand that investing is not a guarantee of quick returns or easy riches. It is a long-term strategy grounded in patience, diversification, and adaptability. Portfolios should reflect a family's financial goals, time horizon, and comfort with risk. A young couple saving for a first home may invest differently than a family approaching retirement. The point is not to mimic others but to develop a coherent, personalised investment plan that supports your specific aspirations.

Teaching children about investing is another powerful benefit of adopting a family-based investment approach. When parents involve their children in age-appropriate discussions about stocks, compounding, or even property values, they plant the seeds of financial literacy early. A teenager who understands how a £100 investment can become £200 or £300 over time is more likely to appreciate the value of saving and less likely to fall prey to consumer debt or impulsive spending. Moreover, witnessing their family's commitment to long-term investing helps normalise the behaviour. It becomes part of their identity, not an abstract ideal.

Many families choose to invest directly for their children's future through tools like Junior ISAs, custodial accounts, or education savings plans. These accounts allow investments to grow tax-free or tax-deferred, providing a substantial head start when children reach adulthood. Beyond the financial benefits, these actions carry symbolic weight—they show children that their family is planning ahead for their future, instilling confidence and a sense of continuity.

It is worth emphasising that investing is not about perfection. Markets fluctuate, mistakes are inevitable, and not every investment will perform as expected. But success in investing does not hinge on flawless execution. It depends on persistence, reflection, and incremental improvement. Families that review their strategies annually, rebalance their portfolios, and adjust to new life circumstances will find that the act of investing becomes not only a financial habit but a philosophical one—a belief in progress, compound growth, and the ability to shape the future through deliberate action.

Furthermore, the act of investing changes how families think about money. It reframes financial decisions from short-term transactions to long-term contributions. The choice to invest is the choice to delay consumption in favour of building something lasting. It teaches patience, resilience, and vision—qualities that transcend money and influence other aspects of life. When a family chooses to invest, they are not just growing assets; they are cultivating values.

The role of investing in creating long-term wealth is indisputable. It is the bridge between effort and independence, between present sacrifice and future abundance. For families committed to a sustainable, values-driven financial life, investing is not optional—it is essential. It allows money to serve not just immediate needs, but broader goals: education, homeownership, generational legacy, and ultimately, the freedom to live with intention rather than necessity.

By embracing investing as a tool for long-term wealth, families position themselves to thrive—not merely to survive. They prepare not only for what they can foresee but also for what they cannot. And in doing so, they elevate financial planning from a reactive activity to a proactive expression of purpose, security, and hope. Investing, when understood and implemented with care, becomes one of the most powerful and empowering decisions a family can make.

Stock Market Basics for Families

For many families looking to take control of their financial future, the stock market often represents a confusing and intimidating landscape—one full of acronyms, flashing figures, and dramatic headlines. But beneath the surface noise lies an accessible and powerful tool for building wealth. Contrary to the perception that investing in the stock market is reserved for financial experts or the affluent, it is entirely possible—and increasingly practical—for everyday families to begin investing confidently with basic knowledge, clear goals, and the right strategies.

Understanding how the stock market works is the first step. In essence, buying a stock means purchasing a small piece of ownership in a publicly listed company. When a person buys shares in, say, a supermarket chain or a technology firm, they become a shareholder entitled to a portion of that company's earnings and a stake in its future. If the company grows and becomes more profitable, its share price typically rises, allowing investors to benefit through capital gains. Additionally, many companies distribute a portion of their profits to shareholders in the form of dividends—another potential stream of income.

However, investing in individual stocks carries a certain degree of risk. Companies, even well-known ones, can experience downturns, and their share prices can fluctuate widely based on market sentiment, earnings performance, or economic conditions. For a family new to investing, this volatility can be unsettling. That's where diversification comes into play—and why index funds and exchange-traded funds (ETFs) are invaluable tools for beginners.

Index funds and ETFs operate on a straightforward but powerful principle: rather than trying to pick winning companies, they aim to replicate the performance of an entire market segment. An index fund tracking the FTSE 100, for example, includes shares from the 100 largest companies listed on the London Stock Exchange. By investing in this fund, families gain exposure to a broad cross-section of the economy in one simple purchase. This diversification significantly reduces the risk associated with investing in a single company, as gains in some sectors can offset losses in others.

ETFs function similarly to index funds but offer greater flexibility. Traded on stock exchanges like individual stocks, ETFs can be bought and sold throughout the trading day, often with low fees and minimal investment thresholds. This accessibility makes them ideal for families starting with modest sums. For example, a family might begin by investing £50 or £100 per month into an ETF that tracks a global index, such as the MSCI World. Over time, these contributions grow not only through market appreciation but also through the compounding effect of reinvested dividends.

The simplicity of these products is one of their greatest strengths. Rather than poring over balance sheets or tracking corporate earnings, families can take a passive investment approach—trusting in the long-term growth of the economy as a whole. Historically, broad-based stock market indices have delivered average annual returns of around 7–10% over extended periods, far outpacing inflation and traditional savings accounts. While past performance is no guarantee of future results, the long-term upward trend of diversified markets remains one of the most compelling arguments for participation.

Getting started with stocks, ETFs, or index funds does not require complex accounts or financial intermediaries. A growing number of platforms allow individuals to set up investment accounts online within minutes. These platforms typically offer user-friendly interfaces, educational resources, and low or no account minimums. For families, selecting a platform that supports regular automatic contributions—sometimes referred to as a "direct debit investing plan"—can make the process seamless and consistent. Automating investments ensures that saving becomes habitual and removes the temptation to time the market based on news headlines or emotion.

One real-world example involves a couple with two children who decide to open a Stocks and Shares ISA. Each month, they contribute £250 to an ETF tracking the FTSE All-Share Index. Over time, they involve their children in monitoring the account's growth, explaining the ups and downs in age-appropriate language. The children learn that investing is about patience, not speculation, and that wealth builds gradually through commitment and strategy.

This practice not only strengthens the family's financial position but also embeds financial literacy into daily life—an invaluable asset for the next generation.

Another consideration for families is deciding between lump-sum investing and pound-cost averaging. While a lump-sum investment involves deploying a large amount of money at once, pound-cost averaging spreads purchases over time—buying more shares when prices are low and fewer when prices are high. This method helps mitigate the risk of investing at a market peak and aligns well with monthly budgeting routines. For most families with steady income and recurring savings goals, pound-cost averaging through a monthly contribution plan is both practical and psychologically reassuring.

Families should also be aware of fees, which can significantly impact long-term returns. While ETFs and index funds are known for their low cost, not all products are equal. Expense ratios—expressed as an annual percentage of the investment—vary, and even small differences can accumulate over decades. A fund with an annual fee of 0.2% will preserve more capital than one charging 1%, especially when compounded across years. Choosing low-cost, well-managed funds is an important element of an effective investment strategy.

Tax efficiency is another crucial aspect of investing in the UK. For families, utilising tax-advantaged accounts such as Individual Savings Accounts (ISAs) or Junior ISAs can significantly enhance returns by shielding investments from capital gains tax and dividend tax. These vehicles are particularly powerful when used consistently over many years. A Stocks and Shares ISA, for instance, allows adults to invest up to £20,000 annually without incurring tax on profits, while Junior ISAs offer similar benefits for children with annual contribution limits and tax-free growth until the child turns eighteen.

Risk tolerance must also be considered. While the stock market rewards long-term patience, it also demands a measure of emotional resilience. Families must prepare for periods of decline—temporary losses that can be disconcerting but are entirely normal. Understanding that market downturns are part of the cycle and staying invested through them is essential. History shows that markets tend to recover, and those who remain invested are often better off than those who sell during a dip and attempt to re-enter later.

Incorporating investment into family discussions can also demystify the process and instil a culture of shared responsibility. Children can be invited to learn about companies they recognise—such as the brands behind their favourite cereals, clothes, or toys—and track their stock prices. This simple exercise links the abstract concept of investing to their lived experience and demonstrates how businesses create value, serve customers, and generate profits. It also teaches them to think critically about where they place their money and the power of ownership in shaping economic outcomes.

Over time, as confidence grows, families can expand their knowledge to include other asset classes such as bonds, property investment, or even entrepreneurship. But the stock market remains a foundational pillar—liquid, scalable, and transparent. It is where compounding takes form, where patience is rewarded, and where ordinary families can grow extraordinary wealth through steady, informed participation.

Ultimately, investing in stocks, ETFs, and index funds is not just a financial decision; it is a mindset shift. It moves families from a short-term, consumption-focused orientation to one that values discipline, growth, and long-term thinking. It turns money from a passive object into an active participant in a family's future. And perhaps most importantly, it creates an environment where children learn not only the mechanics of investment, but also the values of planning, patience, and shared prosperity.

Starting small, staying consistent, and remaining informed are the pillars of success. As with most meaningful endeavours, the hardest part is often beginning. But for families who take that step—who open the account, make the first deposit, and commit to learning—the rewards are significant. Not only in terms of financial return, but in confidence gained, knowledge shared, and futures secured.

The stock market, once viewed with apprehension, becomes a partner in possibility—a place where families build not just capital, but capability.

Real Estate Investing for Generational Wealth

When families begin to think seriously about building enduring financial security, real estate consistently emerges as one of the most reliable and compelling paths. Unlike more abstract forms of investment, property is tangible. It provides both a sense of ownership and a physical asset that can serve practical needs while generating income and appreciating over time. Whether the goal is to purchase a family home, acquire rental properties, or diversify an investment portfolio, real estate offers a unique blend of stability, passive income potential, and legacy-building capacity that makes it exceptionally well-suited to intergenerational wealth strategies.

The first and often most emotionally resonant form of property investment is homeownership. Buying a primary residence does more than provide shelter—it anchors a family, offers predictability in housing costs over the long term, and builds equity with each repayment. For many households, a mortgage functions as a forced savings plan. With each monthly payment, the family reduces their liability while simultaneously increasing ownership in a long-term appreciating asset. Unlike rent, which benefits a landlord, a mortgage payment incrementally enriches the household's net worth.

Yet the real power of homeownership as an investment lies in time and intent. Property values have historically trended upwards over extended periods, driven by population growth, limited housing supply, and inflation. Families who buy wisely, maintain their property, and hold for the long term typically see substantial capital appreciation. Moreover, they benefit from stability—a buffer against the unpredictability of the rental market. Parents can plan for their children's education, commute, and community engagement without the disruption of forced moves or fluctuating lease terms. This continuity contributes not only to financial well-being but to emotional and social stability.

Of course, homeownership requires careful planning. It is not without its risks. Interest rates fluctuate, markets correct, and property maintenance can be costly. For this reason, purchasing a home should be approached not as a speculative venture, but as a strategic decision grounded in affordability, location, and long-term utility. A well-bought home—modest but expandable, located in a growing community, near employment and amenities—often proves to be one of the most resilient investments a family can make.

For those looking to extend their wealth-building efforts beyond their primary residence, rental property offers an avenue for income generation and capital growth. Investing in a buy-to-let property introduces a second revenue stream, potentially covering the mortgage and creating monthly cash flow. Over time, as the mortgage is paid down by tenant income, the equity position improves. The property not only generates passive income but continues to appreciate in value, expanding the family's net worth while offering ongoing financial utility.

Take, for instance, a couple who purchase a two-bedroom flat in a university town. They secure a reasonable mortgage and rent the property to postgraduate students. Over the next ten years, the rental income covers the mortgage, property management fees, and occasional maintenance. Meanwhile, the flat appreciates in value by 30 percent. By the end of the decade, the couple holds a significantly more valuable asset with minimal out-of-pocket cost, and they have the option to continue renting, refinance for another investment, or sell to fund retirement or education expenses. This kind of thoughtful, strategic property investment can be repeated and scaled, forming the backbone of a multi-generational wealth strategy.

Success in rental property investment depends on several critical factors. Location remains paramount. Areas with strong rental demand, low vacancy rates, and access to schools, transport, and employment centres tend to yield more consistent returns. Equally important is understanding the financial model: calculating net rental yields, accounting for periods of vacancy, and planning for repairs and property taxes. Engaging a reputable letting agent can reduce the operational burden, especially for families managing multiple obligations.

The legal and regulatory landscape must also be navigated carefully. Landlord obligations in the UK include ensuring the property meets safety standards, managing deposits appropriately, and complying with evolving housing legislation. While this may seem daunting, families who approach rental investment professionally—with proper due diligence, insurance, and support—can mitigate risks and operate successfully.

Beyond the financial gains, real estate plays a distinctive role in transferring wealth across generations. A well-maintained home or income-generating property can be passed down to children or held within a family trust, providing housing, income, or collateral for future investments. More than just money, property represents continuity. It becomes a symbol of long-term thinking, of sacrifice made for the benefit of those yet to come. When children see their parents investing in property, they learn about stewardship, financial literacy, and the power of long-term commitment.

Some families involve their children in the process early—taking them to property viewings, explaining mortgage statements, or showing how rental income supports household expenses. These interactions embed practical knowledge and demystify wealth-building. A teenager who understands how a flat generates rent or why location matters will be better equipped to enter adulthood with informed confidence. Moreover, when children inherit not just property but the understanding of how to manage it, the wealth is more likely to endure and multiply.

Real estate also provides unique tax planning opportunities. In the UK, the use of property ownership structures—such as limited companies for rental income or trusts for inheritance—can offer advantages in terms of tax efficiency and succession. While these tools require professional guidance, they underscore how property can be more than a financial asset; it can be a platform for strategic, legally sound generational planning.

It is important to acknowledge, however, that property investment is not risk-free. Markets fluctuate, tenants change, and interest rates can rise. Families must plan for contingencies—maintaining emergency funds, purchasing landlord insurance, and avoiding over-leveraging. Diversification across asset types, such as combining property with stocks or pensions, can provide balance and reduce vulnerability to sector-specific downturns. Property should be one part of a well-rounded strategy, not the entirety of it.

That said, few investment classes offer the same combination of income, capital appreciation, and generational continuity as real estate. Unlike shares or bonds, which can feel distant and abstract, a home or rental property is tangible. It can be walked through, renovated, lived in, or rented out. It anchors wealth in the real world and provides options—whether to house a family member, generate income, or serve as a base for future expansion.

Real estate investment also has the potential to influence local communities positively. Thoughtful landlords who maintain their properties and treat tenants fairly contribute to neighbourhood stability. Families who invest in their own communities help improve housing quality, support local economies, and model responsible ownership. This dimension of property investing—rooted in stewardship rather than mere profit—resonates with families seeking to align financial goals with broader values.

For families beginning their exploration of property investment, the first steps involve education and assessment. Understanding mortgage terms, analysing rental yields, visiting local markets, and speaking with estate agents or other investors all build the confidence needed to act. Starting with a single, well-chosen property and scaling over time is a realistic and manageable path. With each step, the family develops not only assets but skills, insights, and shared experience.

Ultimately, real estate is not just about accumulating properties—it is about expanding possibilities. It offers a means to diversify income, hedge against inflation, and secure a more autonomous future. For families committed to building lasting wealth, property investment provides a multi-dimensional tool that grows with them. It fosters resilience, reinforces strategic thinking, and lays a foundation that can support and inspire the generations that follow. When handled wisely, it becomes more than an asset class. It becomes a legacy.

Passive Income Streams for Families

For many families, the notion of financial freedom often feels just out of reach—an elusive state imagined as the result of winning the lottery, inheriting wealth, or working around the clock. Yet in practice, financial security is often achieved not through dramatic windfalls, but by strategically building income that flows without constant, direct effort. This is the essence of passive income: earnings generated by assets or systems that, once established, require minimal day-to-day management. For families seeking to diversify their income, reduce financial pressure, or lay the groundwork for generational wealth, passive income represents not just a tactical advantage but a mindset shift—one that moves from trading time for money to allowing money to work on their behalf.

The concept is compelling in its simplicity. Rather than relying solely on wages or a single salary, families can develop income streams that complement their primary earnings and increase their financial resilience. These streams might begin modestly—a few pounds in dividends each quarter or earnings from a weekend project—but over time, they can grow into meaningful contributions that support education costs, family holidays, home ownership, or early retirement. Passive income transforms financial goals from abstract ambitions into achievable milestones, reached not by working harder but by working smarter.

One of the most straightforward passive income strategies involves investing in dividend stocks. When individuals buy shares in companies that generate consistent profits, those companies often return a portion of those profits to shareholders in the form of dividends. These payouts are typically distributed quarterly and can be reinvested or used as cash flow. For families, dividend investing can offer a relatively accessible entry point into passive income. By focusing on reputable companies with long-standing records of dividend payments—often referred to as dividend aristocrats—

investors can begin building a portfolio that generates reliable, recurring income.

For example, a family might invest in a basket of dividend-paying shares across sectors such as consumer goods, healthcare, and utilities. Over time, the dividends accumulate and grow, especially when reinvested through a dividend reinvestment plan (DRIP). While the early returns may be small, the power of compounding turns those modest beginnings into significant financial growth. Over the span of ten or twenty years, a well-constructed dividend portfolio can yield a sizeable income, providing the family with greater financial autonomy and reducing reliance on employment alone.

Another powerful avenue for passive income is the creation of a side business with scalable potential. Unlike freelancing or self-employment, which depend on active time input, side businesses designed for passive income focus on systems, automation, and repeatable products. This might include selling digital products such as eBooks, online courses, or design templates. Once created, these assets can be distributed through platforms that handle sales, delivery, and even customer service, allowing the business to generate revenue around the clock.

Consider a parent with expertise in a particular subject—perhaps early childhood education or family budgeting. With some initial effort, they could develop a digital course or downloadable resource and host it on a site like Teachable or Etsy. Once the content is live, the work largely shifts from production to promotion, with social media, email lists, and content marketing driving traffic. Sales made while the family is asleep, on holiday, or spending time together feel profoundly liberating. These earnings are not tied to hours worked but to value delivered through a leveraged platform.

Physical product businesses can also be structured for passive income when combined with dropshipping or fulfilment services. A family might create a line of branded home goods or apparel, using platforms like Shopify or Printful to handle inventory, packaging, and shipping. With thoughtful branding and a clear niche, such businesses can become steady income sources with relatively low overhead. While initial setup demands effort and learning, the long-term payoff can be both financial and educational, particularly when older children are involved in the business operations, learning skills in design, marketing, and customer service.

Property investment, while often requiring more upfront capital, remains a cornerstone of passive income for many families. Rental properties, when managed effectively, produce monthly income that can supplement a primary salary or cover major family expenses. Letting agencies or property managers can be hired to handle tenant interactions and maintenance, reducing the day-to-day involvement required. Over time, rental income combined with property appreciation can significantly increase net worth and provide a dependable source of income that persists across generations.

Additionally, families can explore more modern investment vehicles that offer passive income, such as Real Estate Investment Trusts (REITs). These trusts allow individuals to invest in large-scale property portfolios without the complexities of owning physical property. REITs distribute income through dividends, providing a lower-barrier alternative to direct property ownership while still benefiting from the real estate sector's long-term growth potential.

Peer-to-peer lending is another lesser-known but increasingly popular method for generating passive income. Through platforms like Funding Circle, investors can lend money to individuals or small businesses and earn interest on the repayments. This model bypasses traditional banks and allows families to put their money to work supporting real-world ventures. While risk must be carefully considered and diversified across multiple loans, the returns can outperform traditional savings accounts and provide a steady trickle of income.

Beyond financial investments and digital ventures, families can also create passive income through intellectual property. Writing a book, licensing a piece of music, or inventing a product are all ways to earn royalties long after the initial work is completed. While not every family has access to these routes, those with creative or technical skills can explore how their talents might be converted into enduring income sources. Even content shared on YouTube or a well-managed blog, monetised through ads and affiliate marketing, can provide income streams with low marginal effort once established.

It is important to recognise that building passive income requires intention, patience, and often a degree of upfront effort. The term "passive" should not be mistaken for "effortless." The initial stages—whether researching investments, developing a product, or launching a platform—demand time and learning. However, the return on that investment is measured not only in money but in time reclaimed, stress reduced, and freedom gained.

One of the most powerful aspects of passive income is the flexibility it provides. For dual-income households, it might allow one parent to reduce hours or transition to part-time work. For families with young children, it can offer the ability to cover extracurriculars, save for education, or simply afford more quality time. Over time, multiple small income streams—each contributing modest amounts—can accumulate into a meaningful monthly supplement, changing the way a family approaches work, budgeting, and life planning.

Moreover, passive income cultivates a mindset of ownership and innovation. It encourages families to think in terms of assets rather than liabilities, of building systems rather than relying solely on labour. Children raised in households where passive income is part of everyday conversation are more likely to develop entrepreneurial thinking, financial curiosity, and a proactive approach to economic challenges.

As with all financial strategies, diversification is key. No single income stream is infallible. Stock markets fluctuate, rental properties can sit vacant, and digital products may lose relevance. By cultivating multiple avenues—some based in investment, others in creativity or property—families can build a resilient financial ecosystem capable of withstanding change and uncertainty.

Passive income, at its best, is not just about making money while you sleep. It's about reshaping the relationship between effort and reward. It's about creating space—space to pursue passions, to spend more time with children, to travel, to care for ageing parents, or simply to rest without financial strain. It empowers families to make decisions from a place of strength rather than scarcity.

For those just beginning to explore this landscape, the first step may be modest: purchasing a dividend fund, starting a side blog, or researching how to license creative work. Over time, as knowledge deepens and confidence grows, these early efforts expand into a portfolio of income-generating assets—each quietly contributing to the family's future, day after day, year after year.

The journey toward building passive income is not linear or instant. But for families willing to commit to it, the rewards are transformative. It is not merely about increasing income; it is about reclaiming time, building legacy, and creating a financial framework in which every family member can thrive. Passive income is not a promise of easy wealth. It is a practical, proven path to freedom—one that families can walk together, step by thoughtful step.

Investing for Kids' Future

Few responsibilities weigh more significantly on a parent's mind than ensuring their child's future security and opportunity. While nurturing, education, and values form the emotional and intellectual scaffolding of a child's upbringing, financial foresight plays an increasingly vital role in shaping the trajectory of their adult lives. One of the most effective ways families can secure this future is through strategic, long-term investing. By taking advantage of specialised investment tools designed for children—such as custodial accounts, Junior ISAs, and education savings plans—parents can harness the power of time and compounding growth to create lasting financial support systems that empower rather than encumber.

Investing for a child is fundamentally different from saving. Whereas saving focuses on short-term preservation, investing is about long-term growth. Time, which is often in short supply for adult investors approaching retirement, is the most abundant and valuable asset for a child. Starting early, even with modest sums, allows families to unlock exponential returns through compounding interest. The earlier the seed is planted, the larger the tree it can grow into.

In the UK, one of the most accessible and tax-efficient vehicles for investing on behalf of children is the Junior Individual Savings Account (Junior ISA). Introduced in 2011, the Junior ISA allows parents, guardians, and even extended family members to contribute up to an annual limit into an account held in the child's name. The funds grow tax-free, and once the child turns eighteen, they gain full access. While this may raise concerns about financial readiness, it also offers a valuable opportunity for teaching responsibility and decision-making in the context of real assets.

There are two types of Junior ISAs: cash and stocks and shares. While cash ISAs offer safety and predictability, they often provide modest returns that struggle to outpace inflation. For families investing over a long time horizon—fifteen to twenty years—a stocks and shares Junior ISA can be significantly more effective. By allocating contributions to a diversified portfolio of index funds, ETFs, or managed investment products, families can harness market growth without the complexity or volatility of individual stock picking. Many platforms now offer simple, automated investment options tailored for children's accounts, making the process user-friendly even for those new to investing.

Outside the UK, similar mechanisms exist, such as custodial accounts in the United States. These accounts—commonly structured under the Uniform Gifts to Minors Act (UGMA) or Uniform Transfers to Minors Act (UTMA)—allow adults to invest on behalf of a child, with the assets becoming fully accessible to the child upon reaching the age of majority. Like Junior ISAs, custodial accounts support a wide range of assets, including stocks, bonds, mutual funds, and even real estate in some jurisdictions. While they don't carry the same tax advantages as education-specific accounts, they offer greater flexibility and can be used for purposes beyond tuition, such as travel, starting a business, or making a deposit on a home.

For families whose focus is squarely on education, dedicated savings plans can offer tailored benefits. In the United States, 529 plans are tax-advantaged investment vehicles specifically designed to fund qualified education expenses. While the UK does not have a direct equivalent, families can still use general investment accounts or Junior ISAs to prepare for future schooling costs. The advantage of a 529 plan lies in its favourable tax treatment: contributions grow tax-free, and withdrawals used for approved educational expenses are not taxed. Many plans also offer investment options with varying risk profiles, allowing parents to tailor the strategy based on the child's age and the family's risk tolerance.

It's worth noting, however, that these tools are not without nuance. In some countries, student financial aid assessments take parental and child-held assets into account, potentially reducing eligibility for needs-based assistance. For this reason, families should consider how each investment type might interact with broader funding strategies. Consulting with a financial adviser or doing thorough research can help ensure that investments are structured to optimise both growth and access.

The act of investing for a child is not merely financial—it is educational. When children are old enough, involving them in discussions about their investment account fosters financial literacy and a sense of ownership. They learn not only the mechanics of money but the discipline of planning, the patience required for long-term goals, and the reward of delayed gratification. A teenager who logs in to see their Junior ISA balance, asks about its performance, and begins to grasp the basics of market returns is better prepared to manage adult financial responsibilities than one who receives a lump sum at eighteen with no context or training.

To make this engagement more meaningful, some parents create joint goals with their children. For instance, saving for a gap year, contributing to a first car, or even investing together in a stock the child is interested in—perhaps a company that makes their favourite video game or mobile app. This bridges abstract financial concepts with personal relevance, turning investment from a passive inheritance into a shared learning experience. It also strengthens family relationships by anchoring values like trust, foresight, and mutual commitment.

Real-world examples underscore the impact of starting early. Consider a family who invests £100 per month into a stocks and shares Junior ISA from the child's birth. Assuming a conservative average annual return of 7%, by the time the child turns eighteen, the account could hold over £38,000. This is not merely a financial cushion; it is a launching pad—whether for university, entrepreneurial endeavours, or as a deposit on a first property. More importantly, it represents intentionality and care. It tells the child: we believed in your potential, and we planned for it.

Even families who cannot commit to large monthly contributions can benefit from consistency. Small, regular investments compound more powerfully than sporadic lump sums, especially when markets fluctuate. The practice of pound-cost averaging—investing a fixed amount regardless of market conditions—ensures that the family buys more shares when prices are low and fewer when they're high, smoothing out volatility and reducing timing risk. Over the course of a child's upbringing, this method can result in significant, low-maintenance growth.

While financial products evolve and investment platforms become increasingly sophisticated, the core principles of investing for children remain remarkably consistent: start early, be consistent, prioritise long-term growth, and engage the child in the process. These are not just techniques—they are habits, embedded in family culture and passed down like any other value or tradition.

Some families formalise these values through written investment charters or family financial meetings, setting clear intentions about how and when funds will be used. Others prefer a more organic approach, weaving money conversations into daily life—discussing shopping decisions, savings goals, or household budgets openly and with age-appropriate transparency. Whichever path is taken, the message children receive is the same: financial wellbeing is not something that happens to us; it is something we create.

For parents and caregivers balancing immediate expenses with future aspirations, investing for children can feel aspirational or even out of reach. Yet the landscape has shifted dramatically in recent years. With low-cost platforms, fractional share investing, and flexible contribution schedules, it is more accessible than ever to begin—even with just a few pounds a month. What matters most is not how much is invested, but that the habit is established, the tools are in place, and the mindset is clear.

Ultimately, investing for a child is an act of hope. It reflects a belief that their future is worth preparing for and that with the right support, they can meet it with confidence and dignity. It is a quiet but powerful expression of love—a way of shaping not only a child's financial foundation but their worldview. When done with thoughtfulness and intention, investing for kids is more than a transaction. It becomes a legacy.

Chapter 5
Teaching Kids About Money — Raising Financially Smart Children

In today's swiftly shifting financial terrain—where paper money is fading, digital spending is frictionless, and consumer temptation is constant—one thing is abundantly clear: if we don't teach our children about money, the world will. And not always kindly. Financial literacy is no longer a nice-to-have; it is a life skill as essential as reading or writing. Still, many young people stumble into adulthood with only a hazy notion of how to handle money, learning through expensive mistakes what could have been taught through simple, intentional conversations. It's an uncomfortable truth, but also a hopeful one. The most potent financial education doesn't begin in the classroom or bank office. It begins at home, often without a textbook in sight.

Parents are, whether they intend to be or not, their children's first financial mentors. Long before a child understands interest rates or compound returns, they are watching—absorbing, mimicking. They see how a household reacts when an unexpected bill arrives, how spending decisions are made (or avoided), how payday feels. Money is as much about mood as it is about maths. When conversations around finances are cloaked in stress or secrecy, children pick up on that anxiety. But when decisions are explained with openness and purpose, something else takes root: a quiet sense of clarity, even confidence. The goal, then, isn't just to teach kids how to budget—it's to cultivate a healthier, values-driven relationship with money itself.

A structured allowance system is one of the earliest tools parents can use to make financial concepts tangible. Now, whether that allowance is tied to chores is a matter of ongoing debate, but that's not the heart of it. What matters more is that the system is consistent and intentional. Give a child a small, regular sum—say £5 a week—and suddenly abstract ideas like saving or planning are no longer hypothetical. They're lived. Children learn not from being told what to do with money, but from feeling the consequences of their own choices.

Break that £5 into buckets: spend, save, give. Immediately, the child is making real decisions. Blow it all on sweets today, and next week's cinema trip might be out of reach. Delay gratification, and perhaps that longed-for toy is within sight. These early lessons aren't just financial—they're emotional. They teach patience, foresight, and even a bit of regret, which, when navigated safely, is a powerful teacher in its own right.

From there, a natural progression leads to banking. A simple savings account, opened in the child's name and managed together, introduces the notion that money doesn't just sit—it can grow. Walking into a bank branch (yes, those still exist) or navigating a child-friendly app together makes the invisible visible. Deposits, interest, tracking balances—these aren't lofty concepts, they're everyday actions. And with them comes an appreciation for the idea that money has purpose, destinations, and momentum.

As children mature, the next step might be a youth debit card or prepaid account. This extension of independence allows them to make real-time decisions and see, often immediately, the effects. Watch that balance drop after a spontaneous purchase? That's a lesson you feel. And because these accounts mirror the tools they'll use as adults—contactless transactions, budgeting dashboards, and even mobile alerts—they gain not just understanding but fluency in the modern financial landscape.

Still, perhaps the most essential principle to impart—sooner rather than later—is the subtle but crucial distinction between wants and needs. In an age of influencers and relentless marketing, this line can be maddeningly blurry. Children, and let's face it, adults too, are bombarded with messages equating worth with what we own. The antidote isn't to scold or deny, but to contextualise. "Why do we need this coat, but not that console? What happens if we wait for a sale? Is this purchase solving a real problem or just filling a fleeting desire?" These questions, gently introduced, build discernment.

Central to all of this is the concept of delayed gratification—that rare and often undervalued virtue of resisting now for something better later. It's not just a money skill; it's a life skill. Save up for a bike, plan a contribution to a family trip, delay buying that gadget—each experience is a small rehearsal for the bigger financial choices adulthood demands. And each successful delay plants a seed: that discipline has dividends.

Yet financial education needn't be confined to saving and spending. Entrepreneurship, even in its most playful forms, can be a game-changer. A lemonade stand, homemade crafts, dog-walking gigs—these aren't just quaint childhood rites. They are miniature economies. Children set prices, assess costs, handle customers, and if they're lucky, earn a little profit. And what happens when they choose to reinvest that profit into their "business"? That's a masterclass in financial strategy, no spreadsheet required.

But the real value of these ventures goes beyond pounds and pence. They foster autonomy, initiative, and resilience. The moment a child earns and spends their own money, something fundamental shifts. They are no longer merely consuming—they are participating. They begin to understand that money is not magic nor malevolent. It's a tool. And tools, once understood, lose their intimidation.

Parents can amplify this learning by weaving it into everyday life. Discuss why a favourite café might raise its prices, or what overhead costs a family friend's bakery faces. Talk about discounts, budgeting for holidays, or why a shop might go out of business. These aren't lectures—they're passing conversations. But their cumulative effect is real: they demystify finance and foster curiosity.

It is vital, however, that we resist framing money purely in terms of rules or, worse, punishment. Children who grow up associating money with guilt, fear, or status are more likely to struggle with it later. Instead, money should be taught as an expression of values. A family that values generosity might set aside part of the budget for charity. One that prizes sustainability could model thoughtful, long-lasting purchases over quick consumer fixes. In this way, financial decisions are not just about affordability—they become aligned with identity and ethics.

And sometimes, the best teaching tool is simply your own story. Tell your children how you saved for your first car, or what you learned from an impulsive spend that backfired. Share the real cost of the family holiday or how long it took to pay off a particular loan. These aren't just anecdotes—they're bridges. They make money real, human, and, crucially, relatable.

As children grow older, their financial world grows with them. Birthday money becomes job income. Part-time wages turn into university savings. And if the foundation has been laid with care, these bigger numbers are less likely to overwhelm. The habits forged with pocket money—budgeting, saving, discerning—scale up naturally. It's no longer about the money itself, but what it enables.

In the end, raising financially capable children isn't about preparing them for crises—it's about preparing them for life. It's about giving them the agency to choose, to plan, to adapt. And perhaps above all, to live not just wisely, but meaningfully. Financial education, when embedded in family life, becomes less a curriculum and more a culture—one that champions integrity, curiosity, and a quiet kind of power.

In this chapter, we'll explore not only the techniques—allowance systems, child-friendly banking, entrepreneurship—but also the mindset shifts and family rituals that make money management a natural, engaging part of childhood. Because it's not just about raising savers. It's about raising thinkers, doers, and, yes, givers. People who see money not as a measure of worth, but as a means to live with purpose.

Why Financial Education Starts at Home

The home is a child's first classroom, and parents are their earliest and most enduring teachers. While schools provide the structure for formal learning, the foundational attitudes and behaviours that govern a person's relationship with money are often shaped long before any economics textbook is opened. These early financial scripts—formed through observation, conversation, and experience—can leave lasting imprints on a child's worldview. Whether money is associated with security or stress, generosity or scarcity, responsibility or recklessness, these associations often trace back to the home environment. It is within this context that financial education finds its truest and most formative starting point.

Children absorb financial behaviours not only from what parents say, but also from what they do. The habits, priorities, and decisions made around money are silently recorded in a child's developing consciousness. A parent who carefully budgets, discusses spending plans openly, or models saving for future goals subtly communicates values of foresight and responsibility. Conversely, a household characterised by impulsive spending, secrecy around bills, or anxiety about money transmits a different kind of message—often internalised by children as either caution or indifference towards finances. Even in families where money is not explicitly discussed, the silence itself conveys a meaning: that financial matters are taboo, inaccessible, or too complex to be understood.

This silent curriculum is more powerful than many realise. Studies in behavioural economics and developmental psychology consistently show that financial attitudes formed in childhood can influence adult financial outcomes. Whether an individual becomes a prudent saver or a chronic debtor is often not solely the result of income level or education, but of early conditioning. The good news is that these patterns are not fixed. Parents who actively engage in financial education at home can shape not only knowledge but also the confidence, discipline, and mindset that underpin healthy money management.

Effective financial education at home does not require formal lessons or expert credentials. It begins with openness. When parents normalise conversations about money—discussing budgets, explaining household expenses, or involving children in small financial decisions—they break down the mystique that surrounds personal finance. Money becomes not a source of anxiety or confusion, but a tool to be understood and managed. This demystification process is particularly important in a cultural landscape saturated with consumerism and credit. Children who grow up understanding how money is earned, saved, spent, and invested are better equipped to navigate the pressures and complexities of adult life.

One of the most impactful ways to embed financial learning is through daily life. A trip to the supermarket becomes a lesson in price comparison and prioritisation. Receiving birthday money turns into an opportunity to discuss saving, spending, and giving. Helping plan a family holiday offers insights into budgeting, goal-setting, and delayed gratification. These moments, though small in themselves, accumulate into a rich, experiential education that no textbook can replicate. They also reinforce the idea that financial decisions are part of everyday life—not something reserved for accountants or bank managers.

Real-world examples underscore the importance of these lessons. Consider a family where the parents involve their children in planning for a new household purchase, such as a washing machine. They research prices together, compare brands, and discuss whether to buy outright or opt for a payment plan. Through this process, children witness critical thinking in action and gain exposure to concepts such as interest, value for money, and the difference between needs and wants. This experience offers more than knowledge; it builds financial literacy through participation, giving children a sense of agency and familiarity with decision-making.

Parents also play a critical role in modelling emotional regulation around money. Children who see their parents respond to financial stress with calm problem-solving are more likely to develop resilience and confidence. Those who witness panic, denial, or conflict may internalise money as a source of fear or shame. Financial education at home, therefore, is not just cognitive—it is emotional. It involves helping children understand not only how money works, but how to manage the feelings that surround it: desire, envy, anxiety, and pride.

An often overlooked aspect of home-based financial education is the role of values. Every family, whether consciously or not, conveys a set of beliefs about what money is for. Is it primarily for security, enjoyment, generosity, independence, or status? Clarifying and communicating these values helps children develop a moral compass around financial choices. For instance, a family that emphasises giving might encourage children to donate a portion of their allowance or earnings. One that values sustainability might explain the financial and environmental impact of fast fashion or disposable products. By linking money to broader ethical and personal frameworks, parents teach that financial decisions are also life decisions—interconnected with character, purpose, and community.

Financial education at home also requires acknowledging mistakes and modelling recovery. No one navigates finances perfectly, and children benefit from seeing that errors are part of the learning process. A parent who openly reflects on overspending, a poor investment, or a budgeting misstep—and then demonstrates how to adjust—teaches far more than a lecture on prudence. They show that financial competence is not about perfection but about adaptability and learning.

Importantly, these lessons must be tailored to a child's developmental stage. A five-year-old might begin with simple saving goals using a piggy bank or jar system. A ten-year-old could manage a small weekly allowance and begin to understand opportunity cost. Teenagers, approaching financial independence, should be introduced to banking, interest, debt, and long-term planning. At each stage, the goal is not to inundate children with information, but to offer age-appropriate experiences that build confidence and competence incrementally.

Incorporating financial education into family life also helps to bridge economic disparities. Children from lower-income households often face more immediate financial stress but receive less formal financial education. By prioritising these conversations at home, regardless of income, parents can help level the playing field. Teaching children how to manage limited resources, avoid debt traps, and build savings habits is not just protective—it is empowering. It equips them with the tools to break cycles of financial instability and to make informed, strategic choices as adults.

Technology can also play a supportive role in home-based financial education. Many apps and digital platforms now offer child-friendly budgeting tools, simulated stock market experiences, and gamified saving trackers. When used judiciously, these tools can reinforce lessons taught at home and offer interactive learning that resonates with younger generations. Parents can guide children in using these technologies not merely as entertainment, but as instruments of financial skill-building.

Perhaps the most compelling argument for financial education at home is its lasting impact. A child who understands how to manage money grows into an adult who can make autonomous, ethical, and confident financial choices. They are more likely to avoid debt, plan for their goals, and contribute meaningfully to their communities. Moreover, they are better positioned to teach their own children, creating a virtuous cycle of financial empowerment that spans generations.

In the wider societal context, financially literate individuals contribute to a more stable, equitable economy. They are less likely to rely on predatory lending, more likely to invest in their futures, and better equipped to advocate for themselves in economic transactions. Teaching children about money at home, therefore, is not only a personal duty but a civic contribution. It prepares the next generation not just to survive, but to thrive—to participate in society with clarity, confidence, and integrity.

Parents need not have perfect finances or all the answers to provide this education. What matters most is a willingness to engage, to learn alongside their children, and to treat money as a subject worthy of honest, ongoing conversation. When financial literacy is woven into the fabric of daily life, it becomes second nature. Children raised in such environments enter adulthood with a quiet strength—one that allows them to navigate financial decisions not with fear or confusion, but with wisdom, perspective, and self-trust.

Financial education begins not with formal instruction, but with everyday choices and conversations. It starts at the dinner table, in the supermarket aisle, and on the high street. It is shaped by the tone in which bills are discussed, the transparency of family budgeting, and the shared excitement of achieving a savings goal. It is a long arc of learning that begins with small seeds—each coin saved, each question answered, each example set. And in time, those seeds grow into the roots of financial capability and the fruits of independence.

Allowance, Chores, and Earning Money

Teaching children about money is far more effective when they have their own to manage. An allowance offers a practical, low-risk platform for this kind of learning, allowing young people to begin making financial decisions in a structured and supportive environment. When thoughtfully designed, an allowance system does far more than distribute pocket money—it nurtures responsibility, embeds core values, and helps children internalise the essential principles of budgeting, saving, spending, and even giving. But to realise its full educational potential, an allowance must be intentional. It must be approached not as a reward or appeasement, but as a tool for development.

One of the most debated aspects of allowances is whether they should be tied to chores. Some families believe children should earn their allowance by contributing to household tasks, reinforcing the concept that money must be earned. Others advocate for a fixed allowance independent of chores, on the basis that participating in household responsibilities is a shared duty, not something to be financially incentivised. Both approaches have merit, and the decision often comes down to family values and goals. The key lies in clarity and consistency—whatever system is adopted must be communicated and maintained in a way that feels fair, logical, and purposeful.

In practice, many families adopt a hybrid approach. Core responsibilities—such as tidying bedrooms, helping with meals, or feeding pets—are considered part of being a member of the household and are not compensated. Additional tasks, which require more time or effort, such as washing the car, mowing the lawn, or helping with a home project, can be linked to optional earning opportunities. This balance preserves the ethos of mutual contribution while still allowing children to make the connection between work and income. It also introduces them to the concept of extra effort leading to increased reward, an idea that mirrors real-world economic dynamics.

When determining how much allowance to give, the decision should reflect both the child's age and what the money is expected to cover. A younger child might receive a small weekly amount to spend on small treats or toys, while a teenager may be given a monthly allowance intended to include clothing, transport, social outings, or even phone bills. The purpose of increasing both the amount and the responsibility as a child matures is not only to prepare them for greater financial independence, but also to foster critical thinking about needs versus wants and to experience the consequences of overspending in a controlled environment.

For example, a twelve-year-old receiving £20 a month may be responsible for buying their own school snacks, contributing to birthday presents for friends, and saving for larger items. They will likely face moments of choice—whether to spend on impulse or save for something more meaningful. Parents should avoid bailing them out too quickly. Learning from small, manageable mistakes is an important part of developing financial resilience. When a child spends all their allowance on a toy and then cannot afford a cinema ticket later, they experience a lesson in prioritisation that will be far more instructive than a verbal warning.

To support learning, many parents find it helpful to introduce a structure to how allowance is used. One popular method is to encourage children to divide their money into categories: spending, saving, and giving. This not only reflects the multifaceted nature of adult money management but also introduces the idea that not all money is meant to be consumed immediately. Saving develops delayed gratification and goal-setting; giving instils empathy and social responsibility. A child who consistently saves part of their allowance for a desired item learns patience and strategic planning, while one who donates a portion to a chosen cause develops a sense of agency and values alignment.

For these habits to take root, the experience must be tangible. Using physical jars or envelopes for each category can be very effective for younger children, while older children may benefit from digital tools that mimic bank accounts or budgeting apps designed for youth. These tools help make abstract concepts concrete and give children visual feedback on their progress. Watching their savings grow—even if slowly—reinforces positive habits and offers a sense of accomplishment.

The regularity of allowance matters as well. A consistent payment schedule mirrors real-world income cycles and helps children develop budgeting skills. Whether weekly or monthly, the key is predictability. Children should know when to expect their allowance, understand what it covers, and be responsible for managing it until the next instalment. This practice encourages planning and helps counteract impulsive behaviour. Additionally, paying allowance in denominations that allow for easy dividing between categories—such as coins or small notes—can make the process more engaging and intuitive.

Parental modelling is crucial throughout. Children are far more likely to respect the allowance system if they see similar principles reflected in their parents' financial behaviour. Discussing household budgeting, explaining savings goals, and being transparent about spending decisions can all help normalise money conversations and create an environment where financial education is ongoing. If a parent saves for a family holiday, discusses trade-offs in spending, or shares why they chose not to make a purchase, these actions contextualise the lessons being taught through the child's own allowance.

One of the greatest advantages of using allowances as a teaching tool is that it creates space for autonomy. With autonomy comes the opportunity to make mistakes, and with mistakes come invaluable lessons. The purpose is not to ensure flawless financial behaviour from the outset, but to cultivate awareness, reflection, and growth. Parents should be available for guidance but avoid micromanaging. When children are given room to make their own choices—within reasonable boundaries—they begin to develop internal decision-making frameworks, rather than relying on external control.

Some families take this a step further by encouraging children to earn beyond their base allowance. Whether through entrepreneurial ventures like a lemonade stand, selling crafts, babysitting, or helping neighbours with odd jobs, these experiences extend financial learning into the broader economy. Children learn about pricing, customer interaction, profit, and reinvestment. They also begin to see that money is not just something that appears, but something that is created through effort, skill, and creativity. This not only deepens their financial literacy but builds confidence and self-efficacy.

Furthermore, an effective allowance system can serve as a bridge to more advanced financial concepts. As children mature, the discussions can evolve to include interest, debt, taxes, and investment. If a child chooses to "borrow" from their savings jar and repay it with interest, or if they invest in a mock stock and track its performance, they begin to encounter the mechanics of adult financial life in a low-risk, developmental context. These gradual exposures ensure that by the time they are legally and practically responsible for their finances, they are not starting from scratch.

Ultimately, structuring an effective allowance system is about more than dispensing money. It is about instilling life skills—discipline, prioritisation, generosity, foresight—and embedding financial competence into everyday behaviour. The allowance is merely a medium; the message is one of agency and intention. By empowering children to manage their own money in a thoughtful and supported way, parents prepare them not only to navigate financial choices but to approach life itself with greater clarity, confidence, and care.

Allowance is not a bribe, nor a mere tradition. When implemented with purpose, it becomes a cornerstone of practical financial education—a formative experience that equips children with the knowledge, judgement, and values they need to thrive in a complex and demanding world. Through a blend of structure, autonomy, and guidance, families can use allowance systems to do what all meaningful education aspires to: transform theory into understanding and action into character.

Introducing Banking to Kids

For many children, money is first encountered in the form of coins slipped into birthday cards or pocket money handed over in person. It is physical, immediate, and tangible—spent quickly, often impulsively, and without much thought for long-term use. However, as the financial world becomes increasingly digital, teaching children about banking is an essential next step in their financial education. Understanding how to navigate accounts, track balances, save securely, and spend wisely forms the bedrock of financial literacy. Introducing banking at a young age not only demystifies a crucial life skill but empowers children with confidence and clarity in an area that many adults struggle to master.

The first experience of banking should be tactile, structured, and aligned with a child's level of understanding. While traditional savings jars provide a visual method for managing money, eventually they outgrow their utility. A child who regularly receives an allowance or birthday gifts in cash may quickly begin to accumulate more than a handful of coins. When the idea of "saving" becomes less about storing and more about growing or protecting, it's time to move from the kitchen shelf to the financial system. Opening a savings account in a child's name marks this transition and should be celebrated as a milestone of maturity.

In the UK, most high street banks offer child savings accounts specifically designed for young users, typically from the age of seven. These accounts often come with passbooks or basic online access that allows for visual tracking of deposits and interest. While interest rates remain modest, the purpose at this stage is not financial gain but experiential education. A child who watches their balance slowly increase through monthly deposits and sees a few pence of interest added each quarter begins to internalise the idea that money can grow over time if it is left alone. This simple but powerful lesson—delayed gratification and the reward of patience—is one of the pillars of responsible money management.

Beyond opening the account, it is crucial to build rituals around its use. Going to the bank together to deposit money creates a sense of importance and ceremony. It reinforces the act of saving as something intentional and valued. For younger children, even handling a deposit slip or talking with a bank teller can demystify what might otherwise seem like an inaccessible adult space. As they grow older, transitioning to online banking—with appropriate supervision—introduces them to the modern tools they will inevitably rely on in adult life. Being able to view their account digitally, track spending, and move money between accounts begins to cultivate autonomy and financial awareness.

As children become teenagers, the conversation can expand to include current accounts or basic debit cards. This is often a parent's first introduction to the idea of giving a child financial independence beyond controlled spending or saving categories. Understandably, many parents are concerned about misuse, overspending, or exposure to scams. These concerns are legitimate, but they also present opportunities for teaching. A bank card is not simply a spending device; it is a key to understanding budgeting, accountability, and digital responsibility. Used properly, it can help children learn the consequences of their decisions in a relatively low-risk setting.

For example, a teenager might receive a monthly allowance deposited directly into their current account. They are responsible for managing this amount, using their debit card for school lunches, personal expenses, or social activities. Parents can guide this process by helping them create a simple budget, identifying fixed and variable expenses, and discussing how to prioritise spending. Should the funds run out mid-month, the lesson is clear and immediate. The goal is not to protect them from every financial mistake, but to allow them to experience the realities of managing money before the stakes are too high.

Introducing online banking and mobile apps into this process adds another layer of sophistication. These tools allow young people to monitor their spending in real time, categorise expenses, set savings goals, and even receive alerts. Financial apps tailored to teenagers often provide dashboards that are more engaging and user-friendly than traditional banking interfaces. By using these tools, children learn to view money not just as numbers on a screen, but as a resource that must be monitored and directed with intention. It also mirrors the way most financial activity is conducted today—digitally, instantly, and with constant data feedback.

Equally important is teaching children how to protect their accounts and understand digital risks. Concepts like keeping passwords secure, recognising phishing emails, avoiding oversharing financial information, and reviewing transactions regularly for errors or fraud are all essential components of modern banking literacy. These topics can be woven into broader discussions about internet safety and personal data, reinforcing the interconnectedness of digital life and financial health.

Another valuable aspect of introducing banking to children is the opportunity to connect it to wider financial systems. Discussions about how banks lend money, why savings accounts pay interest, or how card transactions are processed help children see beyond the surface mechanics of banking. These conversations can be sparked by simple questions: Where does the bank keep our money? What happens when I use my card at a shop? Why can't I take out more money than I have? Through these dialogues, children develop a foundational understanding of the broader financial infrastructure, which can be expanded over time to include topics like credit, mortgages, or investment.

Real-world scenarios offer fertile ground for deepening this education. When planning a holiday, for instance, children can help estimate the cost, observe currency exchange rates, or track how spending accumulates during the trip using an app. If a family is saving for a large purchase, children can be involved in tracking progress, discussing financing options, or understanding interest charges if credit is used. These shared financial experiences foster transparency and trust while embedding practical knowledge through participation.

For parents, introducing banking is not only a technical exercise but a relational one. It signals trust in the child's capacity to take responsibility. When framed correctly, it says: "We believe you're capable of managing this." This affirmation, especially during adolescence, can have a profound impact. It helps shape identity and confidence, positioning financial management not as a burden but as a normal, expected part of personal development.

Of course, banking education must be responsive to a child's personality and maturity. Some children take naturally to structure and are motivated by goals and systems. Others may require more hands-on guidance or frequent check-ins. Flexibility, patience, and a commitment to ongoing dialogue are essential. No single conversation or account setup will suffice. Financial education is cumulative, and the introduction to banking should be seen as a starting point—an entry into a larger, evolving conversation about independence, planning, and future readiness.

In today's fast-paced financial environment, where transactions are seamless and spending can be almost invisible, raising children who understand the mechanics and ethics of banking is more urgent than ever. Without this understanding, young people risk becoming passive consumers rather than informed financial agents. But when families take the time to embed these lessons through action, discussion, and example, they equip their children with more than knowledge—they foster resilience, foresight, and autonomy.

By integrating banking into the rhythm of everyday life, parents create a lasting educational impact. Whether it is a seven-year-old excitedly depositing birthday money into a savings account, a twelve-year-old checking their balance online, or a teenager budgeting their monthly debit card expenses, these experiences shape lifelong habits. They build a generation not only capable of managing their money but of doing so with awareness, integrity, and confidence. In this way, banking becomes more than a service; it becomes a formative experience—one that supports the child's growth into a financially capable and empowered adult.

Smart Spending and Delayed Gratification

Children are born into a world where spending is not only easy, but increasingly invisible. With a few clicks on a screen or a tap of a card, transactions are made without the physical exchange of money. This seamless convenience, while technologically impressive, obscures the mechanics of financial decision-making. For young minds learning how to navigate money, this can pose a significant challenge. Understanding the difference between wants and needs, as well as developing the patience to delay gratification, are essential life skills that form the foundation of smart spending. These skills do not emerge spontaneously—they must be nurtured intentionally, through practice, reflection, and guidance.

Teaching children to distinguish between wants and needs is one of the first—and most important—steps in shaping thoughtful consumers. At first glance, the distinction may seem straightforward: needs are essentials like food, clothing, shelter, and education, while wants include toys, gadgets, sweets, or designer items. However, the real learning occurs in the grey areas. Is a second pair of trainers a need or a want? What about a mobile phone? Or a school trip abroad? These are the kinds of questions that prompt critical thinking and help children develop their own criteria for evaluating purchases.

Children, particularly in their early years, are naturally impulsive. Their world is immediate, emotionally driven, and geared towards gratification. Seeing a toy in a shop window or an advert on television can trigger a strong desire that feels like necessity. This is not a flaw in character but a developmental reality. The role of parents is not to shame these impulses but to help children slow them down, examine them, and consider alternatives. This begins by modelling decision-making aloud. When adults say things like, "I'd like to buy this, but I don't really need it right now," or "I'm saving for something more important," they are demonstrating that even grown-ups experience temptation—and that discipline is a choice, not a denial of joy.

Allowing children to make spending decisions with their own money further embeds these lessons. A child given a weekly allowance and the freedom to spend it will likely make mistakes. They might buy something cheaply made that breaks within hours, or spend it all at once and regret it later. These experiences, while frustrating, are invaluable. They provide real, emotional feedback on the consequences of choices. When a parent resists the urge to intervene or rescue and instead engages in a reflective conversation afterwards—asking what they liked about the purchase, whether it was worth it, and what they might do differently next time—children learn from the process rather than being protected from it.

One effective way to cultivate discernment is to encourage children to develop a list of wants and review it periodically. This practice teaches that not every desire demands immediate fulfilment. By writing down what they want and waiting a few days or weeks, children learn that some impulses fade while others persist. This naturally leads to prioritisation. They begin to ask themselves: which item do I want the most? Is this worth the time it would take me to save for it? Have I done my research? Have I compared quality and price? These questions shift the experience of spending from emotional reaction to thoughtful intention.

Delayed gratification, in particular, has been extensively studied and is widely recognised as a predictor of success in numerous areas of life. The famous "marshmallow experiment" conducted by psychologist Walter Mischel in the 1960s tested whether children could resist eating one marshmallow immediately in order to receive two if they waited. The children who delayed gratification tended, over time, to achieve better academic performance, healthier relationships, and greater financial stability. While the study's findings have been debated and nuanced in recent years, its core insight remains valid: the ability to wait, to tolerate discomfort, and to act with the future in mind is a powerful predictor of resilience and self-regulation.

Real-life application of this principle can begin with small, achievable goals. Saving for a specific item—a new book, a game, or a piece of clothing—provides an opportunity to practise waiting. Parents can support this by helping children calculate how much they need, how long it will take to save, and how to track progress. Visual aids such as savings charts, jars, or apps make the process engaging and concrete. As children witness their savings grow, they begin to see time not as an obstacle, but as an ally. They experience the satisfaction of earning, waiting, and achieving—feelings far more enduring than the fleeting pleasure of spontaneous consumption.

An often overlooked aspect of smart spending is the emotional context in which it occurs. Many adults use shopping as a way to manage stress, boredom, or self-esteem—and children absorb these behaviours. If a parent regularly uses phrases like "I deserve this" after a hard day, or "Let's buy something to cheer up," children may come to associate spending with emotional regulation. To counter this, families can explore non-monetary ways of responding to emotional needs—going for a walk, talking about frustrations, engaging in creative activities. When spending is framed as a choice rather than a coping mechanism, it becomes more deliberate and less reactive.

Technology, while often a complicating factor, can also be a teaching tool. Budgeting apps, prepaid cards, and child-friendly banking interfaces allow children to track their spending, set goals, and receive instant feedback. These tools mirror the financial systems they will encounter as adults and prepare them to manage digital money responsibly. For example, a teenager with a prepaid card linked to a budgeting app can see how their spending is allocated—how much goes to food, entertainment, or savings. This visibility fosters accountability and encourages reflection. It also gives parents a shared language and platform to discuss financial habits in a collaborative, non-punitive way.

Smart spending also includes understanding the concept of value—not just price. A child who learns to ask, "Is this worth it?" begins to consider durability, utility, enjoyment, and long-term benefit. Teaching children to look beyond marketing and hype, to read reviews, compare alternatives, and think critically about what they consume, cultivates not just financial intelligence but consumer awareness. This is especially important in a world where children are increasingly exposed to influencer culture and targeted advertising designed to generate desire rather than need.

One practical method to reinforce value-based spending is to involve children in family purchasing decisions. Letting them compare prices for groceries, calculate discounts during sales, or evaluate product features when buying a household item helps them see spending as a thoughtful process rather than an impulsive act. These experiences encourage curiosity and a sense of partnership. They also help children realise that managing money is not just about restriction—it is about making choices that align with goals, values, and circumstances.

Parents can also frame spending within broader ethical and environmental considerations. Discussing fair trade, local sourcing, or sustainable products introduces children to the idea that how they spend money reflects what they believe. A child who chooses to support a local craftsman over a mass-produced toy is exercising agency and conscience. These discussions make financial decisions richer and more meaningful, turning everyday purchases into acts of intention.

Importantly, none of these lessons are about denying joy or enforcing austerity. Smart spending is not the opposite of enjoyment—it is the practice of mindful enjoyment. It is the ability to recognise when spending enhances life, when it aligns with personal values, and when it creates real satisfaction rather than momentary distraction. A child who saves for something meaningful, plans for it, anticipates it, and then enjoys it fully, gains far more than a product. They gain the understanding that money is not simply to be spent, but to be directed with care.

Parents must also be patient. The development of financial discipline is a gradual process. Children will make impulsive purchases, change their minds, and occasionally feel regret. These experiences, rather than being seen as failures, should be treated as valuable data points. They provide the raw material for learning and growth. A parent who engages calmly and curiously—asking questions rather than offering reprimands—helps transform mistakes into insight.

Smart spending and delayed gratification are not merely about financial literacy. They are about life skills—about shaping individuals who can manage themselves, plan for the future, and act with intention rather than impulse. When families make these lessons part of daily life, through open conversation, modelling, and experiential learning, they raise children who are not only financially competent, but also resilient, thoughtful, and values-driven.

By giving children the tools to distinguish between wants and needs, to wait with purpose, and to spend with wisdom, parents empower them to lead lives marked by clarity and self-determination. Money, then, becomes more than a resource. It becomes a reflection of personal values, a measure of foresight, and a medium through which children can grow into adults who manage their choices with both intellect and integrity.

Encouraging Entrepreneurship in Children

One of the most powerful gifts a parent or educator can offer a child is the belief that they have the capacity to create value in the world. Encouraging entrepreneurship in children is not about preparing them to run a corporation or predicting the next market trend. Rather, it is about cultivating curiosity, initiative, problem-solving skills, and self-reliance—qualities that underpin not only successful ventures but a resilient and adaptive approach to life. In today's rapidly changing economic landscape, where traditional career paths are increasingly non-linear, fostering an entrepreneurial mindset in children equips them to think independently, embrace risk thoughtfully, and pursue financial autonomy with purpose and creativity.

Children are naturally inventive. They build, imagine, experiment, and role-play as shopkeepers, inventors, and creators long before they understand economic systems. These early instincts can be harnessed to build real-world skills when children are encouraged to translate their interests into micro-enterprises. Whether it's a lemonade stand, a homemade jewellery stall, pet-sitting, or designing digital artwork, the act of turning an idea into something others find valuable teaches more than profit-making—it nurtures confidence, initiative, and accountability.

The first step in supporting a child's entrepreneurial spirit is to recognise that entrepreneurship is not solely about business. It is about identifying problems and envisioning solutions. A child who notices that neighbours struggle to bring in their bins and offers to help for a small fee is already thinking entrepreneurially. A teenager who sells second-hand books or designs T-shirts online is engaging with real markets and real consumers. These experiences, though modest in scale, introduce children to fundamental economic principles—supply and demand, pricing, marketing, cost control, and customer service—in ways that are far more effective than passive instruction.

Starting small is crucial. Children do not need a detailed business plan or financial backers to begin. What they need is encouragement, access to resources, and a safe environment to take calculated risks. Parents can support this by providing seed capital in small amounts, offering guidance on basic budgeting, and helping children think through logistics. The goal is not to remove difficulty, but to serve as a sounding board—a trusted advisor who listens, challenges assumptions, and helps navigate challenges without taking over.

Real-world examples can inspire and make the concept tangible. Consider the story of a twelve-year-old who loved baking and began selling cookies to friends and neighbours. With her parents' help, she calculated the cost of ingredients, experimented with recipes, and created simple packaging. Over a school term, she made a small but meaningful profit and gained confidence in her ability to manage money, respond to feedback, and adapt her offerings. Another child with an eye for design might begin making greeting cards or stickers, using digital tools to create and print products at home, then selling them online through platforms with parental oversight. These ventures are not about scale or professional ambition—they are about learning through doing.

Entrepreneurship also teaches emotional resilience. Children learn to face rejection, to try again, to problem-solve when things go wrong. A failed sale, a product that doesn't work, or a miscalculated cost becomes a lesson rather than a source of shame. Parents can model this mindset by sharing their own professional setbacks and how they responded. When children see that failure is not final but part of growth, they become less risk-averse and more willing to challenge themselves.

These experiences offer a natural entry point to broader financial concepts. Revenue, profit, reinvestment, and budgeting all become relevant and necessary. If a child earns £20 from a weekend market, how should it be allocated? How much went into materials? What will be saved? Will any be used to improve the product or advertise the next sale? These are questions that teach not only arithmetic but strategic thinking. They also lay the groundwork for more advanced financial education, such as understanding cash flow, tax, or even investment—all introduced through a child's own interest and momentum.

Entrepreneurial activities also serve as a channel for values education. Children learn about honesty, reliability, fairness, and perseverance. They come to understand that long-term success depends on trust and integrity. If they promise a delivery and fail to follow through, they face the consequences not through scolding, but through lost trust or missed opportunities. These lessons, learned experientially, are retained far more deeply than abstract instruction.

Moreover, encouraging entrepreneurship invites children to explore their identities and talents. A child who starts a photography venture learns not only technical skills but also self-expression and how to communicate their perspective. One who makes and sells jewellery might discover a passion for aesthetics, customer engagement, or branding. Entrepreneurship, when guided thoughtfully, is not a rigid discipline but a space for exploration—a sandbox in which children test ideas, take pride in their work, and discover new interests.

Parents and educators must also be mindful of balance. The goal is not to instil a hyper-competitive or financially obsessive mentality, but to integrate entrepreneurship within a holistic view of growth. Children should be encouraged to pursue business ideas in ways that are enjoyable, ethical, and aligned with their interests. The focus should remain on learning, not on maximising income. An entrepreneurial activity that becomes stressful or overly commercialised too early risks undermining the very sense of autonomy and creativity it was meant to foster.

Technology has made entrepreneurship more accessible than ever. With parental supervision, children can sell crafts online, produce content for YouTube, design digital art, or offer simple services through community groups. These platforms not only provide reach but expose children to real markets and feedback. The process of setting up an online shop, designing a logo, writing product descriptions, and managing orders teaches a wide range of transferable skills—communication, design, time management, and digital literacy.

Entrepreneurship can also be integrated into family routines. A family might set up a weekend market stall together, use dinner discussions to review progress, or allocate part of a holiday budget to help a child explore a business idea. These shared experiences reinforce the idea that entrepreneurship is not a solo pursuit but a collaborative one—part of the family's broader culture of learning and support.

Schools too can play a valuable role by incorporating project-based learning that includes entrepreneurial components. A classroom project to design and market a product, organise a charity fundraiser, or run a mock business fair allows children to apply their learning in a practical, creative context. These activities build not only financial knowledge but teamwork, innovation, and presentation skills. When children are encouraged to think entrepreneurially within their community, they also begin to see themselves as contributors, not just consumers.

Encouraging entrepreneurship in children is ultimately about offering them agency. It is about shifting their perspective from passive participation to active engagement. When a child realises they can create something valuable, respond to a need, and earn through their own initiative, it changes how they see the world—and themselves. They become more observant, more intentional, and more confident. They start to ask different questions, take greater ownership of their decisions, and approach challenges not with avoidance but with curiosity.

These are not just skills for future business owners. They are competencies for life. Whether a child grows up to start a company, work within a team, manage a household, or lead a non-profit, the lessons learned through early entrepreneurship—initiative, problem-solving, ethical reasoning, adaptability—will serve them well. In a world where economic security is increasingly tied to creativity and flexibility, these traits are not optional; they are essential.

By creating environments where children feel supported to take risks, try new ideas, and learn from the outcomes, families help raise a generation of thinkers and doers. Entrepreneurship becomes more than a commercial activity—it becomes a pathway to self-discovery, growth, and meaningful contribution. When children are given the tools and encouragement to start, however small, they begin building not just financial independence, but a sense of purpose and potential that will shape their adult lives in profound and lasting ways.

Chapter 6
Debt Management – Eliminating Financial Burdens

For many households, debt hums quietly in the background—rarely spoken of in polite conversation yet undeniably shaping decisions large and small. It influences what's bought, when it's bought, and sometimes whether it's bought at all. It can feel like a shadow—always there, trailing behind every paycheque, every unexpected bill. Left unexamined, it seeps into the psyche, generating stress, straining relationships, and dimming future prospects. And yet, debt in itself isn't villainous. At its core, it's neutral—a tool, a mechanism. The difference lies in how it's wielded. This chapter delves into the attitudes, behaviours, and practical strategies that can turn the tide—from being at the mercy of debt to establishing a more confident, balanced rapport with borrowing and credit.

It helps to start by disentangling the idea of debt as a singular entity. Not all debt is created equal, nor should it be viewed as such. There is borrowing that, while incurring cost, paves the way for opportunity. This is what's often referred to as "good debt": money used to acquire assets that either appreciate or contribute meaningfully to future income. A mortgage, for instance, may open the door to long-term equity and security. A student loan—taken with forethought—can serve as an investment in earning potential. These are debts taken on with purpose, backed by a vision of future value.

Conversely, "bad debt"—and the term, though blunt, is apt—tends to arise from less considered decisions. Credit card balances that spiral out of control, high-interest payday loans, or financing items that depreciate quickly (think flashy electronics or impulse purchases) are examples. Often, this kind of borrowing is more about immediate gratification than long-term benefit. It piles on quietly, fuelled by interest, and offers little in return. Recognising this divide is not a semantic exercise—it's a lens through which to reassess current liabilities and make more intentional choices going forward.

With clarity comes the imperative to act. And when it comes to tackling debt, there's no one-size-fits-all formula—but there are well-tested approaches. The "snowball" method appeals to those who thrive on tangible progress: debts are paid from smallest to largest, creating psychological wins that propel further effort. The "avalanche" method, on the other hand, takes aim at the most expensive debts first—those with the highest interest—maximising efficiency and savings over time. One strategy leans emotional, the other rational. Both are effective when applied consistently, and ultimately, the best plan is the one you'll stick to. It's progress, not perfection, that matters here.

Debt consolidation can be another helpful lever, merging several debts into one with potentially lower interest and a clearer repayment path. The logic is sound: fewer payments, less confusion, perhaps more favourable terms. But consolidation is not a silver bullet. If the habits that created the debt remain unchanged, the cycle may simply resume with new packaging. Lasting improvement comes not just from reshuffling the numbers, but from reshaping the mindset behind them.

A major part of this shift involves checking lifestyle inflation at the door. As income grows, the reflex to spend more grows with it—often stealthily. A raise becomes a nicer car, a second income stream turns into exotic holidays or an upgraded kitchen. There's nothing inherently wrong with enjoying the fruits of one's labour. But when spending climbs in lockstep with earnings, the space for debt reduction and savings shrinks to nothing. It's worth asking, now and then: does this expense align with our bigger picture? Could restraint today pave the way for more meaningful freedom tomorrow?

When families manage to resist that upward creep, even just a little, the compounding benefits are significant. Holding the line on living costs while earning more generates financial slack—wiggle room. That surplus can go to clearing debts faster, growing emergency funds, or investing in the future. Living below one's means, contrary to popular belief, isn't austere or joyless. It's strategic. It offers breathing space and flexibility—luxuries in their own right.

This broader conversation around debt naturally intersects with how we use and think about credit. Credit is often maligned, but in truth, it's a powerful tool when handled with care. A strong credit history can lower borrowing costs, smooth the path to housing, and even affect employment opportunities in some sectors. Maintaining a healthy credit profile involves a few deceptively simple habits: pay on time, keep balances low, and don't overextend. Parents can demystify this world for their children by involving them in minor but illustrative decisions—explaining, say, how a mobile phone contract affects credit, or how a missed payment can linger like a stain.

Still, vigilance is essential. The temptations of credit run deep, with slick marketing and easy sign-ups masking long-term costs. Store cards, buy-now-pay-later offers, zero-interest schemes—all can look innocuous or even beneficial on the surface. But the ease of access often conceals a trap: the normalisation of consumer debt as a lifestyle. Families must learn to scrutinise these offers with care. A deal is only a deal if it serves your financial interests, not the lender's.

Avoiding future debt isn't just about caution—it's also about preparation. Building an emergency fund is a cornerstone of this preparedness. It's the difference between panic and poise when the boiler breaks or hours are cut at work. Setting aside three to six months of essential expenses may feel ambitious, but even a modest buffer can be a lifeline. It's not dramatic, but it's transformative—especially in turbulent times.

A sound budget forms the bedrock of this stability. Budgets sometimes suffer from bad press—seen as restrictive or joyless—but at their best, they're liberating. A well-crafted budget reflects your values, accommodates your goals, and gives every pound a job. It can be as high-tech or low-tech as you like—from app-based trackers to handwritten ledgers—what matters is that it offers visibility. Knowing where the money is going creates agency, and with agency comes the ability to course-correct.

None of this, however, occurs in a vacuum. The emotional weight of debt—shame, guilt, fear—is often as heavy as the financial figures. These feelings are real, but they need not define the narrative. Families do well to talk about money candidly, without judgement. When children see parents owning their situation, creating a plan, and sticking to it, they witness not just financial recovery but resilience in action. And just as crucially, they learn that debt is not a moral failure. It is a condition, not a character flaw—one that can be resolved through knowledge, effort, and persistence.

Some households go a step further by turning debt repayment into a shared project. A chart on the fridge, a countdown calendar, a family goal with a tangible reward—all these add visibility and a sense of collective purpose. Children can be included in small ways: helping shave a few pounds off the shopping bill, suggesting a home-cooked alternative to a takeaway. These gestures aren't just practical—they're symbolic. They say: we're in this together.

Ultimately, the journey out of debt is about reclaiming control. It's about choosing intentionality over inertia, clarity over confusion. Families who engage with debt openly, who approach it with structure and resolve, do more than fix a balance sheet. They model self-awareness, discipline, and courage. And they gift their children with something far greater than a clean credit score—they pass on the tools to live wisely, with autonomy and purpose.

In a world where borrowing is often encouraged—where consumption is king and restraint is rarely rewarded—choosing a different path is, in its way, a quiet act of defiance. But it is also a deeply empowering one. To live within your means, to chart your own course free from the pull of debt, is not only smart—it is liberating. For families looking to build wealth with wisdom, to raise children who are not only financially capable but also grounded, learning to manage debt is not just advisable—it is essential. Not all at once, not flawlessly—but steadily, one decision, one step, one honest conversation at a time.

Understanding Good vs. Bad Debt

For many families, debt is not only a financial issue but also an emotional one—wrapped in anxiety, uncertainty, and often shame. Yet despite the negative connotations commonly attached to borrowing, debt itself is not inherently destructive. In fact, when used strategically, debt can be a powerful lever for wealth creation and financial advancement. The key lies in distinguishing between debt that serves a long-term, productive purpose and debt that drains resources and undermines financial stability. Understanding this distinction is foundational to building a healthy, sustainable relationship with credit.

Debt, at its most basic, is the act of borrowing money with the promise to repay it, typically with interest. What transforms debt into either an asset or a liability is how it is used, the terms attached to it, and the behaviours that surround its management. So-called "good debt" is generally characterised by its ability to increase a family's net worth or enhance future earning potential. Mortgages, student loans, and certain types of business loans fall into this category when approached thoughtfully. "Bad debt," by contrast, typically involves high-interest consumer borrowing used for items that depreciate quickly or provide only fleeting satisfaction—credit card balances for non-essential goods, payday loans, or financing for lifestyle upgrades that exceed one's means.

Take, for example, a mortgage. Buying a home often involves taking on substantial debt, yet it is considered a positive form of borrowing when the property is reasonably priced, likely to appreciate, and serves as a stable residence. Over time, mortgage payments build equity, and the home can become both a source of security and a financial asset. A well-structured mortgage with a manageable interest rate and repayment schedule is a classic case of good debt—a form of leverage that facilitates an otherwise unattainable investment in long-term stability and value.

Contrast this with the use of a credit card to finance a holiday or purchase designer clothing. The item is consumed quickly, the cost is often inflated due to interest, and the spending may be driven more by emotion than necessity. When balances are not paid in full, the interest charges can spiral, leading to a cycle of debt that becomes harder to escape. This is bad debt—money borrowed not to improve financial circumstances, but to subsidise a standard of living that current income cannot support.

Student loans occupy a more nuanced position. On the surface, they may seem like a financial burden, especially given rising tuition costs and the time required to repay them. However, when education leads to meaningful career advancement and substantially higher lifetime earnings, the loan becomes an investment in human capital. The return on that investment must be considered carefully. A degree that increases job prospects and offers access to a high-income field can justify the debt incurred. On the other hand, borrowing large sums for a qualification with limited employability or personal relevance may result in a poor financial outcome, even if the intention was sound.

Understanding the potential returns on debt is crucial. Just as one would not invest in a business without considering its profitability, so too should families evaluate whether a debt-financed purchase will deliver tangible, lasting benefits. This requires not only financial literacy but also the ability to think long-term. It involves asking questions such as: Will this borrowing help me build an asset? Will it enhance my ability to earn, save, or invest? Is the interest rate fair and manageable? Are there hidden costs or risks? These reflective practices are essential in making informed, empowered decisions around borrowing.

Another important aspect of distinguishing good from bad debt is interest rate awareness. Low-interest loans tied to appreciating assets generally fall on the "good" side of the spectrum, particularly if the terms are fixed and predictable. High-interest debts, especially those with variable rates or penalty clauses, tend to tip towards the "bad" end, especially when the borrowed amount is used for consumables or depreciating goods. Understanding the true cost of borrowing, including fees, compound interest, and the impact on cash flow, can prevent families from underestimating the burden they are taking on.

It is also important to consider the psychological and emotional dimensions of debt. Good debt, when manageable and strategically applied, can foster a sense of progress and empowerment. It enables families to pursue goals, invest in their futures, and build security. Bad debt, on the other hand, often contributes to stress, guilt, and a feeling of being trapped. These emotional effects can spill over into relationships, parenting, and mental well-being, making it harder to stay focused on broader financial objectives.

Real-world examples highlight these distinctions clearly. A couple who take out a business loan to expand a home-based enterprise, and who subsequently double their income, are using debt as a growth tool. Their borrowing is calculated, purposeful, and rooted in a plan for return. Meanwhile, another family might finance a new vehicle they cannot afford on an extended repayment plan, only to struggle with high interest and depreciation that far outpaces the equity gained. In the latter case, debt becomes a drain—consuming future income for a short-term upgrade.

The proliferation of easy credit has blurred these lines for many households. Retail financing, buy-now-pay-later services, and low introductory credit card offers can make bad debt appear innocuous. The convenience of digital payments often masks the weight of future repayments. This is where financial education becomes vital. Families must be equipped not only to access credit but to evaluate it critically. They must learn to spot marketing disguised as financial advice, to compare loan products, and to resist the urge to measure success by lifestyle consumption.

Children can and should be part of these conversations. By explaining the differences between productive and destructive borrowing in age-appropriate ways, parents lay the groundwork for lifelong financial discernment. Sharing personal stories, both successes and mistakes, helps humanise the issue and makes abstract concepts relatable. A teenager who understands why the family chooses to drive an older car while saving for home improvements is learning values that will guide their own financial decisions in adulthood.

Good debt is not without risk. Any borrowing carries obligations that must be honoured, and even well-intentioned loans can become problematic if circumstances change—such as job loss or illness. This is why all debt, even the "good" kind, should be approached with caution and contingency planning. Emergency funds, insurance, and prudent budgeting form the protective layers that prevent manageable debt from becoming unmanageable.

Bad debt, conversely, is not beyond redemption. With the right strategies—such as prioritised repayment, interest negotiation, or consolidation—it can be addressed and eventually eliminated. The experience can also serve as a powerful teacher. Many financially secure individuals have passed through periods of indebtedness and emerged with stronger discipline, sharper decision-making, and a renewed commitment to living within their means.

Ultimately, the distinction between good and bad debt is not only technical but philosophical. It speaks to a family's relationship with time, value, and purpose. Good debt respects the future, aligning today's choices with tomorrow's opportunities. It is grounded in intentionality and supported by a plan. Bad debt, by contrast, prioritises immediacy, often at the expense of long-term wellbeing. It bypasses discipline in favour of instant gratification and, left unchecked, erodes the financial foundation that families work so hard to build.

Navigating these nuances requires more than avoiding mistakes. It demands clarity of goals, honesty about limitations, and a willingness to learn. When families adopt this mindset, they transform debt from a source of fear into a tool of empowerment. They move from reactive to proactive, from overwhelmed to informed. They teach their children not to fear borrowing, but to understand it—to see it as one of many financial instruments that, when used wisely, can help build a life of stability, opportunity, and shared achievement.

Strategies for Paying Off Debt Faster

Debt can be a quiet but relentless presence in family life—its effects manifesting not only in financial terms but in emotional weight, strained relationships, and a reduced sense of autonomy. While borrowing may sometimes be necessary or even beneficial, lingering debt often becomes a barrier to financial freedom. The sooner it is addressed with deliberate and structured action, the more families can redirect their income and energy towards goals that truly reflect their values. Paying off debt faster is not just a mathematical exercise; it is a behavioural and psychological shift. It requires strategy, consistency, and clarity of purpose. Among the most effective methods are the debt snowball, the debt avalanche, and debt consolidation—each offering a different route to the same destination: financial liberation.

The debt snowball method is grounded in behavioural psychology. Rather than focusing purely on interest rates, it prioritises debts by size—starting with the smallest balance and progressing towards the largest. The logic is simple: quick wins build momentum. When individuals or families see a debt cleared in full, even if it carries a lower interest rate, they gain a sense of accomplishment that can propel them to tackle the next. This method appeals to the emotional dimension of debt repayment. It replaces the fatigue of long-term struggle with the satisfaction of steady, visible progress.

Imagine a family with five debts: a small store card, a larger credit card, a car loan, a personal loan, and a lingering student loan. Under the snowball method, they would direct extra funds toward the smallest—perhaps the store card—while making minimum payments on the rest. Once the store card is paid off, they would apply that payment amount toward the next smallest debt, and so on. Over time, the amount allocated to debt repayment "snowballs," growing larger with each paid-off balance, accelerating the process. It's a method well-suited to those who need early reinforcement and prefer psychological momentum over numerical optimisation.

The debt avalanche method, by contrast, is structured to save the most money over time. It prioritises debts by interest rate—paying off the most expensive debt first, regardless of balance size. Mathematically, this method is more efficient. The faster one eliminates high-interest debt, the less total interest will be paid. It is a rational approach that appeals to individuals who are motivated by optimising results rather than incremental achievements.

Consider the same family mentioned earlier. Suppose their credit card carries an interest rate of 21%, while their car loan is at 6%, and their student loan is fixed at 3.5%. Under the avalanche strategy, they would focus on aggressively reducing the credit card debt first, even if it is not their smallest balance. This might take longer to achieve a first "win," but it will reduce the overall cost of debt significantly in the long run. For families with limited resources and substantial high-interest debt, the avalanche method can make a profound difference in preserving income that would otherwise be lost to interest.

The choice between snowball and avalanche is not merely a technical one—it reflects individual personality and financial behaviour. Some thrive on the motivation of early victories, while others are more comfortable with logical optimisation. In practice, the most effective strategy is often the one that can be sustained. Debt repayment is not a sprint; it is a disciplined, often emotionally charged process. Whichever method keeps a family engaged and consistent over time is likely the best fit.

In addition to snowball and avalanche, another approach that many families explore is debt consolidation. This strategy involves combining multiple debts into a single loan, ideally with a lower interest rate or more favourable terms. The appeal is immediate—simplified payments, possibly lower monthly obligations, and reduced psychological clutter. Rather than juggling five due dates and five interest rates, families have one predictable payment. This can be particularly helpful for those who feel overwhelmed and disorganised in their debt management efforts.

However, consolidation is not a cure-all. It requires scrutiny and self-awareness. Transferring multiple high-interest debts into one loan will only be helpful if it comes with lower costs and if spending behaviours are addressed. Otherwise, families may find themselves back in debt within months, having added another layer to an already complex situation. A consolidation loan or a balance transfer credit card must be viewed as a bridge—not a destination. It buys time and clarity, but only if it is paired with discipline and a commitment to change.

For example, a couple with several credit cards might use a zero-interest balance transfer offer to move their balances onto a single card. If the offer is valid for eighteen months and they divide their balance by eighteen, they can establish a clear repayment plan that avoids further interest. However, this only works if they stop using the card for new purchases and ensure the balance is fully paid before the promotional period ends. Consolidation can also take the form of a personal loan used to pay off other unsecured debts. Again, the key is to make sure the new loan has better terms, and that the freed-up lines of credit are not used to accumulate more debt.

Beyond specific repayment methods, accelerating debt clearance requires a broader shift in financial behaviour. Increasing income, reducing expenses, or using windfalls strategically can all amplify results. Side hustles, freelance work, or even seasonal employment can provide the additional funds needed to move the needle. Simultaneously, small lifestyle adjustments—such as cancelling unused subscriptions, cooking at home more frequently, or delaying discretionary purchases—can free up more cash for repayments. Families who review their spending line by line often discover leakage in unexpected areas. Plugging these leaks can significantly bolster their efforts.

Psychological readiness plays an essential role as well. Families must confront the feelings that often accompany debt—shame, denial, fear—and replace them with empowerment and purpose. This may involve open discussions between partners, setting joint goals, or seeking external support from a financial coach or adviser. A shared vision—such as becoming debt-free before a child starts school or eliminating credit card debt within twelve months—can create motivation and accountability. Children, too, can be part of this transformation. Age-appropriate conversations about budgeting, saving, and mindful spending can reinforce family values and create a culture of financial awareness.

Technology can also serve as a powerful ally. Many budgeting apps now include debt-tracking features, visual progress charts, and payment reminders. These tools offer not only structure but also visibility—turning the abstract task of "getting out of debt" into a measurable, achievable plan. Families can use such platforms to simulate repayment scenarios, compare methods, and celebrate milestones. The very act of logging into an app and seeing a reduced balance or checking off another paid month reinforces the habit loop that leads to long-term success.

It's equally important to protect the progress that is made. As debts are cleared, families should consider reallocating those funds toward savings, investments, or emergency buffers. The same monthly amount once used to pay down credit cards can, without interruption, become a contribution to a rainy-day fund or a child's education account. This continuity helps cement the behaviours that led to success, while building a safety net that prevents regression.

Moreover, families must remain vigilant against the common temptation to celebrate debt freedom with significant spending. The relief of no longer having repayments can create a psychological sense of surplus that leads to lifestyle inflation. A better approach is to acknowledge the achievement while maintaining the habits that made it possible. A modest reward—a family outing, a symbolic gift, or a meaningful experience—can mark the moment without undermining financial stability.

Debt repayment is not just about arithmetic—it is about agency. It is about reclaiming control over one's financial story, reducing stress, and opening doors to new possibilities. Families who commit to structured, accelerated debt reduction experience benefits that go beyond their bank accounts. They report improved communication, reduced conflict, greater confidence, and a renewed sense of purpose. The act of paying off debt becomes a shared project, a symbol of resilience and cooperation.

Whether one chooses the snowball, the avalanche, or a well-structured consolidation, what matters most is taking action with clarity and consistency. There will be setbacks, unexpected expenses, and moments of doubt. But each payment brings progress, each decision reflects growth, and each milestone affirms the power of persistence. In time, the weight lifts. Not because of a windfall or luck, but because a deliberate, human decision was made—to turn towards responsibility, to stay the course, and to build something stronger for the future. That is the true value of paying off debt faster. It is not merely about numbers—it is about freedom, integrity, and the quiet power of choosing better.

Avoiding Lifestyle Inflation

For many families, an increase in income is greeted with relief and celebration. A pay rise, promotion, side hustle revenue, or business success can feel like the long-awaited answer to financial pressure. Yet paradoxically, greater earnings do not always lead to improved financial health. In fact, unless managed with foresight and discipline, increased income often triggers a pattern of spending that absorbs the gains as quickly as they arrive—a phenomenon widely known as lifestyle inflation. Left unchecked, lifestyle inflation can silently erode opportunities for saving, investing, and building long-term security. Understanding its mechanisms and adopting proactive strategies to prevent it is essential for families seeking sustainable wealth and financial freedom.

Lifestyle inflation occurs when a person or household increases their spending in direct proportion to income growth, rather than preserving or expanding the gap between earnings and expenses. The most common signs are subtle but telling: upgrading cars, moving into larger homes, dining out more frequently, purchasing designer brands, or committing to costlier holiday plans—all justified by the sense that one has "earned" the right to enjoy the fruits of their labour. While none of these decisions are inherently wrong, problems arise when they become reflexive and unexamined, replacing financial progress with temporary satisfaction.

One of the challenges in recognising lifestyle inflation is that it often masquerades as improvement. Upgrading to a newer car with better features or moving to a more desirable neighbourhood feels like a sign of advancement, not regression. Social comparison adds further pressure. As income rises, so too may the social circles and environments in which people operate, subtly shifting perceptions of what is normal or necessary. The result is a cycle where expenses rise just enough to keep financial breathing room minimal, even when gross income has substantially increased.

Consider the case of a family whose combined income grows by £10,000 over a year. If this entire increase is allocated to new spending—higher rent, additional subscriptions, increased dining out, or new gadgets—their financial position remains unchanged. They may feel more comfortable, but they are not saving more, investing more, or insulating themselves against future risks. By contrast, a family who maintains their previous lifestyle and channels the added income into debt repayment, retirement funds, or their children's education is actively building financial resilience and future capacity.

Avoiding lifestyle inflation requires intention. The default tendency for many is to allow expenses to rise in tandem with income because of deeply embedded beliefs about success, reward, and identity. Money, for many people, is not just a medium of exchange—it is a symbol. It communicates status, security, and achievement. The desire to upgrade, to live in line with perceived success, is as much psychological as it is financial. This makes the work of resisting lifestyle inflation not only practical but emotional and philosophical.

One of the most effective ways to mitigate lifestyle inflation is to establish clear financial goals that serve as anchors for new income. When a family knows that their top priority is becoming debt-free, saving for a home, or investing for retirement, it becomes easier to view additional income through that lens. Instead of thinking, "We can now afford a new car," the mindset shifts to, "This raise brings us one step closer to our financial goal." Framing money in terms of purpose rather than consumption empowers families to make decisions that are aligned with their values, not their impulses.

Another key tactic is automation. Setting up automatic transfers into savings or investment accounts as soon as income increases helps redirect funds before they are mentally or emotionally claimed for spending. This pre-emptive decision-making supports discipline and limits temptation. It also fosters a sense of satisfaction, as progress towards goals becomes visible and consistent. Over time, these contributions compound—not just financially but psychologically—building a growing sense of control and capability.

Real-world examples demonstrate the long-term impact of these choices. A couple earning £50,000 each who consistently invests £5,000 per year from their incremental raises over a decade could amass a substantial financial cushion, even without major lifestyle sacrifices. On the other hand, a similar couple who channels each raise into ever-more-expensive conveniences may reach midlife with little to show in terms of net worth, despite having earned significantly more over time. The difference lies not in income, but in the ability to contain lifestyle expansion.

Of course, avoiding lifestyle inflation does not mean living in austerity or denying oneself enjoyment. It means making spending intentional rather than automatic. Choosing to increase one's standard of living in select areas, based on thoughtful priorities, is a healthy and fulfilling practice. The problem arises when every new pound earned is immediately allocated to consumption, with no thought given to saving, investing, or giving. Families can enjoy lifestyle upgrades—nicer holidays, a more comfortable home, quality experiences—without allowing those upgrades to become permanent obligations or the default response to every financial gain.

Another aspect worth considering is the relationship between consumption and happiness. Research consistently shows that beyond a certain threshold of income—enough to cover needs, reduce stress, and provide some discretionary spending—the correlation between more spending and greater happiness is surprisingly weak. Experiences, relationships, and a sense of purpose tend to offer more enduring satisfaction than material goods. A family that celebrates a raise with a shared experience—

like a meaningful trip or a new family tradition—may derive more lasting value than from a series of purchased items that quickly fade into the background of daily life.

To embed these principles, families can benefit from holding regular financial check-ins. These meetings create space for reflecting on current expenses, aligning spending with values, and revisiting long-term goals. They also provide an opportunity to acknowledge progress, recalibrate habits, and make decisions collaboratively. Involving children in age-appropriate ways helps cultivate financial literacy and normalise discussions about money. When children grow up in homes where income increases are managed wisely and discussed openly, they are more likely to replicate those behaviours in their own adult lives.

The danger of lifestyle inflation extends beyond missed savings opportunities. It often leads to overextension—higher fixed expenses that create vulnerability in times of crisis. A job loss, medical emergency, or unexpected expense becomes far more destabilising when a family is living at or near their financial limits. Avoiding lifestyle inflation, then, is not just about wealth-building—it is also a form of risk management. It preserves margin, flexibility, and resilience.

Debt is frequently a consequence of lifestyle inflation. As spending habits become more entrenched and expectations rise, credit is often used to bridge the gap between desires and means. This can create a false sense of affordability, encouraging families to take on instalment payments or finance deals that add to long-term obligations. Recognising the role of advertising, peer pressure, and emotional triggers in these decisions is crucial. By fostering awareness and applying simple tools—such as waiting periods before major purchases or spending fasts during specific months—families can create intentional buffers against impulse spending.

Ultimately, avoiding lifestyle inflation is about embracing financial maturity. It means recognising that increased income is not an invitation to spend more, but an opportunity to live more freely. Freedom, in this context, is not about acquiring more possessions—it is about having more choice, less stress, and greater control over one's time and future. It is the ability to weather storms, seize opportunities, and invest in what matters most.

Families who adopt this mindset often find themselves not only financially stronger, but emotionally more grounded. Their spending reflects thought rather than compulsion, and their financial trajectory becomes upward in both net worth and confidence. Over time, they build lives that are not only richer in material terms but also in depth, security, and meaning.

Income growth should be a cause for celebration, but it should also be a catalyst for intention. By resisting the pull of lifestyle inflation and choosing instead to direct new resources toward lasting goals, families can transform short-term gains into lifelong assets. The result is not just wealth—but wisdom, resilience, and the quiet assurance that comes from living below one's means while building a life of real abundance.

Using Credit Wisely

Credit is one of the most powerful tools in the modern financial landscape. It opens doors to opportunity—enabling home ownership, supporting business ventures, providing flexibility during emergencies, and offering convenience in everyday transactions. Yet when misused or misunderstood, credit becomes not a facilitator but a burden. High-interest debt, missed payments, and overextension can swiftly spiral into long-term financial strain. The difference between harnessing credit as a strategic asset and falling victim to its pitfalls often comes down to education, awareness, and consistent discipline. For families aiming to build resilience and prosperity, mastering the principles of using credit wisely is essential.

At the heart of this endeavour lies the concept of the credit score—a numerical representation of an individual's creditworthiness based on their borrowing history. While the precise algorithms vary by credit bureau, the fundamentals remain consistent. A strong credit score is built on timely repayments, low credit utilisation, long-standing accounts, diverse types of credit, and minimal recent credit enquiries. Understanding how these elements interact provides a roadmap for cultivating a robust credit profile.

Timely payment of credit obligations is the single most influential factor in a credit score. Whether it's a mortgage, credit card, utility bill, or phone contract, paying on or before the due date demonstrates reliability. Each missed or late payment is recorded on a credit report and can remain visible for up to six years, with the impact on one's score varying depending on severity and frequency. For families managing multiple financial commitments, setting automated reminders or direct debits can help ensure punctuality and preserve credit health.

Equally important is credit utilisation—the percentage of available credit currently in use. Ideally, this should remain well below the total limit, with many experts recommending staying under 30% as a general benchmark. For example, if a credit card has a £5,000 limit, carrying a balance of no more than £1,500 signals responsible use. Consistently maxing out credit lines, even if repayments are made on time, can suggest financial pressure and diminish one's score. Maintaining low balances relative to limits reflects control and restraint—two qualities highly valued by lenders.

The length of one's credit history also plays a role in credit evaluation. Older accounts offer a longer track record, allowing lenders to assess behaviour over time. Closing long-held accounts can inadvertently shorten one's credit history and potentially reduce a score. This is why, even when certain credit products are no longer actively used, keeping the accounts open (especially if they're free of fees) can be beneficial. It signals stability and demonstrates the capacity to manage credit over the long term.

Credit mix and recent activity further influence scoring. A healthy credit profile often includes a variety of account types—such as credit cards, instalment loans, and a mortgage—each reflecting different types of borrowing behaviour. Applying for multiple new lines of credit in a short period, however, can raise red flags, indicating potential financial distress. Each application typically triggers a hard inquiry, which may slightly reduce the score temporarily. Strategic spacing of credit applications and focusing only on necessary credit products helps maintain credibility and avoids unnecessary impact.

Beyond building and maintaining a credit score, using credit wisely also means avoiding high-interest traps. The most common of these is revolving credit card debt. While credit cards offer convenience and perks such as rewards or cashback, they often carry steep interest rates, particularly when balances are not cleared in full each month. A purchase of £1,000 at a 20% annual interest rate, if left unpaid, could balloon significantly over time due to compound interest. This cost is easily underestimated and, when coupled with minimum repayments, can lead to years of servicing the same debt without making meaningful progress.

One common pitfall is using credit to finance lifestyle upgrades rather than needs or investments. Retail financing schemes, buy-now-pay-later platforms, and zero-percent introductory offers can all encourage spending beyond one's means. These options can be harmless when used strategically and repaid promptly, but they often come with terms that trigger high penalties or interest if not managed precisely. Missing a payment or failing to settle the balance before the end of the interest-free period can result in sudden and substantial charges. Education about the fine print—interest rates, penalties, late fees—is vital before engaging with these schemes.

To mitigate these risks, families can adopt a proactive and intentional approach to credit. One effective method is to use credit only when there is a clear plan for repayment. Charging a necessary expense to a credit card, such as a car repair or school expense, is justifiable if the family has already allocated funds to cover the cost within the month. The card then functions as a temporary tool for transaction, not a long-term borrowing mechanism. This preserves cash flow while preventing interest accumulation.

Building credit intentionally can also involve using low-limit cards for small, recurring expenses—like groceries or fuel—and repaying them in full each month. This approach keeps utilisation low, demonstrates reliability, and fosters discipline. For families with teenagers or university-age children, adding them as authorised users to a parent's account can help them begin to establish credit while being guided in responsible practices. It is an opportunity to model and teach, rather than waiting until adulthood when mistakes carry more serious consequences.

Another strategy for avoiding credit pitfalls is the use of budgeting and financial tracking tools. Apps that categorise spending, send alerts, and project upcoming expenses can help families maintain visibility and avoid overspending. When credit cards are used, integrating them into the overall budget—treating them as cash rather than "extra money"—prevents the illusion of affordability. This mindset shift is fundamental. Credit is not income. It is a temporary advance that must be repaid, often with interest.

Real-world examples can illustrate both the dangers of misused credit and the benefits of sound management. A young couple, for instance, might start their life together with multiple credit cards used to furnish their home. Initially manageable, the debt grows as they rely on cards for everyday expenses. With minimum payments and high interest, they find themselves paying hundreds each month with little reduction in principal. After seeking advice, they implement a consolidation loan with a lower interest rate, close unnecessary accounts, and commit to repaying the loan ahead of schedule. Within three years, they are debt-free, with improved credit scores and stronger financial habits.

Contrast this with another family who uses a credit card solely for planned purchases—bills they were already intending to pay. They earn rewards, pay off the balance monthly, and maintain an excellent credit rating. When they later apply for a mortgage, their favourable score secures them a lower interest rate, reducing the overall cost of the loan by thousands. In both cases, the outcome is not dictated by the credit products themselves but by the behaviours and understanding behind them.

Credit, when used with knowledge and discipline, is not a threat but a facilitator. It enables strategic borrowing, builds trust with lenders, and supports flexibility when life presents unexpected challenges. But this power must be respected. Ignorance or complacency can transform a useful tool into a long-term liability. Families that build credit literacy—understanding scores, terms, interest structures, and repayment strategies—position themselves to make informed, confident decisions.

Teaching these principles early and modelling them consistently lays the foundation for generational change. Children who see their parents using credit intentionally, speaking openly about financial decisions, and taking responsibility for repayment are more likely to grow into adults who do the same. They inherit not only a financial framework but a mindset—one that views credit not as a crutch, but as a carefully managed asset.

Ultimately, using credit wisely is about alignment. It requires that borrowing decisions reflect a family's true priorities, values, and long-term plans. It is a discipline that calls for reflection, restraint, and resilience. And when approached with those qualities, credit becomes a source of empowerment rather than entrapment—a lever that can help lift families toward stability, opportunity, and lasting financial well-being.

Preventing Future Debt

Debt has a way of creeping quietly into financial life. Often it begins with a modest loan or a manageable credit card balance—nothing alarming, just a temporary measure to address a need or desire. But left unexamined, borrowing can evolve into dependency, consuming future income and eroding peace of mind. Families who have worked hard to become debt-free often describe the experience as liberating, even transformative. The challenge then becomes maintaining that freedom over time. Preventing future debt is not about perfection or strict denial; it's about building systems, habits, and mindsets that foster resilience and intentionality in financial decision-making.

One of the most powerful strategies to avoid returning to debt is the establishment of a realistic, dynamic budget. Budgeting is not a restrictive exercise—it is a way of clarifying priorities, making space for joy, and planning proactively. When families allocate their income with a purpose, rather than reacting to spending as it arises, they gain control over their financial landscape. The budget becomes a mirror, reflecting values and revealing hidden patterns. Importantly, it should not be static. Life circumstances change, and a sustainable budget must evolve with them. A growing family, a job transition, or an unexpected windfall all warrant budget reviews to ensure spending and saving remain aligned with current realities.

Beyond budgeting, maintaining an emergency fund is essential. One of the leading causes of consumer debt is the absence of savings when life delivers a financial shock—a medical bill, car repair, or job loss. When no buffer exists, families often turn to credit as a lifeline, re-entering a cycle they had worked hard to escape. A well-stocked emergency fund—ideally covering three to six months of essential expenses—acts as a cushion, preserving financial stability during periods of disruption. The very act of building this fund, slowly and deliberately, reinforces discipline and signals a long-term commitment to staying out of debt.

Preventing future debt also requires addressing the psychological drivers behind overspending. Emotional spending, social comparison, and the desire for instant gratification are all deeply human tendencies. Marketing and technology exacerbate these impulses, offering one-click purchases and aspirational imagery designed to lower resistance and stimulate consumption. Families must cultivate awareness around their spending triggers and create boundaries that support healthy decision-making. This might mean implementing waiting periods before large purchases, unsubscribing from promotional emails, or setting monthly spending caps on discretionary categories. These are not punitive measures—they are supports for intentional living.

Real-world examples help illustrate how these principles play out in everyday life. Consider a young couple who, after paying off £20,000 in combined credit card and car loan debt, decide to shift their focus towards building financial security. They allocate a portion of each paycheque towards an emergency fund, set clear saving goals for upcoming expenses like holidays and school fees, and agree not to use credit for any purchases unless they can pay the balance in full at month's end. When their car breaks down unexpectedly, they are able to cover the repair without relying on a loan. The stress is still present, but it doesn't compound into financial strain. Over time, these small acts of preparation become habits, shaping a financial life that is stable and empowering.

Another key aspect of debt prevention is learning to distinguish between good and poor timing for purchases. Many families fall into debt not because of extravagance, but because of poor planning. School uniforms bought all at once in August, winter heating bills, or holiday expenses can throw a budget off balance if not anticipated. By forecasting expenses—looking ahead a few months and identifying likely financial demands—families can begin saving in advance. Sinking funds, where small amounts are set aside regularly for irregular expenses, turn predictable costs into manageable ones. When needs are anticipated, they lose their power to derail.

Staying debt-free also requires careful use of credit products. It is not necessary—or even wise—for most people to avoid credit entirely. In fact, responsible credit use helps maintain a healthy credit score, which can lead to better loan terms and financial flexibility when borrowing is strategically necessary, such as for a home purchase. The difference lies in how credit is approached. Families who treat credit as a tool—one to be used deliberately and paid off consistently—retain control. Those who see it as an extension of income or a fallback for poor planning are more likely to fall into trouble. Practising disciplined credit use while avoiding dependence ensures credit serves its purpose without becoming a liability.

Another overlooked dimension of debt prevention is fostering financial transparency within the household. When partners or family members do not communicate openly about spending, income, and goals, misalignment often leads to tension or missteps. Joint financial reviews, monthly check-ins, or shared budgeting apps can help ensure everyone is informed and on the same page. These conversations also provide opportunities to celebrate progress, acknowledge sacrifices, and reaffirm commitments.

Financial wellbeing is not solely about numbers—it is about clarity, trust, and collaboration.

Financial education plays a preventative role as well. Families that invest time in understanding basic economic principles, personal finance management, and the mechanics of credit are better equipped to navigate complex decisions. This education should be extended to children, who absorb money habits from a young age. Teaching children about saving, responsible spending, and the cost of borrowing prepares them to make informed choices later in life. When a child sees their parents save for a family holiday rather than putting it on a credit card, they internalise a valuable model of delayed gratification and planning.

Lifestyle management is another cornerstone of debt prevention. As income rises, there is often a temptation to upgrade housing, cars, wardrobes, and other aspects of daily life. While modest lifestyle improvements can be enjoyable and even deserved, unchecked lifestyle inflation can quietly absorb income that could otherwise be directed toward savings or investments. A family that continues living as though they earn £40,000 even after their income increases to £60,000 creates a gap that can be used for long-term goals. This restraint doesn't require living in deprivation. Rather, it means making deliberate choices about what matters and preserving flexibility for the future.

Technology offers both risk and opportunity in the context of debt prevention. On one hand, digital platforms make it easier than ever to spend impulsively. On the other, they offer tools for tracking, planning, and automating good habits. Apps that categorise spending, visualise savings progress, or remind users of upcoming bills can provide structure and accountability. When families use these tools to create visibility around their financial behaviours, they reduce the likelihood of unpleasant surprises or unconscious drift.

Preventing future debt also involves recognising the emotional triggers that often accompany spending. Stress, boredom, peer pressure, and the desire to reward oneself can lead to unplanned purchases that gradually accumulate. Cultivating alternative coping mechanisms—exercise, hobbies, social connection—can reduce the reliance on spending as a form of comfort. Encouraging mindfulness around money—asking whether a purchase aligns with values or long-term goals—creates a pause between impulse and action.

Importantly, debt prevention is not about never encountering financial difficulty. Life is unpredictable, and even the best plans can be upended by circumstances beyond one's control. What matters is building enough resilience to absorb those shocks without collapsing into long-term debt. This resilience comes from preparation, discipline, and adaptability. Families who have put safeguards in place, cultivated strong financial habits, and maintained open communication are far better equipped to recover quickly and return to stability.

Ultimately, preventing future debt is a practice, not a finish line. It is a way of engaging with money that prioritises foresight over reaction, values over image, and empowerment over dependency. It does not require perfection, but it does require attention. It asks families to pause, reflect, and decide—not just about what they want now, but about the future they are building. When families commit to these principles, they don't just avoid debt—they construct lives that are guided by intention, protected by planning, and enriched by the freedom that comes from living within their means.

Chapter 7
Planning for Children's Education Without Debt

The escalating cost of education has become, for many families, not just a budgetary consideration but a source of deep unease—one that quietly shapes long-term decisions and family aspirations. For parents, the desire to provide their children with a quality university education isn't merely practical; it carries a powerful emotional weight. It speaks to the promise of opportunity, self-determination, and a life better than the one before. And yet, this hope is increasingly tempered by the sobering realities of student debt—an ever-growing figure that shadows young adults well beyond graduation. In the UK, it's not uncommon for students to emerge from university burdened with debts north of £50,000. In the US, the student loan system has ballooned into what many now call a national crisis. So the question, though uncomfortable, must be faced: how can families pave the way to higher education without jeopardising their children's financial stability—or their own?

This chapter takes a closer look at how families can approach education costs with both intention and ingenuity. Avoiding debt isn't the only goal here; it's about reshaping the way we think about paying for education. Too often, student loans are resignedly accepted as a standard part of the university experience—just another line on life's ledger. But must they be? Reframing this assumption involves early planning, open dialogue, and a re-evaluation of what's possible when families and students act together, rather than separately.

Among the most effective long-term strategies is the use of dedicated, tax-advantaged education savings plans. In the United States, parents may open 529 Plans or Education Savings Accounts, which allow investments to grow tax-free if used for qualified education expenses. These accounts aren't just about financial efficiency—they serve as a tangible signpost of intent. There's clarity, too, in having a clearly marked fund set aside solely for education, away from the volatility of general savings or emergency cash. When started early, even modest, regular contributions can accumulate powerfully over a decade or more, thanks to the quiet magic of compounding.

Across the Atlantic, British parents have their own set of tools—Junior ISAs, for example—which can be structured to keep tuition savings both tax-efficient and inflation-resistant. The principle remains constant: start sooner than feels necessary, stay consistent even when progress seems slow, and separate these funds from other financial obligations. And in homes with more than one child, clarity matters all the more—without it, it's easy to unintentionally prioritise one child's future over another's.

But let's not pretend that saving alone can cover everything. For most families, savings provide a base—but not the full structure. That's where non-repayable financial aid steps in: scholarships, bursaries, and grants. These funds—sometimes called "free money"—can drastically reduce the burden of tuition and related costs, yet they remain underutilised. Why? Often it's down to timing. Too many families wait too long, assuming that scholarships are either out of reach or too obscure to be worth the effort.

The truth is, applying for scholarships takes effort and strategic thinking. It's rarely a one-click process. Many require thoughtful essays, letters of recommendation, or a record of leadership, service, or artistic talent. But the rewards can be considerable. And the criteria are broader than people think—there are scholarships for academic excellence, financial hardship, niche hobbies, cultural backgrounds, and everything in between. Parents can support this process not just by proofreading applications but by encouraging children to build a well-rounded profile from an early age—volunteering, pursuing interests deeply, and embracing opportunities outside the classroom.

Work experience, too, can play a pivotal role in managing education costs. Encouraging teenagers to earn their own money—through summer jobs, part-time roles, or university-based work-study programmes—can lighten the financial load and deepen their engagement with their studies. It's not about pushing young people into adult responsibilities prematurely, but about letting them develop a sense of agency and ownership over their education. A student who helps pay for their own books or accommodation will almost certainly think more carefully about how they spend their time and money.

The knock-on benefits are significant. That weekend café shift or summer internship may teach budgeting, tax basics, and time management more effectively than any classroom ever could. And the habits formed—saving a portion of income, planning for larger expenses, keeping track of spending—lay a foundation for lifelong financial competence.

Still, perhaps the most neglected piece of the puzzle is the loan itself. Too many students sign loan agreements without understanding what they're agreeing to. Interest rates, repayment schedules, grace periods, penalties for missed payments—these are often glossed over, sometimes not even read. And yet they dictate the financial terms of the next decade, or longer. In many systems, interest begins accruing while the student is still in lectures, and compound interest can quietly double the original amount borrowed before the graduate even enters full-time work.

Families must take time to decode these documents—together. Debt, when treated as a serious financial commitment rather than a vague future worry, becomes something students can prepare for strategically. Yes, loans may be necessary—particularly when scholarships fall short or when the degree in question promises strong returns—but they should never be entered into lightly. The decision to borrow must be informed, deliberate, and always accompanied by a clear plan to minimise the total cost.

Equally transformative is involving children in the financial planning process from the outset. Conversations about money, far too often, are kept behind closed doors. But when students are included—when they understand the costs, the preparations, and the potential consequences—they are better positioned to make wise, informed choices. And they begin to see university not just as a right, but as a shared family investment.

There's a great deal young people can do, once they're invited into the conversation. They can apply for scholarships, contribute savings, evaluate course and university options through both academic and financial lenses. They can weigh whether a prestigious university across the country is truly worth the added cost—or whether a strong, more affordable local option might serve them just as well. Some may even consider gap years, apprenticeships, or modular learning, paths that offer flexibility and cost-efficiency without compromising intellectual growth.

The cultural script often suggests otherwise. We're conditioned to see elite universities and traditional degrees as the gold standard, regardless of cost. But success needn't hinge on brand names or high fees. When families broaden the definition of educational success to include financial independence, purposeful study, and a life free from the chains of early debt, the pressure begins to lift. The focus shifts—from outward appearances to inward values, from prestige to practicality.

Planning for education without leaning on debt isn't a single decision—it's a philosophy, a process that unfolds over years. It requires initiative, openness, and adaptability. And above all, it demands that families resist passivity. With every early contribution, every scholarship sought, every honest conversation, the pathway becomes clearer—not just towards a degree, but towards financial resilience.

In the chapters ahead, we'll examine the tools and case studies that bring this approach to life. We'll explore savings instruments, funding streams, and employment strategies that make higher education not just attainable, but sustainable. But more importantly, we'll discuss how to cultivate a family culture that values education while safeguarding financial freedom. Because with the right preparation and a bit of courage, it is entirely possible to help a child pursue their academic dreams without sacrificing the economic wellbeing of the family they come from.

529 Plans and Education Savings Accounts

For families aspiring to provide their children with access to quality higher education, the financial aspect can often feel overwhelming. Tuition fees are rising steadily, alongside the additional costs of accommodation, textbooks, travel, and living expenses. While student loans remain the default route for many, they also represent a long-term financial burden that can limit post-graduate freedom and delay critical life milestones. Against this backdrop, one of the most proactive and effective solutions for parents is to invest in structured education savings accounts—particularly 529 Plans and similar education-specific investment vehicles. These tools, when used wisely, offer families a powerful means of saving for higher education in a tax-advantaged, flexible, and potentially debt-free manner.

A 529 Plan is a tax-advantaged investment account specifically designed to help families save for future education costs. While it originated in the United States, the principles underpinning the 529 model—long-term investment, tax efficiency, and designated use for education—are increasingly relevant in a global context. In the UK, Junior Individual Savings Accounts (Junior ISAs) and other child-specific savings instruments play a comparable role. Though the mechanics may differ, the objective remains consistent: to create a dedicated financial resource that supports a child's educational aspirations without resorting to loans.

What makes a 529 Plan especially powerful is its combination of tax incentives and investment potential. Contributions to a 529 Plan are made with after-tax income, but the money grows tax-free and withdrawals are not taxed when used for qualified educational expenses. This includes not only tuition, but also books, supplies, computers, and room and board for students enrolled at least half-time. In many states, contributions also qualify for state tax deductions or credits, adding another layer of fiscal benefit.

The long-term growth potential of a 529 Plan depends largely on how early the account is opened and how consistently it is funded. The principle of compound interest, when paired with a diversified investment strategy, can transform modest monthly contributions into a substantial education fund. For instance, a parent who invests £150 per month starting from a child's birth, with an average annual return of 6%, could accumulate over £50,000 by the time the child turns 18. This amount could significantly reduce or even eliminate the need for borrowing, offering the student greater autonomy and the family greater peace of mind.

There is also a strategic psychological benefit to earmarking money for education through a dedicated account. It creates clarity of purpose. Funds are not easily accessed for non-educational spending, which protects them from the competing demands of everyday life. Moreover, the very act of contributing regularly reinforces a commitment to the child's future. It becomes a tangible expression of long-term vision, discipline, and hope.

Education Savings Accounts (ESAs), sometimes referred to as Coverdell ESAs in the U.S., offer another tax-advantaged vehicle for education funding, albeit with lower contribution limits and income restrictions. These accounts allow for broader investment choices and can be used for both K–12 and higher education expenses. Though they are less popular than 529 Plans due to their limitations, they may still be useful as a supplementary tool for families with specific educational planning needs or higher-income flexibility.

While these plans are most often used for traditional university tuition, recent changes have expanded their use to include apprenticeships, trade schools, and even student loan repayment (up to certain limits). This diversification reflects a broader recognition that education is not one-size-fits-all. Families who invest in 529 Plans or similar savings accounts are no longer constrained to a single model of higher education. Instead, they are funding future opportunity in its many forms—technical training, professional certification, or advanced academic study.

Some parents hesitate to invest in education-specific accounts because of concerns about flexibility. What if the child doesn't attend university? What if they receive a full scholarship? Fortunately, 529 Plans and similar tools offer options. The funds can often be transferred to another qualifying family member without penalty, including siblings, cousins, or even the account holder themselves. Alternatively, non-qualified withdrawals are permitted with tax implications—earnings are subject to income tax and a 10% penalty—but contributions are never penalised. In practice, this means that money is not lost, merely redirected if plans change.

Real-world examples help to clarify the practical benefits of these tools. Take the case of a middle-income family who begins saving £100 per month in a 529 Plan when their daughter is born. As she grows, her grandparents contribute annually for birthdays and holidays. By the time she graduates from secondary school, the account has grown to £40,000. She secures a partial scholarship for university, reducing her tuition needs, and the family uses the 529 funds to cover room and board, books, and supplies. No loans are needed. She enters adulthood with no education debt, while her parents are free to continue focusing on their retirement and other goals. The foresight they demonstrated eighteen years earlier has produced freedom and choice—not only for their daughter but for themselves.

Another family might use a Junior ISA to build a similar fund for their child in the UK. Although Junior ISAs don't have the same tax benefits as 529 Plans for education-specific expenses, the long-term investment opportunity remains robust. Once the child reaches 18, the funds transfer to them directly, offering flexibility for tuition or other needs. The key is that the family planned early, invested consistently, and treated the account as untouchable for non-essential spending. These behavioural choices made the financial outcome possible.

Of course, education savings plans are not a silver bullet. They require long-term thinking in a culture that often prioritises immediate consumption. They require budgeting and trade-offs in households that may already be stretched. And they require a level of financial literacy that not all parents possess from the outset. Yet these challenges are not insurmountable. With guidance, support, and the right tools, even families of modest means can make meaningful progress. Many financial institutions offer low-cost investment options, automated contributions, and educational resources to help families navigate the process. The first and most important step is simply to begin.

There is also a profound cultural message embedded in the act of saving for education. It tells children that learning is valued, that their potential matters, and that their family is investing not just in academic achievement but in their future agency. This message can be as impactful as the financial support itself. Children who grow up knowing that a fund exists for their education often feel empowered to pursue ambitious goals. They are less burdened by fear of cost and more focused on fit, passion, and purpose.

It is worth noting that families do not need to shoulder the entire financial burden of education alone. 529 Plans and Education Savings Accounts are most effective when used in combination with other resources—scholarships, grants, part-time work, and informed educational choices. What these plans provide is a base: a structured, protected, and intentional reservoir of support. They transform uncertainty into strategy, replacing passive hope with active preparation.

Ultimately, education savings plans are about more than numbers. They are about expanding choice, reducing stress, and fostering independence. They allow families to support their children's dreams while maintaining their own financial health. They are, in essence, a quiet but powerful form of generational planning—a means of handing down not just money, but values, foresight, and freedom.

For families serious about avoiding debt and building a foundation for long-term success, 529 Plans and Education Savings Accounts represent an essential part of the conversation. They are not reserved for the wealthy or the financially elite—they are accessible, adaptable, and profoundly effective when approached with consistency and care. As the cost of education continues to climb, the need for such tools becomes not optional, but essential. And in the broader context of family financial planning, they reflect one of the most meaningful investments any parent can make.

Scholarships, Grants, and Alternative Funding

When families begin to consider the financial implications of sending a child to university, the projected figures can be daunting. Tuition fees, accommodation, books, and general living expenses quickly add up, often reaching tens of thousands of pounds. For many, the prospect of such an investment leads to the uncomfortable conclusion that student loans are not only inevitable but essential. Yet this perception, while understandable, overlooks a vast and often underutilised resource: non-repayable financial aid. Scholarships, grants, and alternative funding streams represent one of the most effective ways to fund higher education—money that does not need to be repaid, thereby preserving a student's financial independence and protecting family resources.

Scholarships are typically merit-based awards offered to students who demonstrate excellence in academics, sports, leadership, or other specific competencies. Grants, on the other hand, are generally awarded based on financial need, though they may also consider factors such as location, background, or intended field of study. Both forms of aid can significantly reduce, or even eliminate, the financial burden of higher education. Yet year after year, millions of pounds in scholarship and grant money go unclaimed—not due to a lack of eligible candidates, but because too few families are aware of the opportunities available, or underestimate their child's potential to qualify.

One of the first steps in pursuing this kind of aid is to shift the family mindset from passive hope to active strategy. Applying for scholarships and grants requires effort—research, documentation, essays, and sometimes interviews—but the return on investment can be immense. A single application might yield a £1,000 award, while a well-targeted effort could result in a full tuition package. Unlike loans, which create long-term repayment obligations and interest accrual, these funds provide immediate financial relief and long-term freedom. They can change the entire shape of a student's educational experience, removing the pressure to work excessive hours, defer graduation, or make compromises based solely on affordability.

What is most encouraging is the breadth of funding sources now available. While many families are aware of high-profile academic or athletic scholarships offered directly by universities, there is a rapidly expanding universe of less publicised opportunities. Foundations, corporations, professional associations, local charities, religious institutions, and even private individuals offer awards for students from particular regions, ethnic backgrounds, career interests, or life circumstances. There are scholarships for first-generation university students, children of veterans, aspiring artists, environmental activists, and future engineers. Some awards are surprisingly specific—targeting students who play a rare instrument, pursue a niche sport, or plan to study a particular dialect. These so-called "niche scholarships" often have less competition than mainstream ones and are well worth pursuing.

To identify and access these resources, families should begin early—ideally by the time a student enters their final years of secondary education. Online databases, school counsellors, and university financial aid offices provide a starting point, but personal networks can also be invaluable. Teachers, mentors, and community leaders may know of local awards that are not widely advertised. Students should be encouraged to keep a record of their achievements, extracurricular activities, volunteer work, and leadership experiences. These records become the foundation of strong applications that communicate not only eligibility but depth of character and commitment.

Real-world examples reveal the impact of these efforts. A student from a low-income background in Birmingham secured over £25,000 in cumulative funding from a combination of local government bursaries, a foundation supporting women in science, and a community scholarship awarded for volunteer work. She entered university with minimal out-of-pocket costs and graduated debt-free. Another student, passionate about music, won multiple small awards from different sources—one from a local symphony foundation, another from a cultural heritage group, and a third from a corporate sponsor supporting arts education. None of the awards alone would have covered his tuition, but together, they made a significant contribution that reduced his reliance on part-time work and allowed him to focus on performance and academics.

In addition to traditional scholarships and grants, alternative funding methods are emerging as viable supplements or stand-alone solutions. One growing trend is income-share agreements (ISAs), in which an educational institution or private investor funds a student's education in exchange for a percentage of future earnings for a set period. While ISAs are not universally available and require careful scrutiny of terms, they reflect an evolving landscape in which education funding is being reimagined beyond conventional debt models.

Crowdfunding has also gained traction, especially for students pursuing unique projects or degrees with strong community value. Platforms such as GoFundMe and ScholarMatch allow students to tell their story, set financial goals, and receive direct support from individuals moved by their aspirations. Though success varies, and these platforms should not be relied on as a primary strategy, they offer an outlet for creativity and community engagement that can yield unexpected support.

Employer-sponsored education is another promising avenue. Some parents work for organisations that offer education benefits for dependents, while older students themselves may qualify for tuition reimbursement through part-time or full-time employment. Encouraging teens to research and pursue such employers—particularly those in the healthcare, technology, or retail sectors—can result in both work experience and significant financial aid. Even government programmes designed to support specific career paths, such as teaching or public health, often offer forgivable loans or grants in exchange for a service commitment after graduation.

One of the most underappreciated aspects of securing scholarships and grants is the way it fosters self-development. The application process demands introspection, articulation of goals, and the ability to present oneself compellingly. These are skills that extend well beyond education funding and contribute to career readiness and personal growth. Writing a thoughtful personal statement, assembling references, and preparing for interviews builds confidence and resilience. It shifts students from passive recipients to active participants in their academic future.

For families, supporting this process means more than encouraging children to apply. It involves creating an environment where effort is recognised, resources are shared, and setbacks are met with encouragement. Not every application will succeed. Rejections are part of the process. But each attempt hones a student's ability to express who they are and why their goals matter. With every draft, interview, and revised application, they build the capacity to advocate for themselves—a skill more valuable than any single award.

Preventing education-related debt is not about finding a singular financial windfall. It is about piecing together a mosaic of opportunities—some large, some small—that together reduce reliance on borrowing. Scholarships, grants, and alternative funding form a critical part of that mosaic. They represent not only financial assistance but a powerful message: that the pursuit of knowledge is worthy of investment, that achievement is recognised, and that education need not come at the cost of long-term financial constraint.

Families who approach this process with intention, persistence, and openness to a broad range of possibilities often find that their efforts yield far more than they anticipated. Beyond the money itself, they gain confidence, clarity, and a renewed belief in their ability to shape their future with agency and purpose. For the students who walk into their first lecture hall without the weight of looming debt, the impact is not just financial—it is liberating. It is the foundation of a future defined not by obligation, but by opportunity.

The Role of Work-Study and Part-Time Jobs

For many families, the idea of their teenager juggling coursework with employment raises questions: Will it detract from academic performance? Is it appropriate at such a young age? Can part-time work genuinely contribute meaningfully to education costs? These are valid concerns. Yet when approached thoughtfully, part-time employment and work-study arrangements can play a transformative role in a young person's development—not only easing the financial burden of higher education, but also cultivating responsibility, independence, and a grounded understanding of money's value.

There is a significant difference between financial literacy taught in theory and financial understanding gained through experience. A teenager who earns their own wages, tracks their spending, and saves for a goal learns lessons that no textbook can adequately convey. The regularity of paycheques, the deductions listed on a payslip, the choice between spending on leisure or saving for essentials—these are not abstract lessons, but real decisions with immediate consequences. Such experiences embed financial discipline early, often leading to stronger habits in adulthood.

Work-study programmes offered by educational institutions are one particularly constructive means of integrating employment into a student's academic life. These schemes, typically available in many universities across North America and Europe, match students with campus-based jobs that align with their course schedules. Roles might include assisting in the library, tutoring peers, working in administrative offices, or conducting basic research for faculty members. These jobs are not only more accommodating of students' academic obligations but often expose them to professional environments and networks.

The advantages of work-study extend beyond the paycheque. Students learn to manage their time effectively, balancing coursework with job responsibilities. They acquire workplace etiquette, communication skills, and a sense of professionalism. For first-generation university students in particular, these experiences can provide a valuable bridge into formal work environments that may have previously felt distant or inaccessible. Moreover, the psychological benefits of earning—even a modest amount—should not be underestimated. The act of contributing financially to one's education can foster pride, reduce feelings of dependency, and strengthen a student's sense of agency.

Part-time jobs beyond campus also serve a vital function. Many students find employment in retail, hospitality, childcare, or manual labour—sectors often demanding but rich in life lessons. These jobs build resilience, expose students to diverse people and circumstances, and sharpen interpersonal skills. While the work may not always be glamorous, the discipline it instils is enduring. A student who works ten to fifteen hours a week while maintaining solid academic performance demonstrates not only competence but character.

Take the example of a young man studying engineering who works part-time as a barista. He earns enough to cover his transport and books, reducing the financial pressure on his family. But more importantly, he learns how to work in a team, manage customer expectations, and perform under pressure. These soft skills complement his technical training and enhance his employability. When he graduates, he doesn't just possess a degree—he carries with him years of experience that employers find attractive.

Likewise, a student pursuing a degree in education who works as a tutor or after-school programme assistant gains direct, relevant experience in her field. The income helps her avoid unnecessary borrowing, but the exposure to real-world teaching challenges deepens her academic understanding. She enters her profession not only qualified on paper, but seasoned through practice.

For teenagers still in secondary school, part-time jobs offer early exposure to the responsibilities and rewards of work. Whether it's a Saturday shift at a local shop, babysitting for neighbours, or delivering newspapers, these experiences develop a strong work ethic and a practical understanding of budgeting. They also offer teenagers a sense of autonomy. Earning and managing even a small amount of money builds confidence and encourages goal setting. A teenager saving for a laptop, trip, or university fund becomes an active participant in their financial future, not a passive observer.

Parents can play a supportive role in this process without taking over. Helping teens open a savings account, discussing pay and budgeting, and encouraging reflection on how money is spent teaches financial self-awareness. Importantly, the emphasis should not solely be on earning, but on learning. The purpose of part-time work is not to impose financial pressure, but to introduce financial fluency through real-life experience.

Some families express concern that employment may interfere with academic performance. This risk can be managed through clear boundaries around working hours and prioritisation of studies. Research consistently shows that working a moderate number of hours—generally under twenty per week—does not harm academic outcomes, and may even improve them by instilling better time management. The key is balance and support. When work is structured around educational goals and approached with clarity, it becomes a complement rather than a competitor.

Work experience also enhances access to scholarships and funding. Many scholarships look favourably on applicants who demonstrate initiative, leadership, and community involvement. A student who can articulate what they've learned from employment—how it shaped their perspective, taught them resilience, or connected to their academic interests—often stands out in a competitive field. The narrative of a student who works while studying is compelling because it reflects maturity, discipline, and character.

Beyond individual development, student employment contributes to a larger culture of financial responsibility. When young people see the connection between effort and reward, they become more critical consumers, more thoughtful spenders, and more cautious borrowers. They are less likely to see loans as abstract or benign, and more likely to approach financial decisions with a long-term perspective.

Institutions and policymakers also have a role to play. Universities can expand and promote work-study opportunities, ensure fair wages, and integrate financial education into career services. Governments can incentivise employers to offer student-friendly schedules or tax breaks for educational employment. The goal should not be to burden students with employment, but to empower them through opportunity.

In today's economic landscape, where the cost of education continues to rise and the employment market becomes increasingly competitive, the ability to combine academic study with practical work experience is not just valuable—it is essential. Work-study and part-time employment equip students with more than money. They provide the confidence, competence, and financial grounding that form the basis of long-term self-sufficiency.

The families who recognise this and support their children in seeking balanced, meaningful work opportunities are not diminishing academic focus—they are reinforcing it. They are helping to raise young adults who understand what it means to earn, to plan, and to contribute. These are not just students. They are future professionals, leaders, and citizens with the tools to navigate life with intention and resilience.

By integrating earning into education—not as a burden, but as a feature—families set their children on a path that is not only more affordable but more empowering. It is a model of financial responsibility that honours effort, cultivates character, and prepares the next generation not merely to study for their future, but to shape it with skill and integrity.

The Real Cost of Student Loans

Student loans are often framed as a gateway to opportunity—a means of unlocking the doors of higher education for those without the immediate funds to pay tuition fees or living expenses. For many, borrowing seems not just necessary but inevitable. Universities encourage it, governments facilitate it, and societies normalise it. However, beneath the surface of this seemingly pragmatic solution lies a complex financial instrument that can profoundly shape a graduate's future. The real cost of student loans extends far beyond the headline figures of tuition or termly maintenance—it includes the silent accumulation of interest, the nuances of repayment structures, and the long-term impact on financial stability, decision-making, and mental well-being.

Understanding the full implications of student debt begins with a clear grasp of how interest functions. Interest is not merely a minor add-on to the principal borrowed. It is the engine by which debt compounds, and when misunderstood or underestimated, it can significantly inflate the total cost of a degree. Most student loans begin accruing interest from the moment they are disbursed, even before the student has completed their studies. In some loan systems, particularly those using compound interest, this means that interest is charged not only on the original amount borrowed but also on previously accrued interest, creating a snowballing effect that can double or even triple the initial debt over time.

Take, for example, a student who borrows £30,000 with an interest rate of 6.5%. Over the course of a three-year degree, that loan may grow to over £35,000 by the time they graduate, even if no further borrowing occurs. If repayment is deferred due to low income or further study, the interest continues to accumulate. For many graduates, the amount they end up repaying over the life of the loan can reach £50,000 or more. This burden is not merely academic—it directly affects life decisions, from choosing a job to buying a home or starting a family.

The structure of student loan repayments adds another layer of complexity. In some countries, such as the UK, repayments are tied to income thresholds. Graduates repay a fixed percentage of their earnings above a certain level, and any remaining balance is written off after a set period—typically thirty years. On the surface, this system appears humane and manageable. Yet the psychological weight of carrying debt for three decades, and the economic consequences of paying interest throughout that period, must not be ignored. Even when repayments feel modest month to month, the overall cost of the loan can be disproportionately high, especially for those with moderate to above-average earnings who repay for the full term.

In contrast, fixed-term repayment plans, such as those used in the United States, may require set monthly payments regardless of income. While this can lead to a shorter repayment period and potentially less interest paid over time, it also places considerable pressure on graduates with variable or limited early-career incomes.

In both models, the inflexibility and long-term implications of student debt underscore the importance of making informed, strategic decisions well before the first loan application is signed.

One of the most effective ways to mitigate the cost of student loans is to minimise the amount borrowed in the first place. This requires a multi-pronged approach, combining practical foresight with financial planning. Families should explore all non-loan funding sources available—scholarships, grants, bursaries, part-time employment, and family savings—before turning to borrowing. Even reducing borrowing by £5,000 can translate to substantial long-term savings when interest is factored in. Strategic choices, such as living at home during study, attending a local university, or pursuing a shorter or accelerated degree, can also reduce the need for large loans.

Equally important is selecting a loan structure that aligns with the student's expected future earnings and career path. High-interest, variable-rate private loans should be approached with caution, especially when compared to government-backed loans that offer income-based repayment options and forgiveness provisions. Where multiple loans are involved, prioritising repayment of the highest-interest balances can limit overall cost. Students and their families should not hesitate to consult financial advisers or university support staff to understand the comparative risks and benefits of each option.

Awareness of interest subsidies and deferment opportunities is another tool for debt management. In some systems, interest does not accrue while the student is enrolled full-time or during periods of unemployment. Making small payments during these periods—even if not required—can substantially reduce the amount of interest capitalised into the principal. These seemingly minor actions can have outsized impact over a ten- or twenty-year loan horizon. For example, a student who makes modest interest payments during their degree may graduate with a balance thousands of pounds lower than a peer who deferred all repayment.

Beyond technical strategies, it is crucial to appreciate the psychological dimensions of student debt. Many graduates experience anxiety, guilt, or avoidance around their loans, especially when balances grow despite regular payments. This emotional burden can affect mental health, deter financial planning, and create a persistent sense of limitation. Open, ongoing conversations about debt within families, coupled with honest assessments of earning potential, lifestyle expectations, and repayment timelines, can help students contextualise their debt as manageable and temporary—not a life sentence.

Real-world stories underscore the diversity of experiences with student loans. One graduate, a teacher, borrowed modestly and benefited from a public service loan forgiveness programme after ten years of qualifying payments. Another, pursuing a career in the arts, borrowed significantly but struggled with inconsistent income, making only minimal progress on repayment and watching the balance grow over time. Yet another entered the tech sector with a high salary and cleared their loans within five years through aggressive repayment. These examples highlight that the impact of student debt is not solely determined by the amount borrowed but by the interplay of repayment structure, career choice, and financial literacy.

Financial education, therefore, must be embedded into the process of planning for university. Teenagers and their parents should understand the mechanics of loans—not just the application process, but the repayment obligations, interest mechanics, and options for early repayment. Schools and universities bear responsibility for making this information accessible and transparent, rather than cloaked in jargon or buried in paperwork. The more clearly students understand the financial stakes, the more likely they are to borrow cautiously, budget wisely, and repay effectively.

The narrative around student loans must also evolve. While borrowing may be necessary for many, it should not be normalised to the point of casual acceptance. Debt should be recognised for what it is: a tool that can support long-term investment in oneself, but which requires respect, attention, and a plan. Just as a mortgage is considered a serious financial commitment, so too should student loans be approached with careful deliberation and an understanding of alternatives.

Families can also foster a proactive mindset in students by encouraging them to visualise their financial future. What will monthly repayments look like on a starting salary? How will these payments affect plans for renting, travelling, saving, or entrepreneurship? These conversations ground the abstract concept of debt in tangible lifestyle considerations, helping students to borrow consciously rather than reactively.

Ultimately, the real cost of student loans is not just measured in pounds and pence. It is measured in opportunity cost, financial freedom, mental clarity, and the capacity to make choices without constraint. For many students, the cost is worth it—higher education can open doors, increase lifetime earnings, and cultivate critical thinking and professional skills. But those benefits are maximised when borrowing is strategic, informed, and proportional to realistic outcomes.

Families who engage with these questions early and often are best positioned to support their children through a university experience that is not just enriching, but sustainable. By demystifying the mechanics of student debt and treating it as a manageable—rather than mysterious—element of financial planning, they prepare the next generation not only to study well, but to live well. Thoughtful borrowing is not about avoiding risk altogether. It is about understanding the trade-offs and making empowered decisions that serve both educational goals and long-term wellbeing.

Teaching Kids to Contribute to Their Education

For generations, education has been framed as a gift bestowed by parents upon their children—a sacrifice made in the hope of a better future. This narrative, while noble, often positions young people as passive recipients of support rather than active stakeholders in their academic lives. As the cost of higher education continues to rise and the financial implications of attending university become more complex, families are increasingly rethinking this dynamic. Encouraging children to contribute meaningfully—financially, intellectually, and behaviourally—to their own education is not simply a matter of budgetary necessity; it is a fundamental step in nurturing responsibility, maturity, and lifelong financial intelligence.

Asking a child to contribute to the cost of their education is not about imposing undue hardship. Rather, it's about instilling the value of participation and teaching them that higher education, while immensely rewarding, is also an investment that requires thoughtful planning and ownership. When young people are involved in the practicalities of financing their university experience—saving for tuition, working part-time, applying for scholarships, or budgeting their allowance—they begin to see education not as an entitlement, but as a pursuit that deserves respect, effort, and strategic decision-making.

One of the most effective ways to begin this process is by fostering financial dialogue from an early age. Children who grow up in households where money is discussed openly—where budgeting, saving, and prioritising are visible practices—enter adolescence with a clearer sense of what it takes to afford significant life choices. By the time university becomes a serious consideration, these young people already have a framework for understanding costs, weighing options, and making trade-offs. They are not shocked by tuition fees or mystified by interest rates. Instead, they are prepared to engage with these realities thoughtfully.

Encouraging contribution does not necessarily mean expecting children to pay for their entire education. Contributions can take many forms and should be tailored to the family's financial context and the child's capacity. Some may be able to contribute substantial savings from summer or weekend jobs. Others might cover the cost of books or contribute to living expenses during term. Even symbolic gestures—such as allocating a portion of birthday money to a university fund or committing to a no-spend challenge to save for application fees—can create a sense of involvement and accountability.

Real-world examples illustrate the power of this approach. A student in Leeds began saving 10% of his part-time wages from age fifteen after a conversation with his parents about university expenses. By the time he started his course in graphic design, he had enough saved to cover his first year's materials and studio fees. The financial impact was helpful, but what proved more significant was his attitude—he approached his coursework with a seriousness rooted in his own investment. He didn't view university as a parental obligation; he saw it as a personal mission.

Similarly, a family in Glasgow developed a matching scheme, agreeing to match every pound their daughter saved toward her education. This approach not only incentivised her to work during holidays but reinforced the idea that effort yields reward. She graduated with a modest but meaningful fund she had built herself, which she used for accommodation and postgraduate applications. The matching strategy gave the family a shared goal and allowed both generations to feel involved and respected in the financial planning process.

Another critical aspect of encouraging contribution is guiding children to make smart choices about their education. This means teaching them to look beyond prestige and consider value. Not all degrees or institutions offer the same return on investment. Helping young people understand course structures, employment outcomes, and the financial implications of various options enables them to make decisions grounded in both aspiration and realism. This doesn't require them to abandon dreams, but rather to pursue them with eyes wide open.

For example, a student considering an expensive private university abroad may be encouraged to compare the costs and benefits with a respected domestic programme offering a similar qualification. If they still choose the more expensive path, knowing they will carry more financial responsibility for it, they do so with greater intentionality. They become accountable not only to their parents but to themselves—and this accountability often translates into stronger academic engagement and a deeper appreciation for the opportunity.

Work experience is another channel through which young people can contribute to their education. Part-time jobs during secondary school or university teach more than just money management. They cultivate time discipline, customer service skills, and emotional resilience. Students who balance work and study often become adept at prioritising, focusing, and working towards long-term goals—qualities essential for both academic success and future employment.

Moreover, these students enter the workforce with tangible experience on their CVs, which enhances their employability upon graduation. Employers often view candidates who have supported themselves during their studies as more grounded and responsible. These graduates are less likely to be overwhelmed by professional expectations because they have already practised managing competing demands.

Teaching children to contribute also includes helping them understand the implications of borrowing. Student loans can seem abstract or even inconsequential to a teenager who has never had to make a monthly repayment. Parents can help by illustrating what loan repayments look like in practice—how long they might take, how interest accrues, and how they could affect future lifestyle choices. Rather than using fear as a motivator, the goal is to foster informed decision-making. When students know that borrowing £40,000 for a degree will mean sacrificing £200 to £300 a month from their future income, they are better equipped to assess whether that investment aligns with their goals.

Families might also explore creative alternatives together, such as deferring university to allow time for savings, considering apprenticeships, or pursuing a degree part-time while working. These conversations not only expand the range of options available but communicate a powerful message: there is no single correct path to education or success, and flexibility and ingenuity are valuable assets.

Financial contribution to education can also be framed as a moral and emotional commitment. When students take ownership of even a small part of their funding, they often engage with their education more purposefully. They attend lectures more regularly, complete assignments more diligently, and approach exams with a heightened sense of consequence. The act of contribution builds emotional investment, transforming the university experience from something that is happening to them into something they are shaping.

It is equally important to approach this topic with sensitivity. Not all children will have the same capacity to contribute, and some families may face circumstances that make financial involvement difficult or even inappropriate. The principle of contribution should not become a source of shame or pressure. Instead, it should be an invitation—a way of engaging young people in the practical and philosophical realities of investing in their own growth.

The conversation should be grounded in respect, framed as preparation for adulthood rather than a burden imposed prematurely. It is a chance to affirm that children are capable of understanding complex issues and making thoughtful choices. And it is an opportunity to model values of responsibility, agency, and cooperation.

As education costs continue to rise and the landscape of employment shifts, the need for financially literate, self-aware young people has never been greater. By encouraging children to contribute to their own education, families nurture not just academic success, but the character, confidence, and capability that underpin a meaningful, independent life.

This approach prepares students not only to navigate higher education, but to approach adulthood with strength and clarity. They learn that opportunity is built, not gifted, and that financial decisions are not obstacles to learning but integral parts of the learning process itself. When parents and children work together—each bringing their resources, efforts, and insights to the table—the result is not merely a well-funded degree. It is a life that begins not with debt and dependency, but with collaboration, pride, and purpose.

Chapter 8
Retirement Planning as a Family

Retirement, though often relegated to the distant margins of one's financial planning, stands as one of the most defining—and, in truth, complex—milestones a family will encounter. It's not merely the end of a career or a tidy line item on a spreadsheet; it is a slow, sweeping transition that echoes across generations, reshaping how time, resources, and responsibility are distributed. Too frequently, people imagine retirement as a private concern—something to be quietly sorted out in late middle age, tucked between tax returns and pension statements. But this mindset misses the larger point. Retirement, properly understood, is not just a personal moment; it is a family matter. And one that deserves to be addressed with openness, deliberation, and foresight.

Starting the conversation early is less about cold calculations than about creating a shared sense of orientation—looking down the road together, not peering up at it alone. Yet many families hesitate. Talking about ageing, money, or future decline can be awkward, even taboo. Sometimes, it's simply a case of being 'too busy'. But when the topic is left unspoken, planning becomes fragmented, rushed, or, worse, left too late. Treating retirement as a living, breathing part of the family's financial structure—rather than an afterthought—shifts it from a burden into something empowering, even clarifying.

A natural entry point for this dialogue is to demystify the tools involved. Across the globe, different systems offer different frameworks—whether it's a 401(k) in the United States, an IRA, or the UK's workplace and personal pensions. While the acronyms and contribution rules vary, the core idea holds: these accounts are long-term savings vehicles, often incentivised through tax benefits and, in some cases, employer matches. Take, for instance, the 401(k)—a staple in the American landscape—where workers contribute a slice of their earnings into an account that grows, ideally, over decades. In the UK, auto-enrolment into workplace pensions has made saving more accessible, with contributions from both employee and employer sweetened by government tax relief.

But knowing these structures exist is one thing; understanding how to use them effectively is quite another. A surprising number of employees neglect to contribute enough to receive the full employer match—essentially walking away from free money. Others may set and forget their portfolios, allowing them to drift into allocations that no longer suit their age or ambitions. A thoughtful strategy—reviewed every so often, adjusted for life's inevitable shifts—can spell the difference between comfort and compromise in later years.

Still, retirement planning shouldn't be reduced to charts and compound growth calculators. At its heart, it's a deeply human endeavour. It's about imagining a life of dignity, of autonomy, and, ideally, of continued purpose after work no longer structures one's days. Too often, retirement is painted as a quiet retreat, a fading into the background. But for many, it is—if they've been spared the stress of financial precarity—a chapter filled with travel, creativity, mentorship, or even part-time work done for pleasure rather than necessity. Planning, then, must account not only for expenses but for aspirations. What sort of life is being built toward? What might healthcare or family caregiving require? These are not minor considerations—they are, arguably, the crux of it.

When retirement is woven into broader family financial planning, something else emerges: the beginnings of legacy. That word, often cloaked in legalism, takes on deeper meaning when viewed through the lens of values. Legacy is not merely the transfer of wealth—it's the passing on of stories, habits, intentions. Many parents hope to leave behind more than just money. They want to leave behind clarity, a sense of continuity. But without a plan, even the best intentions can unravel. Families who avoid difficult conversations about wills, inheritance, or care arrangements may unintentionally sow confusion, resentment, or loss. Conversely, when wishes are clearly stated and understood, those same conversations become acts of care—bridges between generations rather than walls.

Examples abound of both paths. Picture a couple in their mid-fifties who had focused almost exclusively on their children's education, only to realise they'd neglected their own retirement planning. That moment of reckoning, though sobering, needn't have been the end of the story. By upping contributions, selling their larger home, and realigning their investments, they found a way forward. On the other side, consider a family with considerable assets but no clear estate plan. What followed was a lengthy legal battle among siblings, money eroded by court fees, and wounds that may never quite heal.

There's a compelling case to be made for bringing children into the picture—not in full financial detail from the outset, but with an eye toward education and transparency. Children who see retirement planning not as a grim topic to be avoided, but as a natural part of responsible adulthood, are better prepared to handle their own financial futures. A teenager watching their parent contribute monthly to a pension, discuss future plans, or adjust their lifestyle deliberately absorbs lessons no textbook could teach.

And it's worth saying—schools, by and large, do not equip young people with this kind of financial literacy. By the time most young adults come to grips with pensions or investment vehicles, they're already managing rent, bills, and perhaps student debt. The earlier this awareness can be cultivated within the home, the better. Parents needn't be experts; they simply need to be willing to talk. Concepts like compound interest, inflation's erosive effects, or the long-term gains of employer contributions are powerful when grasped young—and they aren't beyond the reach of a curious mind.

The psychological dividends of such openness are not to be underestimated. Children who know their parents are preparing for retirement are less likely to feel anxious about the future—less likely to fear being financially responsible for their care. And for the parents, the reassurance that their plans are understood, even supported, brings peace of mind. There is strength in shared understanding. In knowing that one's later years will not be defined by secrecy or surprise, but by trust and intention.

In this way, retirement planning transcends its bureaucratic trappings. It becomes a form of familial stewardship—a collaborative effort built not just on numbers, but on narrative. It asks families to look beyond the now, to ask what kind of future they want to build and what kind of legacy they hope to leave. And perhaps more importantly, it challenges the notion that financial planning must be an isolated task. It needn't be. When retirement is framed as a family value—when it becomes part of the way a household talks, thinks, and prepares—it lays a foundation not just for individual security, but for intergenerational strength.

What follows in this chapter is a deeper dive into how families can engage with the technical instruments of retirement—pensions, tax reliefs, diversified portfolios. But it also moves beyond numbers, into the more elusive, yet no less essential, dimensions: how to retire without fear, how to prepare loved ones for what's to come, and how to instil a financial culture that extends well beyond retirement itself. Because ultimately, retirement is not merely about exiting work—it is about entering a new stage of life with clarity, courage, and connection.

Why Families Should Talk About Retirement Early

Retirement may seem a distant consideration for young adults or even for parents still focused on raising children, managing mortgages, or funding education. Yet delaying conversations about retirement within the family often leads to missed opportunities, misaligned expectations, and avoidable financial stress. Contrary to the traditional view that retirement is a personal milestone best discussed near the end of one's working life, early and ongoing family dialogue about retirement is an essential part of long-term financial wellbeing. It offers a platform for clear planning, emotional preparedness, and intergenerational continuity that extends far beyond the scope of pensions and savings.

The reluctance to talk about retirement can stem from cultural norms, discomfort with discussing money, or the mistaken belief that such planning is reserved for financial advisers and later life stages. Many parents, keen not to burden their children or seem preoccupied with ageing, postpone these discussions until circumstances force their hand. Meanwhile, children—whether teenagers or adults—often feel unequipped or unwelcome in such conversations. The result is a mutual silence that serves neither party well. Addressing retirement openly and early, by contrast, fosters a culture of transparency and shared responsibility that benefits the entire household.

Retirement planning is not merely a matter of numbers; it is fundamentally about vision. It involves deciding what kind of life one wants to live after full-time work ends, and how that life will be funded, supported, and shared. For families, this vision extends beyond the individual to encompass caregiving, housing decisions, inheritance planning, and lifestyle choices that affect everyone involved. Beginning these discussions early allows families to set realistic expectations and design a future that accommodates both independence and connection.

Financially, early retirement conversations allow for the effective use of time—arguably the most valuable asset in retirement planning. Starting contributions to pension schemes, retirement accounts, or long-term investments in one's twenties or thirties can yield dramatically different outcomes than starting in one's forties or fifties. Compound interest rewards consistency and patience. For example, an individual who saves £200 a month from the age of twenty-five could accumulate significantly more by age sixty-five than someone who saves £400 a month beginning at forty, even though the latter invests more overall. Time allows for lower monthly commitments, greater flexibility, and the ability to absorb market volatility without panic.

Beyond the mechanics of saving, early conversations also allow for adaptation and recalibration. Life rarely proceeds exactly as planned. Career paths may shift, health issues may emerge, family structures may change. Families who treat retirement as a dynamic and revisitable topic are better equipped to respond to these changes. A couple who revisits their retirement goals every five years, adjusting for income, expenses, and aspirations, is far more likely to stay on course than one who waits until ten years before retirement to take stock and attempt a rapid course correction.

Real-world examples illustrate the benefits of proactive dialogue. A family in Manchester began retirement conversations early, with both parents in their early forties and their children entering secondary school. They used annual family meetings to review their financial goals, which included university savings, home renovations, and eventual retirement. These discussions were age-appropriate and evolved over time. By the time the children reached adulthood, they had a clear understanding of their parents' retirement timeline, the role pensions and property would play, and the general expectations around support. When one parent faced an unexpected redundancy in their late fifties, the family was able to respond with composure rather than crisis. The children, now in their twenties, were already engaged in their own retirement savings, recognising its importance from both example and direct discussion.

In contrast, another family delayed conversations about retirement until the father developed serious health issues at seventy. The adult children, unaware of the financial state of affairs, were suddenly called upon to help make difficult decisions about care, housing, and legacy—all without context or preparation. Tensions arose, and what could have been a coordinated, compassionate effort became a source of confusion and distress. The difference between these two examples is not wealth but foresight.

These conversations are not only for parents approaching retirement age. Adult children too benefit from understanding the implications of their parents' retirement choices. Will there be an expectation of shared housing in the future? Are ageing parents financially independent, or might they require support? What role will family members play in caregiving? These are sensitive but essential questions, and addressing them early allows for considered planning rather than reactive scrambling. It also gives parents the opportunity to express their wishes, ensuring dignity and autonomy in their later years.

From the perspective of children—particularly adolescents and young adults—discussing retirement helps demystify the financial landscape and underscores the importance of long-term thinking. Many young people are deeply focused on the present, facing student debt, uncertain job prospects, and rising living costs. Retirement may feel irrelevant or unreachable. However, being exposed to their parents' planning process helps them contextualise their own future. They learn that retirement is not an abrupt end, but a gradual shift that requires decades of thoughtful action. Witnessing their parents' contributions to pensions, decision-making about investments, or discussions about lifestyle goals reinforces the habit of strategic planning.

Families can integrate these conversations naturally into the rhythms of life. Annual financial check-ins, estate planning sessions, or milestone celebrations such as turning fifty or becoming grandparents provide opportunities to discuss not only current needs but future intentions. Importantly, these discussions do not have to be exhaustive or overly technical. They can begin with simple questions: What do we want retirement to look like? Where do we want to live? What resources will we need? Who will be involved in key decisions?

The emotional dimension of retirement planning is equally important. For many people, retirement is not just a financial event but an identity shift. Work provides structure, social connection, and purpose. Families that acknowledge this and support each other through the transition—whether through shared hobbies, intergenerational projects, or simply open communication—create a richer and more stable post-work life. Retirement, when thoughtfully anticipated, becomes an opportunity for renewal rather than withdrawal.

Furthermore, early retirement conversations allow families to discuss broader legacy goals. What values do parents want to pass on? How should assets be distributed? What role will philanthropy or community engagement play in later life? These discussions provide clarity and minimise future conflict. A well-articulated retirement and estate plan reduces ambiguity and ensures that resources are used in alignment with the family's values and aspirations.

In multicultural or multigenerational households, these conversations can be particularly nuanced. Retirement expectations may differ across generations or be shaped by cultural traditions. Some families may assume children will care for ageing parents; others may prioritise independence. Financial planning must accommodate these differences, and open dialogue is the only way to align expectations with reality. Early conversations offer space for respectful negotiation, allowing each voice to be heard and for compromises to be reached before decisions become urgent.

Crucially, families must overcome the taboo surrounding money talk. Financial conversations are not impolite—they are essential. When approached with sensitivity, transparency, and mutual respect, they become a means of empowerment. Retirement planning, when undertaken as a collective process, is not merely about preparing for decline. It is about designing a future that reflects the values, aspirations, and needs of the whole family.

Families that engage in these conversations early benefit from clarity, control, and confidence. They are better positioned to build resilience, avoid financial strain, and support each other with dignity and purpose. Retirement, far from being a solitary or silent subject, belongs at the heart of family financial planning. By bringing it into focus sooner rather than later, families lay the groundwork for a more secure, harmonious, and meaningful future—for themselves and for the generations to come.

401(k)s, IRAs, and Pension Plans

The subject of retirement accounts is often cloaked in technical language and riddled with acronyms that can seem abstract to the average individual. Yet understanding these accounts—and how to make the most of them—is essential for anyone who aspires to financial independence in later life. Whether one is just starting out in a career, mid-way through their working years, or approaching retirement, the ability to navigate the nuances of accounts like 401(k)s, Individual Retirement Accounts (IRAs), and pension schemes can make a profound difference in long-term financial security. These tools, when utilised strategically, not only provide tax advantages and investment opportunities but serve as the cornerstone of a sustainable and dignified retirement.

At the heart of retirement saving is the concept of deferred gratification. It requires setting aside income today to fund life tomorrow—often decades into the future. This can be a difficult proposition, especially in a world that rewards immediacy and short-term thinking. However, retirement accounts are designed to encourage this discipline by offering powerful incentives: tax relief, employer contributions, and the potential for compounding growth over time.

The 401(k), a cornerstone of the American retirement landscape, is a defined-contribution plan typically offered by employers. It allows employees to divert a portion of their pre-tax salary into an investment account that grows tax-deferred until withdrawal. This structure achieves two important goals. First, it reduces the employee's taxable income in the present year, offering immediate savings. Second, it permits the invested funds to accumulate without being eroded by annual taxation, allowing for more substantial growth over time.

One of the key features of the 401(k) is the employer match. Many companies offer to match employee contributions up to a certain percentage, essentially providing free money to those who participate. It is difficult to overstate the value of this benefit. For example, an employee earning £50,000 per year who contributes 5% into a 401(k) may receive an additional £2,500 annually from their employer, assuming a 5% match. Over twenty or thirty years, this matching contribution, combined with compound interest, can significantly enhance retirement readiness. Failing to take full advantage of the match is, in effect, forfeiting part of one's compensation package.

Individual Retirement Accounts, or IRAs, offer an alternative or supplementary path to retirement savings. Unlike 401(k)s, IRAs are not tied to an employer and are available to almost anyone with earned income. They come in two main types: Traditional and Roth. A Traditional IRA functions similarly to a 401(k) in that contributions may be tax-deductible and earnings grow tax-deferred. Withdrawals in retirement, however, are taxed as income. A Roth IRA, by contrast, involves contributions made with after-tax income, but allows for tax-free withdrawals in retirement—both of the contributions and their earnings.

The choice between a Traditional and Roth IRA hinges on one's expectations about future tax brackets. Those who anticipate being in a higher tax bracket later may favour Roth accounts to lock in a lower rate now. Others may prefer the immediate relief of a Traditional IRA, especially if current income is high. Whichever route is chosen, the contribution limits and income eligibility rules require careful attention, and those who are able to contribute to both types over time can enjoy tax diversification in retirement—a valuable hedge against future policy changes.

In the United Kingdom and other Commonwealth countries, pensions serve a similar function. These are typically defined-contribution plans in which both employers and employees make regular contributions, often supplemented by government incentives such as tax relief. The funds are invested, and the accumulated balance is used to provide income in retirement, either through drawdown or the purchase of an annuity. Unlike 401(k)s, UK pensions often benefit from automatic enrolment, ensuring that employees are participating by default, though the onus remains on individuals to maximise contributions and monitor their investments.

It is worth noting the fundamental shift over recent decades from defined-benefit pensions—where retirees received a guaranteed income for life—to defined-contribution plans that place the investment risk on the individual. This evolution has increased the importance of financial literacy and long-term planning. With defined-contribution schemes, the size of one's retirement fund depends not just on how much is saved, but on how wisely those funds are invested. This demands active engagement, regular review, and an understanding of asset allocation that evolves with age and risk tolerance.

For example, a 30-year-old may sensibly invest in a portfolio weighted heavily toward equities, accepting greater volatility in exchange for higher expected returns. As that individual approaches retirement, however, they may gradually shift toward bonds and other lower-risk assets to preserve capital. Target-date funds—investment vehicles that automatically adjust asset allocation based on expected retirement year—can simplify this process, though they should not be adopted without understanding their underlying assumptions and fees.

Real-world cases illustrate both the benefits and missed opportunities inherent in retirement account planning. Consider the story of a woman in her mid-fifties who began contributing to her company's 401(k) only in her forties, after prioritising mortgage payments and her children's education for many years. While she benefitted from catch-up contributions and increased her savings rate considerably, she expressed regret about not starting sooner, acknowledging that earlier contributions—even small ones—could have leveraged decades of compound growth. Conversely, her younger colleague, who began investing 10% of his salary from age twenty-five and consistently received a full employer match, was on track to retire at sixty with a portfolio that would comfortably support his lifestyle.

Maximising retirement contributions requires more than setting up automatic transfers. It involves a conscious effort to increase contributions as income grows. Too often, people maintain the same contribution percentage year after year, failing to adjust for inflation, salary increases, or life changes. By indexing contributions to raises—directing a portion of each pay increase toward retirement—families can build substantial wealth without feeling deprived. Regular reviews, ideally timed with annual financial planning or tax preparation, offer opportunities to assess contribution levels, investment performance, and broader goals.

Another consideration is the integration of retirement accounts with other financial priorities. It can be tempting to divert retirement savings to fund university fees or support ageing parents, particularly in households where financial demands are high. While these decisions are deeply personal, it is important to remember that time lost in retirement investing cannot be recovered. Children may have access to loans and grants; retirement does not. Parents who prioritise their own long-term security are not being selfish—they are preserving independence and preventing future dependency.

Education around these accounts is especially vital for younger generations, who may view retirement as a remote concern or believe that saving can wait. Encouraging teenagers and young adults to open their own Roth IRAs when they begin earning—whether through summer jobs, internships, or side hustles—can establish a lifelong habit of saving. Explaining the benefits in practical terms, such as showing how £1,000 invested at twenty could grow to over £10,000 by retirement, helps to make the abstract concrete.

Financial advisers, employers, and educational institutions also have a role to play. Clear communication, low-cost investment options, and access to professional advice can remove many of the barriers that prevent people from engaging with their retirement plans. Technology too can assist, with apps that track contributions, project future balances, and offer scenario modelling. The more accessible and user-friendly these tools become, the more likely individuals are to take ownership of their retirement planning.

Ultimately, 401(k)s, IRAs, and pension plans are not simply financial instruments—they are commitments to the future. They represent the choices we make today to support dignity, security, and freedom tomorrow. By understanding their structure, maximising their advantages, and integrating them into broader family planning, individuals position themselves not just for financial survival, but for a retirement marked by choice and fulfilment. Families who embrace this perspective early, and sustain it consistently, build more than wealth. They build a foundation for legacy, resilience, and peace of mind across generations.

How to Retire Comfortably Without Financial Stress

Retirement is often envisioned as a period of rest, renewal, and reward—the time to pursue passions, spend unhurried moments with family, and finally reap the benefits of decades of hard work. Yet for too many individuals and families, retirement arrives not with ease, but with anxiety. The absence of a structured income, the unpredictability of living expenses, and the rising cost of healthcare can combine to create uncertainty where there should be peace. Retiring comfortably without financial stress does not occur by chance; it is the product of deliberate, long-term planning rooted in discipline, foresight, and adaptability.

The foundation of a stress-free retirement lies in the early establishment of a clear, actionable plan. This does not mean predicting the future with perfect precision, but rather creating a flexible framework that anticipates various possibilities and provides safeguards. A robust retirement plan begins by asking essential questions: What does comfort look like? How much will it cost? How long might retirement last? And what risks need to be accounted for—economic, health-related, or otherwise?

Comfort in retirement is a deeply personal concept. For some, it might mean maintaining their current lifestyle, travelling occasionally, and helping grandchildren through university. For others, it might involve downsizing, relocating, or embracing a minimalist lifestyle. Without clarity on these personal definitions, financial goals can become too vague, making effective planning difficult. Families must take the time to visualise the retirement they want—not the idealised version seen in brochures, but one grounded in their values, needs, and aspirations.

Once that vision is established, the financial components can begin to take shape. Central to this is the identification of income sources. Traditionally, retirement was supported by a combination of three pillars: state benefits, employer-sponsored pensions, and personal savings. However, shifts in employment patterns, longer life expectancies, and the decline of defined-benefit pension schemes have increased the importance of individual preparation. Today, families must build reliable income streams through defined-contribution plans, such as 401(k)s, IRAs, or personal pensions, while ensuring they understand and optimise entitlements from public pension schemes.

The question of how much to save remains one of the most common—and complex—concerns in retirement planning. A useful rule of thumb suggests that retirees may need approximately 70–80% of their pre-retirement income to maintain their standard of living, but this varies widely depending on debt levels, healthcare needs, housing status, and desired lifestyle. Estimating expenses is therefore a critical step. This includes not only essentials like housing, food, and transportation, but also discretionary spending on travel, entertainment, and gifts, as well as contingencies for emergencies or long-term care.

Real-world examples reveal both the pitfalls and successes of retirement preparation. Consider a couple who, despite earning well throughout their careers, failed to account for healthcare inflation and ended up drawing down their retirement savings faster than anticipated. Their stress in later life was not due to insufficient income, but rather due to inadequate forecasting and over-reliance on one income stream. By contrast, another family with modest means but a structured plan—including diversified investments, debt elimination by age fifty-five, and a modest lifestyle—retired with security and confidence. The difference was not income, but planning.

A central element of a stress-free retirement is debt management. Entering retirement with outstanding mortgage balances, credit card debt, or car loans can severely constrain cash flow and limit flexibility. Eliminating debt before retirement, or at the very least reducing it substantially, eases the burden on fixed incomes and reduces exposure to interest rate fluctuations. It also provides psychological relief, freeing retirees from the monthly obligations that erode peace of mind.

Another vital consideration is the sequencing of withdrawals. Many retirees own a combination of taxable, tax-deferred, and tax-free accounts. Drawing from these in the wrong order can result in unnecessary tax burdens or premature depletion of assets. A tax-efficient withdrawal strategy, often best developed with the help of a financial adviser, can extend the lifespan of savings and reduce long-term liabilities. It can also ensure that retirees remain within favourable tax brackets, preserving eligibility for benefits and minimising the impact of required minimum distributions.

Healthcare costs represent one of the most significant and unpredictable elements of retirement. While many countries offer some form of public healthcare for retirees, these systems often do not cover all expenses, particularly long-term care or specialised treatments. Planning for these costs—whether through dedicated savings, long-term care insurance, or integrated retirement accounts—can prevent catastrophic financial outcomes and preserve family assets. Furthermore, maintaining physical and mental well-being in the years leading up to retirement reduces the likelihood of major medical expenses, underscoring the value of holistic planning that includes health as well as wealth.

Lifestyle planning plays a subtle yet important role in managing financial stress. Some retirees choose to relocate to areas with lower costs of living, better healthcare infrastructure, or more temperate climates. This can provide both financial relief and enhanced quality of life. However, such decisions must be made with care. A lower cost of living may come at the price of distance from family, loss of community ties, or reduced access to specialised medical care. These trade-offs should be evaluated not only in economic terms but through the lens of emotional and relational well-being.

Family dynamics are also central to a successful retirement. Many retirees find themselves part of a "sandwich generation," supporting both elderly parents and adult children. Without clear boundaries and open conversations, this can drain both emotional and financial resources. Encouraging financial independence among adult children, preparing for potential caregiving roles, and discussing inheritance plans with transparency can reduce ambiguity and foster stronger intergenerational cooperation. Retirement should be a time of shared stability, not hidden sacrifice.

Building a long-term retirement plan is not a one-time event, but an ongoing process. Life events such as marriage, divorce, illness, and career changes may require recalibration. Regular financial check-ins—preferably at least once a year—allow families to assess progress, revise assumptions, and adapt to changing circumstances. The key is not to achieve perfection but to cultivate responsiveness and resilience.

Psychologically, the most successful retirees are those who view retirement not as an end, but as a new phase of productivity and purpose. Financial security is not only about avoiding hardship; it's about enabling freedom—freedom to pursue meaningful activities, invest time in relationships, or contribute to one's community. A retirement that is financially sustainable supports emotional fulfilment and prevents the loss of identity that can sometimes accompany the cessation of work.

Technology can support this process in powerful ways. Budgeting tools, retirement calculators, and robo-advisers offer increasingly accessible means to monitor and project retirement health. While these should not replace expert advice where needed, they empower individuals to take ownership of their plans and make informed decisions. Families that embrace these tools and normalise their use in everyday life are more likely to build a culture of financial literacy that extends across generations.

Comfortable retirement is not reserved for the affluent; it is achievable for many through clarity, consistency, and intentionality. The critical elements—early saving, debt elimination, diversified income, and careful expense forecasting—are within reach for those who begin planning with purpose. It is not a matter of outguessing the market or winning the lottery, but of treating retirement with the seriousness it deserves while still embracing the life it makes possible.

Ultimately, retiring without financial stress is not about avoiding complexity, but about confronting it head-on with curiosity and resolve. Families that plan together, communicate openly, and adapt as needed are better positioned to turn retirement from a financial question into a life-affirming chapter. This approach doesn't just safeguard assets; it safeguards dignity, peace, and the ability to age with grace and confidence. That is the true hallmark of a retirement well-lived.

Multigenerational Wealth and Legacy Planning

The aspiration to leave something meaningful behind—a legacy that transcends one's own lifetime—is deeply rooted in the human experience. For many families, this aspiration takes tangible form in the idea of multigenerational wealth: the ability not only to enjoy financial security in one's own life, but to create a foundation upon which future generations can thrive. Yet despite its appeal, building and preserving wealth across generations is far more complex than simply accumulating money. It involves thoughtful planning, open communication, and a conscious effort to align values with financial decision-making. Legacy, in this context, is not just about what is left in a will; it is about what is intentionally cultivated and transferred—knowledge, character, and capital alike.

One of the most significant misunderstandings about multigenerational wealth is the assumption that it is reserved for the very wealthy. While vast fortunes may grab headlines, the principles of legacy planning are relevant to families at nearly every income level. Whether a household holds assets worth hundreds of thousands or several million, the central questions remain the same: How can we ensure our resources serve a long-term purpose? How do we protect those assets from erosion or misuse? And how do we prepare the next generation to manage them wisely?

The starting point is clarity. Families must first determine what wealth means to them—not just financially, but philosophically. Is the goal to provide a financial safety net for children and grandchildren? To enable access to education and entrepreneurship? To support causes that reflect the family's values? These questions are not rhetorical; they shape the entire architecture of a family's wealth strategy. Without a defined vision, even well-managed assets can be squandered or lead to division.

Formalising that vision requires practical tools, the most foundational of which is a comprehensive estate plan. This includes a will, powers of attorney, and, where appropriate, trusts and succession structures. A will ensures that assets are distributed according to one's wishes, reducing the risk of legal disputes and unintended outcomes. Trusts, particularly those designed with long-term objectives, can provide control over how and when beneficiaries access wealth, protect assets from creditors or marital claims, and support charitable endeavours. Powers of attorney ensure that financial and medical decisions are made by trusted individuals in the event of incapacity. While these instruments are often viewed as administrative necessities, they are in fact acts of care—tools that safeguard family unity and ensure continuity.

Real-world examples illustrate the importance of structure and foresight. A family in Edinburgh, with modest property and investment holdings, created a trust to ensure that their grandchildren's education would be funded regardless of future economic conditions. By specifying the terms clearly and appointing a responsible trustee, they not only protected the assets from mismanagement but conveyed a clear message about the family's commitment to learning. Another family, following the sudden death of a parent without a will, endured prolonged legal proceedings that strained relationships and consumed a significant portion of the estate in fees. The contrast between these two outcomes underscores the point that legacy planning is not an indulgence, but a responsibility.

Yet documents alone do not build legacy. They must be complemented by education. Far too often, families transfer wealth without context, creating confusion or conflict among beneficiaries. Preparing heirs to receive and steward wealth is as critical as the financial planning itself. This involves teaching financial literacy, fostering healthy attitudes toward money, and gradually introducing children and young adults to the family's financial framework. Simple practices, such as involving teenagers in family budgeting, discussing investment choices openly, or explaining the reasoning behind philanthropic gifts, can instil a sense of responsibility and continuity.

In some families, this education is formalised through structured "family meetings" where values, goals, and expectations are discussed openly. These gatherings can serve as a platform for shared decision-making, updates on financial performance, and the celebration of collective accomplishments. More importantly, they cultivate a sense of ownership and stewardship among younger members, who come to see wealth not as an entitlement, but as a resource entrusted to them for thoughtful use.

Another dimension of legacy planning involves the intentional inclusion of philanthropy. Families who engage in charitable giving—whether through direct donations, donor-advised funds, or family foundations—often find that this practice reinforces shared values and strengthens generational bonds. Philanthropy, when done transparently and collaboratively, offers a compelling way to integrate purpose into financial planning. It also shifts the narrative of wealth from accumulation to contribution, a perspective that many find more fulfilling and sustainable.

Of course, creating and preserving multigenerational wealth requires more than good intentions and family harmony. Economic realities, market volatility, taxation, and legal risks must all be considered. Diversification of assets—across industries, geographies, and asset classes—can mitigate some of these risks. So too can the judicious use of insurance products, tax-efficient vehicles, and professional advisory services. The goal is not to eliminate all uncertainty, which is impossible, but to build a resilient financial structure capable of weathering inevitable challenges.

Taxation, in particular, poses a significant threat to wealth transfer. Without careful planning, estate taxes, capital gains, and inheritance levies can erode a substantial portion of an estate before it reaches the intended beneficiaries. Strategies such as gifting during one's lifetime, setting up tax-advantaged investment accounts, or using life insurance as a funding mechanism for tax liabilities can all play a role in preserving the value of the estate. These measures require technical expertise, but they also demand clarity of purpose. Tax efficiency should serve the family's vision, not override it.

Legacy planning also encompasses the management of non-financial assets, such as family businesses, property, heirlooms, or even intellectual property. These assets often carry emotional significance and can become sources of both pride and contention. Succession planning for family enterprises, in particular, deserves dedicated attention. Whether the intention is to pass the business to the next generation or prepare it for sale, early and honest conversations are essential. Failure to plan can result in leadership vacuums, strategic drift, or unnecessary liquidation. Success, by contrast, often stems from a deliberate process of mentorship, role clarification, and phased transition.

It is also vital to acknowledge that no plan is permanent. Families evolve, laws change, and financial markets fluctuate. Legacy plans must be reviewed regularly and updated as circumstances dictate. Births, deaths, marriages, divorces, and significant financial events all warrant a reassessment of existing structures and intentions. Flexibility is not a sign of indecision—it is a mark of realism and resilience.

At its best, multigenerational wealth planning is an exercise in hope. It represents a belief in continuity, in the capacity of future generations to do good with what they are given, and in the power of preparation to shape outcomes. It challenges the narrow view of wealth as personal and immediate, replacing it with a broader vision of collective flourishing and sustained purpose. Families that embrace this mindset tend to create not only financial capital, but cultural capital—the habits, stories, and rituals that bind generations together in shared meaning.

Perhaps the most powerful legacy one can leave is not merely a set of assets, but a culture of responsibility, generosity, and clarity. When children and grandchildren inherit not just money, but an understanding of how it was earned, why it matters, and how it should be used, they are far more likely to honour it. They are also more likely to preserve and grow it—ensuring that the legacy does not end, but endures.

In the end, multigenerational wealth and legacy planning is not about control from beyond the grave. It is about partnership across lifetimes. It is an invitation to think expansively, act thoughtfully, and plan with both head and heart. And it is through this approach that families can ensure their efforts, values, and aspirations are not only remembered—but continued.

Teaching Kids About Retirement

The notion of retirement is often perceived as a distant, adult concern—something to be pondered once one has a stable job, a mortgage, or grey hair. For children and teenagers, the idea of saving for an event that might be fifty years away feels intangible at best and irrelevant at worst. Yet the seeds of long-term financial habits, including those that shape retirement outcomes, are planted early. Teaching children to understand the significance of saving for the long term—particularly for retirement—is not only possible but essential in creating a financially literate and self-reliant generation.

At its core, retirement is not simply about ceasing work; it is about ensuring that one can live with security and dignity when paid employment is no longer the main source of income. Helping children grasp this concept starts with shifting the narrative from one of deprivation—"you can't have this now"—to one of empowerment: "you are building freedom for your future." Children are far more capable of understanding these principles than they are often given credit for, especially when the teaching is contextual, consistent, and connected to their own experiences.

The key challenge in teaching children about retirement is that the time horizon involved is so abstract. Children are naturally oriented toward the present and the immediate future. Their savings goals tend to revolve around short-term desires—new toys, gadgets, outings—rather than distant needs. Bridging this psychological gap requires relatable analogies and incremental learning. One approach is to begin with the concept of delayed gratification, a fundamental principle that underpins all forms of saving. When a child saves for a desired object over weeks or months, they begin to experience the value of patience and foresight. This simple lesson forms the cognitive and emotional foundation upon which more complex financial concepts, such as retirement, can be built.

Once this base is established, parents and educators can begin introducing the idea of long-term goals and the notion that money saved today can grow over time. The concept of compound interest is particularly powerful here. Even younger children can be introduced to it through visual charts or simulations showing how small, regular savings can become substantial over many years. For example, showing a teenager how saving £20 a month from age fifteen, with interest, could become several thousand pounds by their thirties provides a compelling visualisation of time's financial power.

Real-world examples can make these lessons more tangible. Stories of family members who planned well and now enjoy comfortable retirements, or conversely, those who struggled due to inadequate planning, offer children a concrete sense of consequences and rewards. The goal is not to inspire fear, but to promote awareness and agency. Children who see retirement as a logical part of life's structure—rather than a financial emergency waiting to happen—are more likely to develop a lifelong saving habit.

Encouraging children to open savings accounts is a practical step that reinforces the value of saving for the future. As they grow older, parents might introduce them to junior ISAs, child pensions, or custodial investment accounts—vehicles that, while often managed by adults initially, become increasingly relevant to the child's own financial identity. Involving them in the management of these accounts—showing them how interest accrues, explaining the role of investments, and even allowing them to track progress—demystifies the world of finance and fosters a sense of ownership.

A critical yet often overlooked aspect of teaching retirement readiness is helping children understand the importance of financial independence. Retirement planning is not just about income; it's about autonomy. It is about ensuring that one does not become a financial burden on others, particularly family members. Framing retirement savings as a means of future self-care resonates strongly with children raised in environments where empathy and responsibility are emphasised. It allows them to see saving not as hoarding but as an act of maturity and respect.

Moreover, retirement education can serve as an excellent entry point into broader economic literacy. Conversations about what pensions are, how state and private systems work, and why people need more than one source of retirement income naturally lead to discussions about taxes, investment risk, employment benefits, and inflation. These topics, when introduced gradually and in age-appropriate language, equip children with a toolkit far more valuable than any single financial tip. They begin to see how systems interconnect and why personal responsibility plays such a crucial role in long-term stability.

Teenagers, in particular, are at a formative stage where values and habits solidify. For them, part-time jobs offer a unique opportunity to connect earning with saving and planning. Parents who encourage their teens to save a portion of their earnings—perhaps by offering to match contributions or helping set goals—create powerful reinforcement loops. A teenager who puts aside £50 a month into a long-term savings account is doing more than accumulating money; they are building a mental model in which future needs deserve attention now.

Equally important is dispelling the myth that retirement is something only "rich people" can afford to think about. For children from lower-income households, the idea of saving for retirement may feel irrelevant or even presumptuous. It is vital to teach all children, regardless of socioeconomic status, that small, consistent actions make a difference. Retirement planning is not about luxury but about security, and everyone deserves that dignity. Emphasising inclusivity and realistic strategies—such as saving modest amounts regularly, seeking employer-matched pensions, or learning to live below one's means—ensures that retirement education empowers rather than alienates.

In families with business interests or generational wealth, retirement education also intersects with legacy planning. Children who are expected to inherit businesses, property, or other significant assets must be taught not only how to preserve and grow those assets but also how to plan for their own eventual retirement. This includes succession planning, understanding tax implications, and distinguishing between personal and family resources. Early exposure to these ideas prevents entitlement and fosters stewardship.

Schools have an important role to play as well. While financial literacy is slowly gaining recognition within national curricula, retirement is often still overlooked. Including it in formal education—alongside budgeting, credit, and taxes—would normalise it as part of a complete financial education. Partnerships with banks, credit unions, and financial education charities can provide valuable support in delivering these lessons in an engaging and accessible manner.

Perhaps the most enduring way to teach children about retirement is through modelling. Parents and caregivers who save for their own future, speak positively about long-term planning, and invite children into financial conversations create an environment in which retirement is seen not as a fearsome unknown, but as a natural and achievable life stage. When children witness family members preparing for the future with optimism and clarity, they are far more likely to internalise those attitudes.

Ultimately, teaching children about retirement is not just a financial exercise. It is a profound act of preparation—an investment in their ability to live well, think ahead, and take responsibility for their lives. It shifts the focus from mere accumulation to thoughtful stewardship and ensures that they understand not only how money works, but how to make it work for them over a lifetime.

By cultivating these insights early and consistently, families and educators empower children to navigate adulthood with confidence. They equip the next generation not merely with savings, but with the wisdom and self-awareness to use those savings meaningfully. And in doing so, they plant the seeds of not just secure retirements, but resilient, well-informed lives.

Chapter 9
Insurance and Financial Protection for Families

Every family, at its core, seeks a life that's stable, secure, and filled with opportunities. And while building wealth or investing wisely often garners the spotlight, there's a quieter, less glamorous pillar of financial health that underpins it all: protection. Without it, even the most carefully constructed plans can come undone in a moment. Illness, accidents, disability, death—life, as we know, doesn't wait for us to be ready. That's why insurance and financial safeguards aren't just sensible add-ons—they are, quite simply, essential.

Now, let's be honest: insurance doesn't thrill. It's not the dinner-table topic that gets people fired up. But perhaps it should be, because it's insurance—not speculation or strategy—that often decides whether a family survives crisis intact or buckles under its weight. Far from being a pessimistic hedge, it is the architecture of resilience. It doesn't undo tragedy, but it cushions its blow. In that way, insurance protects more than just money. It protects time, choices, relationships, and the precious bandwidth needed to recover.

At its heart, insurance is a practical expression of responsibility. When parents take steps to insure their lives, their incomes, their homes, their health—they're not obsessing over worst-case scenarios. They're recognising a simple truth: life is unpredictable, but preparation is not. Choosing to protect against that unpredictability is, in many ways, an act of love. A promise, unspoken but profound, that says: *if something happens to me, you'll be all right.*

Picture, for a moment, the sudden death of a family's main earner. Without life cover, the grieving family faces not only loss but also a cascade of hard, unrelenting financial questions. How will the mortgage be paid? Can the children stay in their school? What happens next? Contrast that with a household where a term life policy was already in place—one substantial enough to erase debt, fund education, and give the survivors space to breathe. The difference goes beyond numbers. It's a question of whether grief is compounded by panic or softened, at least a little, by financial stability.

Health insurance tells a similar story. Medical crises, by their very nature, arrive unannounced. And they don't just threaten wellbeing—they threaten the very resources a family relies on. Where public healthcare systems exist, like the NHS, many assume they're fully covered. But there are gaps—waiting times, prescriptions, private options, specialist treatments—that can stretch family finances to breaking point. Supplementary health policies can close those gaps. And far from signalling gloom, purchasing such cover signals realism: an understanding that health and money are deeply entangled.

Other forms of insurance often get relegated to the background—but do so at your peril. A home is, for most families, their largest investment. Home insurance isn't just about bricks and mortar; it's about what happens if fire, theft, or storm takes more than just property. Auto insurance, too, is about far more than replacing a car—it's about liability, injury, and the unforeseen costs of being on the road. And then there's disability insurance—a quiet workhorse of a policy that rarely gets the attention it deserves. When illness or injury halts a person's ability to earn, disability cover can mean the difference between temporary discomfort and long-term derailment.

The real challenge isn't usually in understanding *why* insurance matters. It's in navigating the bewildering range of policies, terms, exclusions, and providers. Policies can be thick with small print and language few would willingly read. Premiums vary wildly. And sales pitches often obscure as much as they explain. That's why informed decision-making—ideally with the help of a trusted adviser—is vital. Insurance should never be bought as an isolated product, but as part of a coherent financial framework. One that reflects the family's unique needs, goals, and risks.

Estate planning, although separate in function, belongs in the same conversation. While insurance addresses what happens *to us*, estate planning addresses what happens *after us*. A will is the starting point: a document that directs how assets should be distributed, who should care for minor children, and who should carry out these wishes. Without one, the state steps in—often in ways that don't reflect the deceased's values or intentions.

And yet, a will is just the beginning. Powers of attorney, healthcare directives, and in some cases, trusts—all play roles in managing affairs if one becomes incapacitated or dies. These instruments don't just protect wealth; they reduce family conflict, avoid court delays, and clarify difficult decisions when emotions are high and time is short. Many young families dismiss such planning as premature. But that's a misreading. In truth, getting your affairs in order early is not about fearing death—it's about honouring life and those who share it with you.

Let's look at how this plays out in real life. One couple, shortly after buying their first home, took the time to write wills, arrange life insurance, and appoint guardians for their young children. A few years later, the husband died unexpectedly. Because they had prepared, his widow wasn't forced to make desperate decisions in the midst of grief. She could focus on healing, not unravelling red tape. Contrast this with a different family, blindsided by a medical crisis—a stroke that incapacitated their primary earner. No insurance, no directives, no access to financial accounts. The resulting scramble depleted savings, strained relationships, and left scars that went beyond the physical.

Another area often pushed to the margins is long-term care. The reality is stark: people are living longer, and extended care—whether at home or in a facility—is expensive. Too many families only confront this when the need is urgent, by which time options are limited and costly. Planning ahead, through long-term care insurance or dedicated savings, can distribute the burden more fairly and prevent resentment among siblings or spouses. Conversations about who will care for whom, and with what resources, are difficult—but they're far more painful when had in crisis.

No protection strategy is complete without addressing emergencies. The pandemic was a painful lesson in just how fragile our sense of normal can be. Job loss, illness, accidents, natural disasters—any one of these can throw a family into disarray. An emergency fund—modest though it may be—serves as a crucial cushion. It buys time, preserves options, and prevents long-term damage from short-term shocks. It doesn't need to be elaborate. It just needs to be there.

Crucially, protection planning is not a one-time event. Life shifts—sometimes gradually, sometimes all at once. Marriages begin and end, babies are born, careers pivot, people move. Each of these milestones calls for a review. Are beneficiaries still correct? Are policies adequate? Are documents up to date? Failing to revisit protection plans is, in effect, placing trust in the version of yourself that existed five or ten years ago—someone with different priorities and perhaps less understanding.

There's also a cultural element here that's worth noting. Many families, out of discomfort or deference, avoid the hard conversations. Talking about illness, money, or death can feel intrusive or morbid. But avoiding the subject doesn't prevent the reality. It simply leaves loved ones less prepared. Framing these conversations as acts of care—rather than fear—can help. They're not about doom; they're about dignity, agency, and peace of mind.

Young people, too, are watching. When children see their parents take these matters seriously, it leaves an impression. They learn that resilience is something you build, not something you hope for. That responsibility isn't just about today—it's about ensuring tomorrow isn't defined by today's silence. Parents who share the *why* behind their choices—why they bought life cover, why they created a will, why they maintain an emergency fund—aren't just shielding their families. They're teaching a philosophy of preparation, foresight, and self-respect.

In the end, insurance and financial protection are not tools of fear, but instruments of wisdom. They accept that life is uncertain and respond not with panic, but with planning. Families that embrace this ethos create something truly valuable—not just a safety net, but a sense of continuity. A belief that, come what may, they've done what they could. They've left nothing to chance they could reasonably control. And that, ultimately, is the quiet strength upon which all other plans can stand.

Why Insurance is Essential for Family Security

At the heart of every strong financial strategy lies one quietly powerful concept: protection. Families may work hard to accumulate assets, build savings, invest for the future, and plan for retirement, but without the right safety mechanisms in place, that progress remains vulnerable. Insurance, though often misunderstood or relegated to the background, plays a foundational role in preserving a family's stability against unexpected disruption. It is the financial equivalent of a seatbelt—rarely noticed when all goes well, but indispensable when life takes an unforeseen turn.

Insurance is not about pessimism or paranoia. It is about foresight. It exists to shield households from events that, although statistically unlikely on a day-to-day basis, could cause severe damage to their financial standing if they were to occur. A sudden illness, a car accident, a house fire, the unexpected loss of income—these are not pleasant topics, but they are realities that every family is susceptible to. The role of insurance is to absorb the financial blow so that the emotional and practical aftermath can be managed without the added burden of financial despair.

To understand why insurance is so essential, it helps to reflect on what families actually stand to lose in a crisis. Consider a young couple with two children, both working full time and paying down a mortgage. They have managed to save consistently and have started investing in their retirement. But they have no life insurance, no income protection, and minimal home cover. One day, the primary earner is diagnosed with a critical illness that requires long-term treatment and time off work. The family's income is cut in half. Medical bills, though partly covered by a public health service, begin to mount. Mortgage repayments strain their diminished income, and the savings intended for the children's education must now be redirected toward living costs. Their progress, hard-won and carefully planned, begins to unravel.

Now imagine the same scenario, but with adequate insurance in place. A critical illness policy pays out a lump sum, allowing the mortgage to be partially or fully paid off. Income protection replaces a portion of the lost earnings, keeping the household afloat. Private health insurance covers alternative treatments, providing quicker access to care. The family faces the emotional hardship of illness, but not the compounded pressure of financial collapse. Their trajectory is preserved. They are not forced to start over.

Such examples are not rare anomalies. Every year, countless families across the world face similar turning points. While it is impossible to eliminate risk from life, it is entirely possible to reduce its impact. That is the promise of insurance: not certainty, but security.

The role of insurance in protecting assets is equally vital. Families work for decades to pay off homes, acquire property, grow investment portfolios, and accumulate wealth. But these assets are not invulnerable. A flood can render a home uninhabitable. A lawsuit can threaten financial reserves. A car accident without adequate liability cover can put savings at risk. Insurance steps in as a firewall between catastrophe and consequence. It preserves the core of what families have built, allowing recovery rather than regression.

Some forms of insurance, such as home or auto cover, are often legally required or commonly understood. Others, like life, disability, or critical illness insurance, are more easily neglected. The reasons vary—perceived cost, lack of understanding, or the simple human tendency to avoid contemplating misfortune. Yet it is precisely because these risks are uncomfortable to consider that they must be addressed with clarity. Planning for adversity is not a sign of pessimism. It is an expression of care.

Life insurance, in particular, plays a critical role in ensuring long-term security. It is the means by which a family's income can continue even if the person earning it is no longer present. For parents, it is the mechanism that ensures their children can remain in the family home, continue their education, and maintain a sense of normalcy in a profoundly difficult time. For spouses, it is the assurance that grief will not be compounded by financial instability. For business owners, it can ensure continuity and protect against the sudden need to sell or dissolve a business in the event of a partner's death. Life insurance is not simply a payout—it is the preservation of options and stability.

Disability insurance is another often underappreciated component of family protection. The risk of being unable to work due to injury or illness is higher, in many cases, than the risk of early death. Yet it receives far less attention. A strong income protection policy can ensure that household bills continue to be paid and that the long-term financial goals remain within reach, even if one's earning ability is temporarily or permanently compromised. It provides a cushion that allows recovery to be the focus, rather than survival.

Health insurance, whether public, private, or a hybrid model, is central to the conversation as well. Even in countries with comprehensive healthcare systems, gaps exist—particularly when it comes to elective procedures, mental health support, or waiting times for critical care. Supplemental health insurance can offer access to faster or broader services, which can make a substantial difference in outcomes and recovery times. For families with specific medical needs, chronic conditions, or vulnerable dependents, the value of this coverage is not hypothetical—it is lived experience.

It is also essential to view insurance not as a one-time decision, but as an evolving component of financial planning. As families grow, move, change careers, or accumulate assets, their insurance needs shift. A newly married couple may begin with term life insurance and renter's cover. With the arrival of children, the need for more substantial life insurance, health cover, and home protection increases. As retirement approaches, the focus may shift toward long-term care, travel cover, and estate planning tools. The effectiveness of insurance lies not merely in its existence, but in its relevance—and that requires regular review.

Real-world illustrations again reinforce this point. A family who reviewed their insurance policies annually was able to identify that their home was underinsured due to rising property values. A simple adjustment meant that, when a fire later destroyed part of the home, their policy covered the full cost of rebuilding. Another couple, having not updated their life insurance since the birth of their second child, found themselves with a cover amount that would not have supported their dependents beyond a few years. A timely review corrected this gap and restored confidence in their future planning.

At its best, insurance is not just about payouts or paperwork—it is about peace of mind. It allows families to move through life with greater assurance, knowing that they are protected from financial ruin by structures they themselves have chosen. This confidence has psychological benefits as well. It reduces anxiety, fosters a sense of control, and strengthens decision-making. Families that feel protected are more likely to take positive risks—starting a business, relocating, investing in education—because they know their downside is managed.

Insurance also reinforces family cohesion. By removing uncertainty and disagreement about what would happen in a crisis, it creates clarity. Parents can rest assured that their children will be looked after. Spouses can make decisions together with confidence. Adult children caring for ageing parents can do so knowing that long-term care or critical illness provisions are in place. Financial protection thus becomes an expression of love, woven into the fabric of everyday life.

Finally, insurance plays a societal role in reducing dependence on public systems and charity in times of crisis. When families are adequately insured, they are less likely to require emergency support, drain public resources, or experience the social fragmentation that often follows financial catastrophe. This benefits not only the insured family, but the broader community. Insurance, then, is both a private safeguard and a public good.

In a world characterised by uncertainty, families cannot control all that life may bring—but they can control how well they are prepared to withstand it. Insurance is the mechanism by which financial security is preserved, assets are protected, and futures are defended. It is not an afterthought or a luxury. It is a critical pillar of responsible family finance. To neglect it is to leave the door open to chaos. To embrace it is to fortify the foundation upon which stability, resilience, and hope are built.

Types of Insurance Every Family Needs

Insurance is often treated as a background fixture of adult life—something purchased out of obligation or recommended by financial advisers but rarely discussed with real engagement. Yet for families aiming to establish long-term security, insurance is not merely an auxiliary product. It is a strategic shield, one that absorbs financial shocks, prevents wealth erosion, and allows life to continue with some degree of normalcy even in times of disruption. While the modern insurance market offers an almost bewildering array of policies, there are a few core types that no family should overlook. Among them, life, health, auto, home, and disability insurance stand out as fundamental to any responsible financial plan.

Life insurance is perhaps the most emotionally charged of these, touching as it does on mortality and loss. But its role in safeguarding a family's future is irrefutable. When a parent or income-earner dies unexpectedly, life insurance ensures that their financial contributions do not vanish with them. A well-structured life policy can pay off a mortgage, fund children's education, or provide the surviving family members with time and stability to reorganise their lives. Term life insurance, which covers a fixed period and is typically more affordable, is often suitable for families in their income-earning years. Whole-of-life insurance, though more expensive, offers lifelong cover and may be appropriate in legacy planning or for families with estate tax considerations.

Real-life situations often underscore the quiet but pivotal value of life insurance. A family in Birmingham, with two young children and a modest household income, lost the father to a sudden heart attack. Because they had maintained a £300,000 term policy, the mother was able to stay in their home, continue part-time work, and support her children emotionally without facing immediate financial pressure. In contrast, another family without life cover faced mounting debt and a forced relocation following the death of their primary earner—compounding grief with financial chaos.

Health insurance is another pillar of family financial protection, particularly in systems where public provision is limited or stretched. Even where a national health service exists, private medical insurance can provide faster access to specialists, elective procedures, and a broader range of treatment options. For families with ongoing medical needs or concerns about waiting lists, private cover offers peace of mind and tangible benefits in terms of care quality and timing. Beyond hospital visits, health insurance can cover diagnostics, mental health support, physiotherapy, and alternative therapies—helping to maintain wellness rather than just treat illness.

Practical applications of health insurance are wide-ranging. Consider a family with a child requiring specialised therapy for a developmental condition. While some services may be available publicly, private insurance can dramatically shorten wait times and improve outcomes. Or take the example of a self-employed couple without employer-sponsored health cover: an accident or illness could significantly derail their income. By maintaining comprehensive health insurance, they protect not only their physical wellbeing but their financial viability as well.

Auto insurance may seem mundane by comparison, but it remains a critical necessity. Most countries require some form of vehicle cover by law, typically third-party liability, which protects others from damage caused by the insured driver. However, families often benefit from more comprehensive cover, which includes damage to their own vehicle, theft, fire, and legal assistance. Families with teenage drivers, multiple vehicles, or a long commute have even more to gain from reviewing and tailoring their policies carefully. The financial consequences of a serious accident can include repair costs, medical bills, legal fees, and temporary loss of mobility—costs that can escalate rapidly without proper cover.

Auto insurance also intersects with broader family considerations. For instance, if a working parent relies on a vehicle to commute or to drop children at school, even a minor accident can disrupt family logistics. Comprehensive cover that includes courtesy cars or rapid repair services reduces this friction. Likewise, families that travel often—whether domestically or abroad—should ensure their policy extends to rental vehicles or includes appropriate international coverage.

Home insurance is another form of protection that operates quietly in the background until it is suddenly needed. Whether a family owns or rents, property insurance ensures that one of life's most significant financial and emotional assets is safeguarded. Buildings insurance covers structural damage from events like fire, flooding, or subsidence, while contents insurance protects the belongings inside—furniture, electronics, clothing, and valuables. Together, they form a bulwark against physical loss that might otherwise require years to recover from financially.

The need for home insurance becomes painfully clear in moments of disaster. A couple in Leeds experienced a burst pipe while they were on holiday, returning to find substantial water damage throughout their flat. Their contents and building insurance not only covered the repairs and replacement of damaged items but also paid for temporary accommodation while the work was carried out. Had they neglected to update their policy or underinsured the value of their possessions, the financial setback would have been considerable.

Perhaps the most overlooked but critical type of cover is disability insurance. While life insurance addresses the financial implications of death, disability insurance addresses the far more likely event of long-term illness or injury that inhibits one's ability to work. It replaces a percentage of income—typically 50 to 70 percent—if the policyholder is unable to perform their usual occupation. For families reliant on a single income or those with minimal emergency savings, this kind of protection can mean the difference between continued stability and financial collapse.

Disability insurance becomes particularly pertinent for individuals in physically demanding jobs, self-employed professionals, or anyone without a robust sick-pay benefit. One case in point involves a carpenter in Nottingham who, after a serious fall, could not return to work for over a year. His income protection policy covered monthly expenses and allowed his family to maintain their lifestyle during his rehabilitation. Without it, they would have had to rely on state benefits and personal loans, likely falling into debt in the process.

Beyond these core areas, families may consider additional coverages depending on their specific circumstances. Travel insurance, pet insurance, and legal protection plans can all provide useful layers of security. However, they should be viewed as supplementary rather than essential. The foundational policies—life, health, auto, home, and disability—form the baseline of any robust family risk management strategy.

What makes insurance powerful is not merely its ability to provide financial compensation, but its capacity to restore order amid chaos. It allows families to grieve without financial panic, to recover without bankruptcy, and to continue dreaming without fear that one misfortune will erase all that they have built. Its presence may go unnoticed in everyday life, but its absence is felt acutely when misfortune strikes.

Of course, insurance is not a set-it-and-forget-it affair. Policies must be reviewed regularly, especially after major life events—marriage, the birth of a child, a home purchase, or a career change. Coverage that was appropriate five years ago may now be inadequate or misaligned with a family's evolving risks and priorities. The market itself also changes, with new products, revised terms, and shifts in pricing. Staying engaged with one's insurance portfolio is not merely advisable; it is essential.

Families should also approach insurance decisions collaboratively. Both partners, where applicable, should understand what policies are in place, what they cover, and how to make a claim. Transparency helps prevent unpleasant surprises and ensures that, in an emergency, everyone knows how to act. It also creates a culture of shared responsibility—one where protection is seen not as a burden, but as a gift to each other and to future generations.

Insurance, at its best, is not a reactive expense but a proactive investment. It is an act of planning, of stewardship, and of love. It acknowledges that while we cannot predict life's disruptions, we can build a buffer between them and our most important commitments. For any family intent on preserving not just wealth, but wellbeing and continuity, these essential types of cover are non-negotiable. They are the silent scaffolding that holds everything else in place.

Creating an Estate Plan and Will

Few financial tasks are as routinely delayed—and as critically important—as creating an estate plan and will. Often dismissed as an issue for the elderly or the wealthy, estate planning is, in truth, a universal responsibility. It is not about preparing for death so much as about protecting the living. For families of all sizes and incomes, a well-constructed estate plan provides clarity, reduces legal and emotional stress, and ensures that assets are preserved and distributed according to the values and wishes of the individual. It is an act of foresight and care, grounded in practicality but deeply rooted in personal legacy.

An estate plan is a comprehensive legal strategy that dictates how an individual's affairs will be managed both during life and after death. While the will is a central component, a complete estate plan also typically includes powers of attorney, advance healthcare directives, guardianship provisions, and, in some cases, trust structures. The aim is to leave nothing to ambiguity. Without such planning, decisions about property, finances, dependants, and medical treatment may fall to the courts or to individuals who are neither prepared nor informed.

A will is often the cornerstone of this planning process. It is a legal document that outlines how a person's assets—such as property, savings, investments, and personal items—are to be distributed upon their death. It can also name guardians for minor children and appoint executors who will oversee the administration of the estate. Despite its simplicity and affordability, a staggering number of people do not have a valid will. The result is intestacy, a legal condition in which the state decides how to divide the deceased's estate according to a fixed hierarchy. This often leads to outcomes that the deceased would not have intended, including disputes among surviving family members.

The absence of a will can be particularly problematic in blended families, unmarried partnerships, or situations involving dependent relatives. For example, in many legal systems, an unmarried partner may have no automatic right to inherit, regardless of the length or depth of the relationship. Without a will stating otherwise, that partner could be left without housing or financial support. Similarly, adult children from a first marriage could find themselves in conflict with a stepparent over the division of an estate. These scenarios, while emotionally fraught, are entirely preventable with even basic estate documentation.

Real-world experiences often illuminate the consequences of poor estate planning. Consider a middle-aged couple who, after purchasing a family home and having two children, assumed that their modest assets would automatically pass to their next of kin. When the husband died unexpectedly without a will, the estate entered probate. Legal fees accumulated, administrative delays ensued, and tensions surfaced between relatives. What could have been a straightforward process turned into an 18-month ordeal. Contrast this with another family who had a clearly written will, designated guardians, and stored all relevant documents in an accessible location. When the matriarch passed away, her wishes were enacted with minimal dispute, and her children were able to grieve without administrative distraction.

Beyond the will, an effective estate plan addresses incapacity as well as death. A lasting power of attorney for property and financial affairs allows a trusted individual to manage the principal's finances if they become mentally or physically unable to do so. Similarly, a power of attorney for health and welfare designates who can make medical decisions on the individual's behalf. These roles are not just administrative—they are deeply consequential, involving everything from bill payments to choices about life-sustaining treatments. Without these provisions, families may be forced to apply to the court for authority, a process that is often slow, invasive, and expensive.

Trusts are another component that can provide significant advantages, particularly in complex family situations or where asset protection and tax planning are priorities. A trust allows a settlor to transfer assets to a trustee, who manages them for the benefit of designated beneficiaries. Unlike a will, a trust can take effect during the individual's lifetime and continue beyond death. It can provide for minor children, support relatives with special needs, or shield assets from creditors or spendthrift behaviour. Trusts are also commonly used to reduce inheritance tax liabilities or to manage business succession. While they require legal and financial expertise to set up properly, their flexibility and control make them a powerful estate planning tool.

Estate planning is not solely about wealth transfer. It is also a platform for articulating values. Letters of wishes, though not legally binding, can be included to provide guidance on how the estate should be managed, what the testator hopes the assets will achieve, or how relationships among heirs should be respected. These documents add a human dimension to the legal framework, reminding beneficiaries that their inheritance is not merely transactional but imbued with purpose and thoughtfulness.

For families with young children, perhaps the most urgent reason to create a will is the designation of guardians. In the absence of clear instructions, courts will decide who should raise surviving children. This may not align with the parents' preferences and can lead to custody disputes that are traumatic for all involved. Naming a guardian ensures continuity and provides the chosen individual with the legal authority to make decisions on behalf of the children. It also allows parents to articulate their hopes for how their children will be raised, including educational goals, religious beliefs, and lifestyle preferences.

It is equally important to ensure that all estate planning documents are current and accessible. Life changes—marriage, divorce, the birth of a child, the acquisition of new property—necessitate updates. A will drafted a decade ago may no longer reflect the family's reality or priorities. Regular reviews, ideally every three to five years or after major life events, help keep plans aligned with present circumstances. Moreover, it is crucial that executors, guardians, and key family members know where to find these documents and how to act upon them. A will that cannot be located, or one contested due to ambiguity, can be nearly as problematic as having none at all.

Taxation is another consideration that underscores the importance of deliberate planning. Inheritance tax thresholds vary by country and can significantly reduce the value of an estate if not managed properly. Gifts made during one's lifetime, the use of trusts, and other legal strategies can mitigate these liabilities. For example, in the United Kingdom, assets left to a spouse or civil partner are generally exempt from inheritance tax, and there are thresholds for passing on a primary residence to direct descendants. Awareness of these rules enables families to optimise their legacy rather than see it diminished by avoidable taxation.

Digital assets now also form part of the estate planning landscape. Emails, social media accounts, cloud-stored documents, and cryptocurrency wallets often contain not only financial value but sentimental significance. Without clear instructions and access credentials, these assets may be lost or irretrievable. Including a digital estate plan—detailing login information, account inventories, and instructions for online content—ensures that digital legacies are not overlooked in an increasingly virtual world.

Ultimately, creating an estate plan and will is not about anticipating tragedy—it is about eliminating uncertainty. It is about affirming control, communicating wishes, and minimising the burden on those left behind. Families who plan in advance demonstrate a level of care and responsibility that transcends financial management. They create not only a legal roadmap, but an emotional anchor for loved ones navigating a difficult time.

Estate planning requires honesty, not only with professionals but within families. Open discussions about intentions, expectations, and responsibilities can prevent misunderstandings and foster trust. These conversations may be uncomfortable, but they are essential. They transform estate planning from a private act into a shared process—one that empowers the next generation with both clarity and continuity.

Every family, regardless of wealth or complexity, deserves the stability that comes from knowing their affairs are in order. A well-crafted estate plan ensures that what has been built over a lifetime is not lost in transition. It preserves not just assets, but dignity, agency, and intention. And in doing so, it provides one of the greatest gifts a person can offer their loved ones: certainty amidst the unknown.

Long-Term Care and Elderly Financial Planning

As life expectancy continues to rise, families across the world are increasingly confronted with a challenge that is both financial and deeply personal: how to prepare for the long-term care of ageing parents and the medical, emotional, and logistical complexities that come with it. Planning for elderly care is not simply about anticipating frailty or illness—it is about preserving dignity, ensuring continuity, and maintaining the quality of life for those who once provided the same care to others. It is also about recognising that the need for sustained support in later life is not hypothetical; it is a probability that every responsible family must address with thoughtfulness and intention.

The ageing process does not occur in a straight line. While many individuals remain active and independent well into their seventies or eighties, a significant proportion will eventually require assistance with daily tasks, medical supervision, or full-time residential care. This progression can be gradual or abrupt, predictable or unforeseen. The cost of such care—whether delivered at home, in assisted living facilities, or in nursing homes—can be substantial. Without advance planning, these costs can quickly erode savings, strain family relationships, and compromise the wellbeing of both the elderly and their carers.

Understanding the scale of the challenge is the first step. In the United Kingdom, for instance, the average cost of residential care exceeds £35,000 annually, with nursing care costs considerably higher. While some support may be available through the NHS or local authorities, eligibility is often means-tested, and coverage is far from comprehensive. The threshold for receiving financial aid is relatively low, meaning that many families fall into the uncomfortable middle ground: not wealthy enough to absorb care costs without impact, but not poor enough to qualify for full support. Planning, therefore, becomes not just advisable but essential.

Effective long-term care planning begins with open conversation. It requires family members—often adult children and their parents—to speak candidly about preferences, resources, and expectations. These discussions are often postponed out of discomfort or a desire to spare elderly parents from confronting their vulnerability. Yet avoidance only delays difficult decisions until they must be made under pressure. Talking early and regularly about future care preferences—whether to remain at home, move in with family, or consider professional care settings—allows for decisions to be made collaboratively rather than reactively.

Such conversations also provide an opportunity to review the elderly individual's financial position and prepare for future needs. This includes evaluating pensions, savings, insurance policies, investments, and the potential role of assets such as property. Families might consider the sale or rental of a home to fund care costs, or the use of equity release schemes in certain circumstances. Understanding these options well in advance enables a structured, non-emotive approach to what can otherwise be distressing choices.

One powerful yet underutilised tool in this space is long-term care insurance. While more commonly available in countries like the United States, some British providers also offer versions tailored to the UK system. These policies are designed to offset the cost of care should the need arise, either by providing a regular income or reimbursing specific expenses. As with all insurance, the best time to purchase such a policy is before it is needed, ideally in one's fifties or early sixties, when premiums are lower and eligibility criteria more accessible. However, these products are complex and require careful scrutiny, including an understanding of benefit caps, waiting periods, and coverage exclusions.

Real-world examples illustrate both the benefits of foresight and the pitfalls of neglect. A couple in their late seventies, having downsized from a large family home to a smaller bungalow, used the proceeds to establish a fund specifically for their future care. They also created lasting powers of attorney and communicated their wishes to their children. When the husband's Parkinson's disease progressed, the family was able to act swiftly, securing high-quality in-home care without compromising their financial stability. In contrast, another family faced crisis when their mother suffered a fall, resulting in immediate hospitalisation and the need for round-the-clock support. Without any financial preparation or formal documentation, the adult children scrambled to find suitable care, eventually taking unpaid leave from work and depleting personal savings to fill the gap.

This disparity highlights a central truth: the emotional weight of caring for an elderly loved one is significant enough without the added burden of financial uncertainty. Families that plan ahead can focus on what truly matters—companionship, comfort, and quality of life—rather than logistical firefighting.

The legal aspects of elderly planning are equally important. Establishing lasting powers of attorney for both property and health allows trusted individuals to act on behalf of ageing parents when they are no longer able to make decisions themselves. Without these instruments, families may have to apply to the Court of Protection to gain control over finances or care decisions, a process that is time-consuming, costly, and intrusive. Powers of attorney not only simplify administration but offer reassurance to the elderly that their affairs will be handled by people they know and trust.

Families must also navigate the ethical terrain of balancing autonomy and protection. Ageing individuals may be reluctant to accept help or acknowledge cognitive decline. They may resist the idea of moving into care facilities or handing over control of financial matters. Navigating this requires empathy, patience, and often professional guidance. Involving a financial adviser or eldercare specialist can depersonalise sensitive discussions and provide an objective framework for decision-making.

One particularly delicate area is the intersection of care and inheritance. Children who provide care for ageing parents may feel entitled to compensation, especially if they have reduced working hours or foregone opportunities. At the same time, siblings may disagree on the value of such contributions or how they should be reflected in the estate. Addressing these issues proactively, through legal agreements or explicit provisions in a will, can prevent rifts and ensure fairness. Some families establish care agreements that formalise the responsibilities and compensation of caregiving relatives, aligning expectations and protecting all parties.

Technology also offers new avenues for elderly care. Remote monitoring systems, telemedicine, and wearable health devices can extend the period during which older adults remain safely at home. These tools, while not a substitute for human care, offer valuable support, particularly when family members live far apart. They also provide data that can inform medical decisions and reassure carers. Investing in such technologies, where appropriate, should be part of the broader care planning discussion.

It is also worth noting that long-term care planning is not solely the responsibility of adult children. Many ageing parents actively want to shape their own future and will welcome the opportunity to participate in these decisions. When families adopt a collaborative approach, involving all relevant voices and respecting individual dignity, the process becomes one of empowerment rather than loss.

Preparing for long-term care is, at its heart, about embracing the full arc of life. It is about acknowledging that ageing is not a problem to be solved but a phase to be honoured. Financial planning for this phase does more than cover costs—it upholds independence, eases burdens, and allows for choices that align with deeply held values.

As societies continue to age, the need for thoughtful, comprehensive long-term care planning will only grow. Families who engage with this task early—who see it not as morbid but as a natural extension of love and responsibility—are better positioned to face the future with confidence. They build not just financial resilience, but emotional strength. And in doing so, they offer their elders what they have always given in return: safety, comfort, and respect.

Emergency Planning for Unexpected Situations

Crises rarely knock before they enter. They arrive uninvited—sometimes in the form of a sudden illness, at other times as a job loss, an accident, or a family emergency—and they almost always carry a financial impact. Despite their unpredictability, such events are not uncommon. What distinguishes those who recover from those who struggle is not luck, but preparation. Financial readiness for unexpected situations is not about anticipating every possible disaster; it is about building a system that allows a household to absorb shocks without unraveling.

Emergency financial planning is not the exclusive domain of the wealthy or the hyper-organised. It is an accessible, practical approach that every family can undertake with deliberate effort. At its heart lies a simple premise: life is uncertain, but our ability to navigate it need not be.

A critical starting point is the creation and maintenance of an emergency fund. This reserve of liquid savings serves as a buffer, enabling a family to continue meeting essential expenses when income is disrupted. While the recommended amount varies depending on individual circumstances, most financial experts suggest setting aside three to six months' worth of living expenses. This fund should be easily accessible—ideally held in a high-interest savings account—and separate from everyday spending accounts to avoid erosion through casual use.

The value of an emergency fund is best understood in real terms. Consider a family where both parents are employed, and the household is financially stable, with a manageable mortgage, school fees, and modest savings. When the father is unexpectedly made redundant, the family initially panics. However, because they have an emergency fund covering five months of expenses, they are able to maintain their lifestyle while the father searches for new employment. There is no need to rack up credit card debt, no delay in paying the mortgage, and no disruption to the children's activities. The redundancy, while deeply stressful, does not escalate into a financial crisis.

Contrast this with another family of similar means but without a financial cushion. A sudden illness forces one parent to take extended unpaid leave. Within weeks, bills begin to mount. Credit card balances grow, and the family dips into retirement savings just to cover medical costs. By the time recovery arrives, they are dealing with long-term financial consequences that far outlast the crisis itself.

Beyond building an emergency fund, effective crisis planning involves understanding the specific types of risks a household may face and taking proactive steps to mitigate them. For many, job security is a significant concern. Economic downturns, company restructurings, and automation all contribute to a volatile employment landscape. Households reliant on a single income source are particularly exposed. In these cases, diversification becomes not only a career strategy but a financial safeguard. Encouraging multiple income streams—whether through part-time work, freelancing, investment income, or a small side business—can provide resilience when one source dries up.

Insurance plays a complementary role in this landscape. Income protection policies, critical illness cover, and health insurance are tools designed to provide financial support during periods of personal crisis. While they involve a recurring cost, their value becomes clear when unexpected events threaten the household's economic stability. An income protection policy that pays out 60 percent of a salary during a period of incapacitation, for example, can mean the difference between recovery in dignity and a descent into debt. Likewise, a health insurance plan that covers private treatments can enable faster access to care, reducing downtime and associated income loss.

One often overlooked aspect of emergency planning is the structure and visibility of household finances. In a time of crisis, clarity is essential. Families should ensure that all key members understand the location and purpose of important financial documents: bank account details, insurance policies, mortgage statements, wills, and powers of attorney. In dual-income households, both partners should be familiar with all accounts, even if one typically manages day-to-day finances. In the event of illness or incapacity, this familiarity ensures continuity and reduces the emotional toll of an already difficult period.

Technology can aid significantly in this process. Budgeting software and cloud-based document storage make it easier to keep financial information updated and accessible. These tools can help track expenses, alert users to unusual activity, and consolidate financial accounts for easier review. In a crisis scenario, such systems save time, reduce errors, and offer a degree of control when circumstances feel unstable.

Families should also consider establishing a basic crisis response plan—one that outlines the immediate steps to take if a financial shock occurs. This plan might include a list of non-essential expenses that could be paused, a schedule for reviewing benefits eligibility, or a checklist for notifying creditors. Having this prepared in advance reduces the paralysis and confusion that often accompany emergencies.

Creditors, in fact, often have procedures in place for supporting customers experiencing hardship. Mortgage lenders may offer payment holidays or modified terms; utility companies might provide emergency relief programmes. These options are far more effective when accessed early, before arrears accumulate. Families who communicate proactively with creditors are more likely to receive support, whereas those who delay until their situation is critical may face more rigid responses.

Emergency planning is not solely financial, however. It includes the emotional and relational dynamics that play out during a crisis. Financial stress is one of the leading causes of tension within families, particularly between partners. Establishing a clear protocol for how decisions will be made, who will take on what responsibilities, and how communication will be maintained can mitigate conflict. In times of uncertainty, transparency and collaboration are essential. When everyone understands the plan, feels heard, and contributes to the response, the household functions more cohesively under pressure.

Moreover, teaching children about financial preparedness—even in age-appropriate ways—builds resilience across generations. Explaining why a family is cutting back temporarily, why certain expenses are postponed, or how savings help in emergencies normalises the idea that setbacks are part of life and can be managed. Children who witness calm, strategic responses to adversity are more likely to develop similar attitudes themselves.

Real-world examples show that even modest preparations can dramatically shift outcomes. A single parent who set up a contingency budget and maintained a modest emergency fund was able to navigate an unexpected car breakdown without resorting to payday loans. A couple who kept up-to-date wills and powers of attorney avoided protracted legal processes when one spouse suffered a stroke. These cases highlight that emergency planning is not reserved for the affluent; it is a discipline that benefits everyone.

The psychological impact of having a plan cannot be overstated. Even if the plan is never used in its entirety, its existence reduces anxiety and enables clearer thinking when real crises arise. It allows families to make decisions from a place of stability, not desperation. It also fosters a proactive mindset—a belief that, while not every event can be controlled, our response to it absolutely can be.

As families continue to face global uncertainties—from economic instability and job displacement to climate-related disasters and public health emergencies—financial preparedness becomes not a luxury but a necessity. Households that build adaptability into their finances are better equipped not only to endure hardship but to recover from it with strength and clarity.

Emergency planning, at its best, is an affirmation of care: care for one's family, one's future, and one's peace of mind. It allows us to honour our responsibilities, protect our progress, and ensure that when life becomes unpredictable, we remain anchored. It is not fear that drives preparation; it is love, expressed through action. And in that, there is immense power.

Chapter 10
Creating a Family Wealth Plan — The Roadmap to Financial Independence

Financial independence is rarely a fixed point on a map; rather, it's an ongoing journey—fluid, evolving, and shaped by the choices we make along the way. For families, the idea of wealth stretches far beyond mere numbers on a bank statement or the growth of an investment portfolio. True wealth involves something more intangible yet vital: stability, opportunity, shared purpose, and that quiet confidence that comes with steering one's future deliberately, not leaving it to the whims of fate. A comprehensive family wealth plan weaves these threads together, turning hopes into tangible goals and daily habits into lasting outcomes. It's the strategic crescendo of the financial principles laid out across this book.

Starting such a plan demands clarity. Too often, families find themselves caught in a reactive cycle—patching financial holes as they appear, adjusting to sudden income shifts, or responding to market fluctuations without a clear compass. What separates a sound wealth strategy is its proactive stance. Central to this is the establishment of long-term goals that are not only precise and measurable but shared openly among all members of the family. Whether the target is owning a home, funding higher education, retiring early, giving generously, or building wealth that spans generations, having everyone on the same page brings a coherence to every financial choice.

But setting family financial goals isn't just ticking off a list. It's a conversation—sometimes a challenging one—that demands reflection, prioritisation, and often compromise. Divergent values come into play: the tug-of-war between security and aspiration, or reconciling lifestyle desires with the discipline of saving. One couple may debate whether to pour resources into property investment or channel them into expanding a business venture; parents might wrestle with the trade-offs between private schooling and a sabbatical abroad. These aren't purely numbers on a spreadsheet—they touch the very fabric of family life, and so any wealth plan must honour both the practical and emotional landscapes it inhabits.

With a clear vision in place, the plan moves from theory to practice. Cultivating multiple streams of income becomes not just a means of accelerating growth, but a buffer against uncertainty. Dependence on a single paycheck, especially in today's volatile job market, invites risk. Diversification—be it through rental properties, dividends, freelance projects, small businesses, or intellectual property—builds resilience. It provides a safety net, ensuring that if one income falters, others will hold steady, keeping long-term ambitions intact.

This idea isn't reserved for entrepreneurs alone. Salaried workers can participate fully. A teacher might author educational materials; a nurse could offer training courses; a stay-at-home parent might run a blog or online store. The key is leveraging existing skills, passions, and networks into sustainable ventures. And here's a subtlety worth noting: these side endeavours needn't be scaled to blockbuster proportions to matter. Modest, steady supplemental income, when reinvested thoughtfully, can substantially enhance savings and investments over time.

Keeping a wealth plan on track requires more than good intentions—it demands structure and accountability. Regular family finance meetings serve this purpose well. These gatherings aren't just about crunching numbers or juggling bills; they're moments for reflection, recalibration, and renewed commitment. Families that embed financial conversations into their routine—be it monthly, quarterly, or at key milestones—foster a culture of openness and responsibility. Children learn early that money is a shared concern, not a taboo topic. Partners strengthen their financial literacy and deepen their sense of shared ownership. Even when conversations turn uncomfortable—discussing overspending, setbacks, or shifting goals—the very act of coming together fortifies trust and unity.

Examples from real life illustrate this power. A family in Manchester, facing a downturn in their small business, began quarterly finance meetings. These sessions became a forum for debt management, brainstorming new income ideas, and celebrating progress, however small. Within two years, not only had they recovered financially, but their communication as a couple had blossomed. Elsewhere, a family with teenagers turned Sunday breakfasts into informal budget talks, giving their children hands-on roles in managing family outings. This simple practice cultivated in the young ones a strong sense of financial agency and accountability.

Tracking progress remains essential. No matter how carefully crafted, a wealth plan cannot remain static. The world changes, family circumstances evolve, and what once fit perfectly may no longer serve. Budgeting tools, investment trackers, and apps provide useful data, but the real skill lies in interpretation. Are savings growing as expected? Is debt declining? Are income streams stable, or in need of new diversification? Is the portfolio balanced for current life stages and appetites for risk?

These questions demand more than cold numbers. They require context and thoughtful judgement. For instance, rising income can sometimes bring lifestyle inflation—slowly eroding gains. Or a portfolio may swell in value while liquidity shrinks, leaving a family vulnerable in emergencies. By making reviews a regular feature of the family's financial rhythm, such issues can be caught early and addressed before they cause harm.

Perhaps the most profound part of a family wealth plan is legacy. Far from being an afterthought, planning for future generations lies at the very heart of meaningful wealth. Leaving a legacy is about much more than dividing assets—it's about passing on values, opportunities, and a framework for enduring prosperity. This encompasses wills and trusts, but extends further—to teaching financial literacy, setting philanthropic intentions, and preparing heirs to handle both the benefits and burdens that come with inherited wealth.

Legacy invites a family to reflect on a simple yet profound question: "What do we want our wealth to represent beyond ourselves?" For some, this may mean setting up educational funds for grandchildren; for others, endowing community projects or establishing family foundations. What truly matters is that the plan stretches beyond the present, embodying the family's enduring principles.

Consider the example of a family who, having built a thriving business, created a charitable trust now managed by their adult children. This structure not only guarantees long-term charitable impact but also offers a collaborative space for the next generation to engage with shared values and governance. Another family entrusted their young adults with real investment decisions through small portfolios—an education in compound interest, risk, and stewardship that has left these children financially savvy and personally invested.

Ultimately, the success of any wealth plan lies not in its complexity but in its clarity and consistency. Families who approach finances as a cohesive unit—rather than a collection of isolated individuals—are far better placed to weather storms, seize opportunities, and build a legacy that endures.

Creating a family wealth plan is not a one-off exercise to tick off a list, but a living, breathing framework. It evolves alongside changing circumstances, deepening relationships, and a growing understanding of what it truly means to live well and give well. It marries the rigor of numbers with the nuance of human experience, the precision of spreadsheets with the warmth of shared dreams. When done right, it becomes more than a pathway to financial freedom—it stands as a testament to foresight, cooperation, and the enduring strength of family.

Setting Long-Term Financial Goals as a Family

Creating long-term financial goals as a family is one of the most powerful steps a household can take to secure its future, yet it is often approached with less intentionality than it deserves. Families tend to plan for immediate needs—monthly expenses, school fees, holidays—but when it comes to designing a multi-year or multi-decade financial vision, many struggle to articulate what they truly want to achieve. The absence of a long-term plan does not merely lead to inefficiency; it undermines the sense of shared purpose that makes a family financially resilient. Clarity of vision, combined with defined milestones, provides a structure that not only guides decisions but strengthens unity, accountability, and confidence.

Financial goals are not abstract numbers. They are representations of values—what a family prioritises, aspires to, and wants to protect. These could include owning a home without debt, funding university education for children, achieving early retirement, travelling extensively, supporting charitable causes, or leaving an inheritance that fosters opportunity rather than dependence. Such goals require careful articulation and, crucially, the agreement of those affected. Without shared understanding, even the most meticulously crafted plan can unravel under the weight of misalignment.

The process begins with open dialogue. Every family has its own dynamics, but the principle remains the same: financial goals are more sustainable when they are co-created rather than imposed. For couples, this means discussing individual visions for the future—what financial independence looks like, what level of risk is acceptable, and how lifestyle choices align with long-term objectives. For families with children, it means introducing financial conversations early and consistently, not necessarily in technical terms, but in ways that invite understanding and participation.

A family from Bristol, for example, began their planning by holding a simple discussion one weekend: where do we want to be in five, ten, and twenty years? From that conversation, they identified four primary goals—paying off their mortgage, building a travel fund, contributing to their children's education, and retiring by age sixty. They used these goals to reverse-engineer a strategy: calculating how much needed to be saved or invested each year, how expenses could be adjusted to support those savings, and which milestones would help track progress. What made their plan effective was not its complexity, but its clarity. Every family decision—whether to upgrade a car, switch jobs, or make a large purchase—was weighed against their long-term vision.

Such clarity does not arise by chance. It is the product of honest reflection and a commitment to structure. Families must be willing to ask fundamental questions: what does success look like for us? What are we willing to sacrifice in the short term to achieve long-term peace of mind? How do we manage competing priorities between parents and children, between lifestyle and savings, between ambition and contentment?

A major challenge is balancing the aspirational with the realistic. It is one thing to say "we want to be debt-free in ten years," but another to build a budget, debt-reduction plan, and lifestyle adjustments that make it possible. The best goals occupy the space between comfort and stretch—they demand discipline, but remain within the realm of attainability. This is where financial literacy becomes invaluable. Families that understand compound interest, investment growth, amortisation schedules, and inflation can make more informed decisions about what is needed to reach their objectives. This also fosters autonomy and confidence—members of the household understand not just what they are doing, but why.

Tracking milestones along the way provides both motivation and accountability. These can take many forms: reaching a specific net worth, reducing debt by a certain amount, hitting a savings percentage each year, or reaching a property down payment goal. Celebrating these milestones, even modestly, reinforces the family's progress and keeps the momentum alive. Just as athletes track performance metrics to refine their training, families who monitor their financial markers are better equipped to adjust course when necessary.

This tracking is not only about numbers. It should include regular reflection: has our vision changed? Are we still committed to the same goals? Has a life event altered our priorities or capacity? A new child, a job loss, an inheritance, or a health diagnosis can all require recalibration. The best wealth plans are living documents—rigorous but flexible. A family in Edinburgh revised their financial goals after one parent shifted from corporate work to self-employment, which brought less income but more time with the children. Though the timeline to early retirement was extended, the quality-of-life improvements were deemed more valuable. The plan adjusted accordingly, without compromising the overarching sense of direction.

Long-term goals also benefit from specificity. Vague intentions—like "save more money" or "invest better"—tend to fizzle out. Clearer goals—such as "accumulate £50,000 for university fees in ten years" or "achieve a passive income of £1,500 per month by age fifty-five"—provide a reference point for decision-making. They also invite problem-solving: what rate of return is needed? How much must be saved each month? What tools—ISAs, pensions, real estate, side businesses—are best suited to the task?

The psychology of goal-setting also plays a role. Families are more likely to stick with financial plans when those plans are framed positively and emotionally. Rather than focusing solely on constraints ("we can't afford this"), it is more motivating to frame goals in terms of empowerment ("we're choosing not to spend here so we can achieve that"). This language shift transforms budgeting from a chore into a mission. Children, especially, respond well to this framing. Teaching them that every pound saved today brings a step closer to the family's travel adventure or new home fosters not only discipline but excitement.

Moreover, the process of goal-setting cultivates habits that extend beyond finance. It reinforces communication, responsibility, delayed gratification, and collective thinking. Families that plan together often report stronger relationships, as financial clarity reduces conflict and builds a sense of shared achievement. Even setbacks—missed savings targets, unforeseen expenses—become learning opportunities when viewed through the lens of a long-term plan.

Technology can also aid the process. Budgeting tools, investment tracking apps, and goal-setting platforms allow families to visualise their progress, simulate scenarios, and share access in real time. These tools, while no substitute for discipline, make it easier to stay engaged and informed. They also provide an educational platform for children and teens, who can learn financial concepts in a hands-on, real-world context.

Perhaps the most important insight in setting long-term goals is that the process itself is as valuable as the outcomes. Even if circumstances change and some goals are revised or delayed, the act of planning ensures that the family is thinking intentionally about its future rather than drifting aimlessly. It transforms finances from a source of stress into a domain of agency. It reframes money as a tool to support values, not an end in itself.

Ultimately, families that invest the time and effort to articulate a shared financial vision position themselves to make better choices, adapt to uncertainty with greater resilience, and pass on not just wealth, but wisdom. The milestones they reach are not merely financial—they are markers of commitment, collaboration, and clarity. And in that, they find not only financial security, but a deeper sense of unity and purpose.

Building Multiple Income Streams

In an increasingly unpredictable global economy, the concept of a single income sustaining an entire household is not only outdated—it is inherently precarious. While previous generations often relied on one stable job to fund all expenses, modern families face a far more volatile landscape, shaped by technological disruption, global competition, economic downturns, and evolving employment models. In this environment, building multiple income streams is not merely a strategy for accelerated wealth creation; it is a form of financial risk management. By diversifying where income originates, families protect themselves from income shocks, enhance their resilience, and create greater opportunity for long-term growth and independence.

The idea of cultivating more than one stream of income may initially appear daunting, especially to those already stretched by full-time work, parenting, or caregiving. However, income diversification is not about working multiple jobs around the clock. It is about structuring sources of revenue that, collectively, provide stability, scalability, and in many cases, passive or semi-passive earnings over time. With thoughtful planning and a clear understanding of options, families can begin to lay the groundwork for additional income that complements their primary employment and serves their broader financial goals.

The most accessible place to begin is often within one's existing skill set. Many professionals overlook the fact that their expertise has market value outside of traditional employment. A graphic designer, for example, may offer freelance services in the evenings or license digital templates online. A teacher could create educational resources or run private tutoring sessions. A project manager might consult for small businesses or teach online workshops. These side incomes, while initially modest, can grow into substantial contributions over time—particularly when reinvested or used to pay down debt or acquire assets.

One family in Cardiff, for instance, decided to explore income diversification after experiencing the financial strain of a job redundancy. The mother, a speech therapist, began offering private sessions via video call during evenings and weekends, gradually building a loyal client base. Her husband, who had previously worked in IT support, launched a tech-help YouTube channel that, over time, generated advertising revenue. Neither of these ventures replaced their previous income immediately, but together they allowed the family to maintain stability, avoid dipping into savings, and eventually transition both ventures into ongoing income sources with flexible hours.

Another avenue for diversification lies in investment-based income. Dividend-paying stocks, real estate rental properties, peer-to-peer lending, and interest-bearing savings products all generate income that is not tied to hourly labour. These assets, once established, can provide cash flow with relatively low time input, making them particularly attractive for busy families. While these forms of income often require capital to begin, they offer long-term benefits and scale well over time.

Property investment remains one of the most popular paths in the UK, although it comes with its own set of challenges and responsibilities. Families who own additional properties can generate consistent monthly income through rental arrangements, provided that the property is well-located, maintained, and responsibly tenanted. Buy-to-let investments, holiday lettings, or renting out part of a primary residence can all serve as means to generate additional income. A family in the Midlands, for example, converted their unused garage into a self-contained studio, which they now rent to university students during the academic year. The monthly income goes directly into their children's education fund.

However, investing for income requires a level of financial literacy and due diligence. Mismanaging rental properties or speculating in high-risk assets can result in financial losses rather than gains. Families should begin by educating themselves on basic investment principles, seeking advice from certified professionals, and aligning investment choices with their risk tolerance, time horizon, and ethical considerations.

Online platforms have also democratised the process of building additional income streams. The digital economy offers opportunities in content creation, e-commerce, print-on-demand services, affiliate marketing, and digital product sales. While these options are not passive at the outset, they offer low barriers to entry and, if approached with a long-term view, can yield considerable returns. A couple in Glasgow, both primary school teachers, started a blog sharing lesson plans and classroom resources. Over time, they monetised it through sponsored posts and downloadable content, turning a hobby into a profitable venture that also enriched their professional community.

It is essential, however, to separate genuine income strategies from internet myths. Many online schemes promise quick returns but rely on unrealistic assumptions or unsustainable practices. Building income streams—especially those that require upfront effort or capital—is not instant. It requires consistent work, patience, and a willingness to learn from failure. Families must approach this space with discernment, distinguishing between credible models and speculative distractions.

A lesser discussed, but equally valuable, source of income diversification is within the household itself. Encouraging all capable family members to contribute, in ways appropriate to their stage of life, can significantly strengthen the family's economic foundation. Teenagers might take on part-time jobs or monetise creative skills, learning invaluable lessons in the process. Retired grandparents might use their time or expertise to generate modest income or reduce outsourced household costs, such as childcare. Income diversification, in this sense, becomes a family ethos—a way of life where financial participation is shared, understood, and appreciated.

There are also strategic considerations for couples. In dual-income households, spreading risk across different sectors or industries can mitigate exposure to sector-specific downturns. A household where one partner works in a volatile field, such as sales or media, might benefit from the other partner pursuing a more stable role in education or healthcare. This form of diversification doesn't always appear on spreadsheets but can offer real protection when market forces shift.

Managing multiple income streams also requires operational discipline. With several financial inputs, it becomes vital to track income accurately, separate business and personal accounts, prepare for tax obligations, and maintain adequate records. Some families find it useful to set up a holding structure or limited company once their side incomes reach a certain level, offering both tax efficiency and legal protection. These decisions should be made with the guidance of financial and legal advisers who understand the family's goals and context.

Crucially, building multiple income streams should not undermine family wellbeing. There is a temptation to pursue income at the expense of time, health, or relationships. While short bursts of effort are sometimes necessary, long-term financial planning should be anchored in balance. The goal is to create a sustainable, enriched life—not simply to accumulate more money. Families must be vigilant against burnout, ensuring that every income stream adds value not just to their bank accounts, but to their broader vision of success and fulfilment.

At its best, income diversification is empowering. It shifts a family from a passive financial posture—reliant on external employers or singular cash flows—into a more active, agile position. It allows for faster debt repayment, greater savings, and enhanced opportunities. It fosters creativity, encourages entrepreneurship, and builds intergenerational capability. Children raised in households where income generation is diverse and deliberate are more likely to think resourcefully, take initiative, and develop the financial confidence needed for adulthood.

In the current era of economic uncertainty, cultivating multiple income streams is no longer optional for families who want to thrive. It is a necessary evolution of traditional financial planning—one that responds to new realities with adaptability, imagination, and resilience. As with all meaningful endeavours, it requires commitment. But for families willing to think beyond the traditional paycheck, the rewards can be substantial, not only in financial terms, but in independence, peace of mind, and the freedom to choose how to live and how to give.

Regular Family Finance Meetings

Few practices offer more consistent, transformative impact on a household's financial health than the simple habit of holding regular family finance meetings. These meetings are not just about spreadsheets or savings—they are a forum for dialogue, a structure for accountability, and a ritual that reinforces the family's collective goals. They serve as a mechanism for transparency, a safeguard against drift, and a platform for teaching the next generation how to engage with money in a deliberate, empowered manner. In households where financial silence is the norm, introducing regular discussions about money may feel uncomfortable at first. Yet it is precisely in that discomfort that some of the most powerful growth occurs.

The primary function of a family finance meeting is to create alignment. In the absence of regular financial communication, even the most well-intentioned families can fall out of sync. One partner might assume they are saving for a house deposit, while the other prioritises paying down debt. Parents may be planning to support a child's university education, while the child remains unaware of expectations or limitations. Over time, these misalignments erode trust and efficiency. Meetings provide a structured space to clarify priorities, revisit objectives, and ensure that everyone is pulling in the same direction.

Consistency is more important than complexity. A monthly or bi-monthly cadence often works well, although some families opt for weekly check-ins or quarterly reviews depending on their goals and availability. The point is not frequency for its own sake but regularity that allows habits to form. When financial matters are addressed predictably, they lose their emotional charge. Conversations become more neutral, less reactive. The money talk becomes just that—a talk, not a confrontation.

In families with dual incomes, these meetings are critical for equalising participation. It is common for one partner to manage most financial decisions, either out of preference or habit. Over time, this dynamic can create an unhealthy dependency and increase risk if the primary manager becomes unavailable. Joint meetings ensure that both partners remain informed, involved, and capable of stepping in if needed. They also allow for shared decision-making, which strengthens the sense of partnership. When financial wins are celebrated together, and setbacks navigated as a team, the relational bond deepens.

Children benefit immensely from being included in these meetings, provided the content is age-appropriate. For younger children, this might involve discussions about saving for a family trip or deciding on a charity to support. Teenagers can learn about budgeting, managing mobile phone bills, or contributing to their own education savings. Involving children fosters financial literacy not through instruction but through observation and engagement. It demystifies money, presents it as a tool to be stewarded wisely, and normalises the process of goal-setting and compromise. A family in Norwich, for example, began including their teenage children in finance meetings when planning for a summer holiday. By jointly deciding how much the family could afford to spend and how they might save together, the children learned about opportunity cost, budgeting, and shared responsibility—all in the context of a goal they cared about.

Accountability is the second major function of these meetings. Without periodic review, it is easy for spending to drift, goals to be forgotten, or agreements to be overlooked. Regular meetings provide a gentle but firm structure for checking progress against targets. Have savings contributions been made? Is spending aligned with the budget? Have debt payments stayed on track? Are investments performing as expected? These questions, addressed routinely, prevent small oversights from becoming chronic issues. They also reduce the likelihood of financial surprises—a major source of stress in many households.

Importantly, accountability is not about blame. When treated as a space for reflection rather than interrogation, finance meetings become supportive rather than punitive. They allow each member to speak honestly about challenges—unexpected expenses, impulse purchases, job insecurity—and receive support rather than criticism. This fosters a culture of openness, where mistakes are learning opportunities rather than sources of shame.

One powerful example comes from a couple in Birmingham who decided to introduce monthly finance reviews after encountering mounting credit card debt. Their initial meetings were tense, marked by frustration and defensiveness. But over time, as they adopted a more collaborative tone, they began to feel like co-managers of their future rather than adversaries. Within a year, they had paid off a significant portion of their debt, created a sinking fund for annual expenses, and began saving for a home. What made the difference was not just the numbers—it was the conversation.

Structure is key to maintaining momentum. While the tone should remain conversational, a consistent agenda helps ensure that nothing is overlooked. Topics might include reviewing bank statements, updating budgets, checking in on short- and long-term goals, discussing upcoming expenses, and setting action items for the next period. Over time, families can expand these meetings to include financial education—reviewing insurance coverage, understanding investment options, or discussing pension planning.

Technology can play a useful role in facilitating these meetings. Budgeting apps, shared cloud documents, or financial dashboards can provide visibility and help track progress visually. These tools reduce friction by providing real-time data and eliminating the need for manual tracking. However, technology is a supplement, not a substitute. The real value lies in the dialogue—the understanding that comes from sitting down together and taking ownership of the family's financial wellbeing.

Families should also use these meetings to look beyond the numbers. Money is a reflection of values, and finance meetings are an opportunity to revisit those values regularly. Are we spending in a way that reflects what we care about? Are we using our resources to support our wellbeing, our relationships, and our purpose? Are there areas where we can simplify, redirect, or give more generously? When these questions are part of the discussion, financial planning becomes holistic rather than mechanical. It integrates with life rather than sitting apart from it.

For families with adult children or ageing parents, finance meetings can be expanded into intergenerational discussions. This may involve reviewing estate plans, planning for long-term care, or coordinating support for education and housing. These conversations are often delicate but incredibly important. When addressed early and openly, they prevent misunderstandings, reduce stress during transitions, and ensure that everyone understands expectations and intentions.

Introducing finance meetings may require an initial shift in mindset, especially if money has historically been a source of tension or secrecy. But with patience and persistence, they can become a source of connection and clarity. They reduce the emotional volatility often associated with money, replacing it with structure, visibility, and purpose.

Ultimately, regular family finance meetings are not just about managing pounds and pence. They are about stewardship—of time, of values, of shared vision. They remind us that wealth is not merely what we accumulate, but how we communicate, how we collaborate, and how we care for the people we love. When families commit to meeting regularly about money, they do more than protect their financial future. They invest in trust, understanding, and the quiet discipline that turns good intentions into real progress.

Tracking Progress and Adjusting Strategies

Financial planning, no matter how meticulous at its inception, cannot remain static. Life changes, markets shift, goals evolve, and what once seemed like an ideal strategy may become outdated or ineffective. That is why tracking progress and adjusting strategies is not merely a prudent financial exercise—it is a critical discipline for any family aspiring to long-term financial independence. Without ongoing evaluation, even the best-laid financial plans risk becoming irrelevant, misaligned with current realities, or insufficient in the face of new opportunities or emerging risks.

At the core of effective financial evaluation is the ability to distinguish between movement and progress. A family may be earning more, investing regularly, and paying down debt, but unless those actions are moving them closer to clearly defined goals, they risk mistaking activity for achievement. That is why a periodic and structured review is necessary—not just to confirm that things are being done, but to assess whether they are being done well, and whether they still serve the overarching vision.

Evaluating financial plans begins with reference to benchmarks. These benchmarks might be tied to savings targets, debt reduction goals, investment returns, or cash flow management. A family that set out to save £60,000 for a home deposit over five years, for instance, should expect to see measurable progress annually. If two years into the plan only £12,000 has been saved, this is not necessarily a failure, but it is a signal—one that prompts inquiry into whether the original goal was realistic, whether spending habits have veered off course, or whether income constraints need to be addressed.

The discipline of tracking requires accurate data and, ideally, visualisation tools that provide a clear picture of the financial landscape. This does not necessitate complex software—simple spreadsheets or budgeting apps can often suffice. What matters most is consistency. Income, expenses, assets, liabilities, and net worth should be tracked regularly, and family goals should be overlaid on these metrics to show whether the current trajectory aligns with desired outcomes.

A couple in Leeds offers a compelling example of this principle in action. After setting a five-year goal to pay off their £20,000 personal loan, they used a basic spreadsheet to track monthly payments, income changes, and unexpected expenses. Each quarter, they reviewed their progress. During one review, they noticed that although they were making steady payments, their lifestyle inflation—particularly dining out and subscription services—had eaten into their surplus, slowing repayment. Rather than abandoning their goal, they recalibrated: they introduced a monthly cap on non-essential spending and redirected the surplus to their loan. As a result, they not only stayed on course but shaved six months off their repayment timeline.

Adjustment is not a sign of failure—it is the essence of responsiveness. Financial strategies must be flexible enough to absorb setbacks and adaptable enough to incorporate new insights. A young family may initially prioritise aggressive savings but discover after the birth of a child that their capacity to contribute has changed. Rather than abandoning the goal, they might extend the timeline, revise the target, or seek supplementary income to maintain momentum. The act of reassessing does not weaken a plan; it strengthens its realism.

Another critical aspect of strategy adjustment is recognising when external conditions have shifted. Inflation, interest rate changes, tax policy reforms, or shifts in market performance can all impact the effectiveness of a given plan. A family investing heavily in bonds may find their returns eroded by inflation, while those with adjustable-rate mortgages may experience a spike in housing costs as rates rise. Awareness of the broader economic environment allows families to pivot intelligently—rebalancing portfolios, renegotiating terms, or seeking alternative strategies.

Periodic evaluations should also include qualitative reflections. Financial plans are not only mathematical; they are deeply human. Has the family's vision changed? Have priorities shifted? Perhaps early retirement is no longer as compelling as funding a sabbatical year, or maybe supporting ageing parents has become more urgent than upgrading a home. By making space for these reflections during financial reviews, families ensure that their strategies remain aligned not just with numbers, but with purpose.

This human-centred lens is particularly important in families with multiple generations or stakeholders. Adult children may need to be brought into conversations about inheritance planning, parental care, or shared investments. As the family structure evolves—children leaving home, marriages, deaths, or relocations—the financial strategy must evolve too. These transitions often introduce emotional complexity, which is why a scheduled review framework helps maintain focus and clarity during times of upheaval.

Tracking also introduces an opportunity for celebration. Too often, financial progress is acknowledged only when major milestones are hit. Yet recognising smaller wins—a fully funded emergency account, the first £10,000 saved, a credit score improvement—boosts morale and reinforces good habits. It also engages younger family members, who may feel disconnected from abstract long-term goals but resonate with visible achievements.

One particularly effective practice is to establish annual family financial reviews. These more comprehensive sessions differ from monthly budget meetings in that they take a wide-angle view. Families might assess how their financial position has changed over the past year, what goals were met or missed, how investment accounts have performed, and what personal events affected the household financially. They might also use the time to set new goals, revise projections, and assign responsibilities. In one family based in Edinburgh, this annual meeting became a December tradition, held just after the holidays. Over hot drinks and without distractions, they would review the year's finances, reflect on lessons learned, and set fresh intentions for the coming year. It became a cornerstone of their family culture—an anchor point between celebration and strategy.

Making adjustments, however, sometimes requires uncomfortable choices. A financial plan that no longer serves the family's reality may need to be abandoned altogether. A business that was once promising may have become a financial drain. An investment property may no longer be producing reliable returns. These decisions are not easy, but they are necessary. The willingness to course-correct, even radically, reflects maturity and foresight. Clinging to a failing strategy for fear of admitting error only compounds the damage.

Equally important is the discipline of doing nothing when warranted. Not every deviation from the plan requires intervention. Markets fluctuate, life has unpredictable rhythms, and some goals unfold slowly by design. Evaluating a financial plan does not mean constantly tweaking it. The art lies in distinguishing between noise and signal—between natural variance and structural misalignment.

In the final analysis, tracking progress and adjusting strategies is the mechanism through which financial planning becomes a living practice rather than a one-time event. It ensures that the family remains in dialogue with its own intentions, navigating complexity with clarity and confidence. It transforms financial stewardship from a passive hope into an active responsibility. And perhaps most meaningfully, it ensures that the pursuit of financial independence remains anchored to the values and realities of the people it is meant to serve.

Families who embrace this discipline find themselves not only more resilient to adversity but more energised by progress. They know where they stand, what needs to change, and how to act. They become, over time, not just better with money, but wiser in its use. And in doing so, they build not just wealth, but a model of accountability, foresight, and adaptability that future generations will be proud to inherit.

Leaving a Legacy – Ensuring Future Generations Thrive

Creating a legacy is often misunderstood as a concept confined to the affluent—those with significant estates, vast businesses, or philanthropic foundations that bear their names. But legacy is not limited to the wealthy. At its heart, it is about intention. It is about shaping the future in a way that reflects one's values, priorities, and care for those who come next. For families striving toward financial independence, the question is not only how to accumulate wealth, but how to ensure that it endures with purpose—empowering future generations rather than simply enriching them.

Leaving a financial legacy begins with understanding that assets alone are not enough. Inheritance, when transferred without education, structure, or context, can burden rather than benefit. Many families have witnessed wealth dissipate within a single generation due to mismanagement, lack of financial acumen, or conflicting expectations among heirs. Conversely, families who pair financial gifts with guidance and preparation often see those assets grow, support meaningful opportunities, and sustain family wellbeing for decades.

The first step in ensuring a lasting legacy is clarifying the goals behind it. What is the wealth intended to achieve? Is it to provide educational access for grandchildren? To support a child's entrepreneurial aspirations? To fund charitable initiatives? To guarantee long-term security for dependants? When a family understands the purpose of its wealth, it becomes easier to structure it accordingly and communicate those intentions clearly.

Real-world examples illustrate this point with striking clarity. Consider a family in Bristol who built a successful construction business over thirty years. As they approached retirement, they did not simply divide their assets equally among their three children. Instead, they established a trust that would allocate funds in phases—supporting university education, funding deposits for first homes, and eventually providing capital for each child to pursue either a business venture or retirement savings. Importantly, the parents spent several years involving their children in financial discussions, educating them about investments, tax implications, and the values that had guided their wealth-building. When the eventual transfer occurred, it came not as a surprise, but as a responsibility the children were prepared to carry forward.

Legacy also includes intangible assets—less visible but arguably more enduring. These include the family's ethos around work, stewardship, generosity, and resilience. A family culture that prizes living below one's means, giving back to the community, and learning continuously around financial matters is a form of inheritance in itself. It prepares future generations not only to receive wealth, but to build upon it wisely.

Practical steps help bridge these ideals into tangible plans. Drafting a will is a foundational act. Yet many families stop there, believing it sufficient. A will alone may direct where assets go, but it does little to explain why, how, or what recipients are expected to do with them. This is where additional instruments—such as letters of wishes, family constitutions, or structured family meetings—add essential depth. They articulate the story behind the wealth and provide guidance on its stewardship.

Some families go further by creating what is often termed a "family mission statement." This document lays out the shared vision, values, and goals that guide financial decisions across generations. While not legally binding, it serves as a moral compass and can be especially useful when assets are held jointly, or when philanthropic decisions are to be made collectively. For example, a family in Manchester with a multi-generational investment portfolio used their mission statement to define the criteria under which funds would be withdrawn. These included educational advancement, health-related needs, and socially impactful business ventures. The document also encouraged younger members to seek financial education before accessing larger distributions.

Education, in fact, is the linchpin of any lasting legacy. Financial literacy is not inherited through DNA; it must be taught deliberately and over time. Children and grandchildren need to understand compound interest, budgeting, risk, taxation, and economic cycles. But more than this, they need to grasp the mindset of stewardship—that wealth is not merely for consumption, but for cultivation. A family from Glasgow integrated this into their parenting by assigning each child a mock investment portfolio at age twelve, with annual review meetings where they discussed performance, economic trends, and ethical investing. By the time those children inherited real assets in their twenties, they were not overwhelmed—they were engaged, capable, and invested in the broader vision.

There are also legal and financial instruments that support legacy-building in a structured manner. Trusts, for instance, allow for assets to be distributed over time or under certain conditions, protecting them from mismanagement, creditors, or matrimonial disputes. Life insurance policies can be used not only to cover end-of-life costs but to create tax-efficient wealth transfer mechanisms. Pensions, when structured thoughtfully, can provide generational income. Even modest estates can benefit from such strategies, especially when guided by professionals who understand the interplay of family dynamics, law, and finance.

Charitable giving is another dimension of legacy. Families may choose to establish donor-advised funds, endow scholarships, or support causes that reflect their values. Such giving not only benefits society but also shapes how younger generations perceive wealth—not simply as a means of personal gain, but as a resource for good. When children see their parents engage in philanthropy—not as a tax strategy but as an expression of purpose—they internalise a deeper sense of responsibility and privilege.

Yet it is important to acknowledge that legacy planning is not without challenges. Families may disagree about priorities. Older generations may fear losing control, while younger members may chafe under restrictive structures. Inheritance can stir complex emotions—entitlement, guilt, rivalry, or even apathy. That is why communication is paramount. Regular, honest, and inclusive conversations about expectations, concerns, and values can prevent conflict and build trust. These dialogues do not always come naturally, but with patience and facilitation, they can become a cornerstone of family unity.

Leaving a legacy also requires a long view. Short-term sacrifices may be necessary to sustain long-term goals. Families may need to delay gratification, resist lifestyle inflation, or make choices that prioritise stability over spectacle. But these decisions, grounded in purpose, often yield rewards far greater than immediate indulgence. They create a throughline that connects generations—not only in finances but in meaning.

At its best, legacy is about continuity. It is the assurance that what has been built will not vanish with the passing of time, but will serve, uplift, and empower. It is not about imposing a rigid path on future generations, but about offering them the tools, context, and freedom to build lives of their own with dignity and confidence. It is about laying stepping stones, not carving routes in stone.

Families who commit to legacy planning are engaging in an act of profound hope. They are saying, through every policy, conversation, and investment, that the future matters—and that it can be shaped with care, wisdom, and intention. They are not merely passing on wealth, but offering a framework for its use, a story for its origin, and a vision for its potential. And in doing so, they ensure that their impact extends far beyond their own lifetime—into the decisions, values, and wellbeing of those who follow.

Conclusion
Achieving Financial Freedom Together

Financial freedom is often imagined as a solitary endeavour—one person, steadfast and resolute, climbing the steep slopes of wealth accumulation against all odds. Yet, for families, the reality is far richer and more intricate. It is not a solitary climb but a collective journey, a shared mission where goals, values, and cooperation intertwine. When approached with clarity, persistence, and genuine commitment, financial freedom ceases to be a mere endpoint. Instead, it becomes a lived experience, shaped by intention, trust, and a unifying purpose.

True financial independence does not hinge on a singular moment—like clearing every debt or reaching a certain savings milestone. Rather, it is woven into the fabric of everyday decisions, those quiet, consistent acts of patience and prudence. Patience, it must be said, is among the most underrated virtues in personal finance. In a culture obsessed with quick wins and instant gratification, the slow, steady accumulation of wealth can seem almost old-fashioned. Yet, the wealth built over time tends to be sturdier, more meaningful, and aligned with the deepest values we hold.

Take the example of a family from Yorkshire who embarked on a fifteen-year plan, saving steadily but modestly. Their story wasn't one of dramatic success or bold ventures. No headlines, no empire-building, just a deliberate choice to live within their means, invest thoughtfully, and prioritise their aims. Progress wasn't smooth—there were setbacks, health scares, and surprise expenses along the way. But their quiet, steadfast approach eventually bore fruit. They retired with comfort, supported their children through university without the burden of loans, and now volunteer their time mentoring younger couples on financial literacy. Their victory wasn't glamorous, but it was solid—rooted deeply in consistency and a shared vision.

This kind of long-term dedication requires more than technical knowledge; it demands a mindset that prizes delayed gratification over immediate reward, security over spectacle. Crucially, it also calls for trust within the family. Everyone must feel heard and invested in the journey. When children grasp why saving takes precedence over spending, or why a second-hand car was preferred to a brand-new one, they begin to absorb more than just the practical reasons—they learn the values behind those decisions. Such early lessons plant seeds of financial wisdom that last a lifetime.

Passing on this wisdom, empowering future generations, is among the most precious gifts a family can offer. True legacy isn't simply about handing down money; it's about equipping heirs with the tools to manage it wisely. Too often, financial assets are squandered because recipients lack the skills or understanding to steward them well. On the other hand, children educated in budgeting, investing, planning, and philanthropy are far likelier to enhance what they inherit. Financial literacy, like character, is best cultivated through example. A child observing their parents navigate budgets, set goals, and make trade-offs internalises these behaviours far more effectively than through lectures alone.

Consider a London family who integrated money talks into daily life. Around the dinner table, they discussed the cost of groceries or the reasoning behind financial decisions. On weekends, the children were given small allowances, encouraged to divide these into spending, saving, and giving pots. As teenagers, they joined family finance meetings, contributed ideas to savings goals, and helped explore investment options. Now adults, these young people handle money with confidence, independently investing and saving for their own milestones. Their experience highlights the power of financial modelling—not perfection, but openness and steadiness.

As you reach the close of this book, it's important to recognise that financial freedom is not a one-size-fits-all destination. It looks different in every household. For some, it's about owning a home outright and enjoying retirement travel; for others, it might mean supporting charitable causes, funding education, or growing a family business. What unites these varied visions is agency—the power to make choices from a place of strength rather than necessity. It is about choosing work over obligation, giving generously without fear, and meeting life's uncertainties with quiet confidence.

Moving towards financial freedom requires action. Learning and reading lay the groundwork, but real transformation happens through doing. This might start with a simple family meeting to clarify goals, a review of spending habits, or exploring investment options. Perhaps it involves setting up a will, opening a savings account for a child, or seeking expert advice. Whatever the first step, it need not be perfect—just deliberate. Progress is not born from flawless execution but from steady refinement.

And remember, the journey never truly ends. Financial plans need tending—maintenance, revision, and flexibility. Life evolves: children grow up, careers change, health fluctuates. A robust family wealth plan is not a rigid blueprint but a living document, adapting to new circumstances while staying anchored in principle. The capacity to reflect, adjust, and endure through shifting seasons is what ultimately marks success.

This final chapter is not a conclusion but an invitation—to transform ideas into habits, values into practices, and hopes into achievements. Throughout these pages, we have explored the cornerstones of family financial health: mindset, budgeting, saving, investing, debt management, education, retirement, insurance, and legacy. Each element is a tool; together, they form a framework. Now the true work begins—not in reading, but in acting.

Financial freedom is no exclusive privilege of the wealthy or extraordinary. It is within reach of every family willing to act with purpose, collaborate openly, and persevere. It demands not perfection but intention. It requires not genius but belief in the cumulative power of small, consistent choices.

So as you close this chapter, reflect not only on what you have learned but on what you will do next. Have that conversation. Review your finances. Set a clear goal. Teach a child. Take one step today that your future self—and your family—will quietly thank you for. Because the most enduring financial legacy is never the money left behind. It is the mindset, discipline, and vision you embody day after day. Through that, your family will do more than survive—they will truly flourish, for generations yet to come.

The Power of Patience and Consistency

In an age of instant gratification, the principles of patience and consistency stand as quiet yet formidable counterweights to the noise of quick wins and overnight success. Nowhere is this truer than in the pursuit of financial wellbeing. The reality, often underappreciated, is that building genuine financial security and independence is not about speed or spectacle. It is about steady progress, maintained with discipline, over time. While markets fluctuate, jobs change, and life throws its share of unpredictability, it is those who persist—calmly, repeatedly, and without undue distraction—who ultimately reach their goals.

Financial success is not merely about income. It is about how that income is managed, directed, and sustained across decades. And that kind of success cannot be rushed. The power of compound interest, for example, is only fully realised when given enough time to unfold. A consistent saver, investing modest amounts monthly over thirty years, will often outperform the sporadic high earner who saves erratically. The magic lies not in the magnitude of each contribution, but in the unwavering regularity with which it is made.

Consider the case of a couple from Birmingham who began investing £250 per month into an index fund at age thirty. Over the years, they rarely increased their contributions, nor did they chase high-yield strategies. They simply automated their deposits and let the investments grow. By the time they reached sixty, their portfolio had exceeded £300,000—built not through windfalls, but through consistent deposits, market growth, and the unshakable power of time. Their story is unremarkable in its glamour, but extraordinary in its outcome. It demonstrates a truth that is all too easily lost amid the hyperbole of financial media: wealth builds slowly, quietly, and usually without drama.

Patience is not passive. It is an active choice—to stay the course, to resist the allure of short-term gains that compromise long-term potential. It is the decision to weather downturns without panic, to delay purchases in favour of more meaningful goals, and to continue contributing even when the rewards are not yet visible. This kind of resolve is particularly difficult in times of uncertainty, when markets dip or expenses surge. But it is precisely in these moments that the most significant financial gains are forged—not through aggressive tactics, but through unwavering consistency.

Take, for instance, the 2008 financial crisis. Investors who panicked and withdrew their funds locked in losses that took years to recover. Those who stayed invested, continued contributing, and maintained their long-term perspective were often rewarded with substantial gains as markets rebounded. The lesson is not about market timing, but about temperament. Financial success favours those who plan over those who predict. And planning, at its heart, is about showing up repeatedly—regardless of circumstances.

Consistency is also the antidote to financial fatigue. Families often begin with enthusiasm—drafting budgets, setting goals, and implementing new strategies. But over time, enthusiasm wanes. Setbacks arise. The novelty wears off. This is where routines matter most. Just as brushing one's teeth daily ensures oral health, engaging regularly with finances—tracking spending, reviewing goals, adjusting strategies—builds long-term stability. These small acts, performed consistently, create a compound effect that mirrors the financial principles they serve.

One family in Glasgow took this idea seriously. They began with weekly financial check-ins, often lasting no more than fifteen minutes. Each session involved reviewing the previous week's spending, assessing any upcoming expenses, and discussing how their current actions aligned with their broader goals. Over time, this practice became a fixture in their household rhythm, like grocery shopping or family meals. The benefits were tangible: fewer disagreements about money, a stronger sense of control, and a shared understanding of progress. Their net worth grew steadily—not just because they earned more, but because they managed their money with unwavering attention.

In parenting, too, the lessons of patience and consistency yield profound dividends. Teaching children about saving, budgeting, and spending wisely is not a one-off conversation. It is a continuous process, reinforced by example and everyday engagement. When parents model long-term thinking—saving for holidays rather than using credit, planning for retirement rather than relying on vague assumptions—they instil values that outlast the numbers in any account.

The benefits of consistency extend beyond finances. They influence behaviour, self-perception, and family dynamics. A consistent saver begins to see themselves not merely as someone who saves, but as a disciplined person. This identity shift influences other areas—health, relationships, productivity—because consistency builds confidence. Each successful repetition strengthens belief in one's capacity to follow through. And that belief becomes a powerful asset, particularly during challenging times.

Yet none of this is to suggest that the path is without obstacles. Life is unpredictable. Job losses, illnesses, market downturns, and unexpected costs will all test one's resolve. The key is not to avoid these challenges, but to build systems that absorb them. An emergency fund, for instance, does not prevent hardship, but it cushions its impact. A diversified income stream does not guarantee stability, but it reduces dependence. These strategies, built patiently over time, allow families to continue forward even when setbacks occur.

Adjustments, too, are part of the process. A consistent financial strategy is not a rigid one. There will be times when contributions must pause, when goals must be revised, or when priorities shift. But what distinguishes successful families is that these deviations are seen as detours, not derailments. They return to the path, recalibrate, and continue. The long view sustains them—not the illusion of control, but the commitment to progress.

In a culture obsessed with hacks, speed, and shortcuts, the virtues of patience and consistency can feel almost quaint. But they remain among the most effective, time-tested principles in personal finance. They require no advanced degrees, no insider information, and no elaborate tools. They ask only for commitment, humility, and the willingness to act in service of a future that cannot yet be seen, but is being shaped with every decision.

Families that internalise these principles will find themselves not only more secure, but more grounded. Their goals will feel less overwhelming, their progress more tangible, and their sense of agency more robust. Financial freedom, after all, is not a finish line to be crossed, but a condition to be cultivated. It is built not by what is done once, but by what is done repeatedly.

So the invitation, now, is to begin—or to continue. Not dramatically, but consistently. Not perfectly, but persistently. Because in the end, it is not the boldest action, but the most consistent one, that delivers the richest reward. And for families seeking not just wealth but wellbeing, there is no more powerful truth to embrace.

Empowering Future Generations

Wealth, when unaccompanied by wisdom, can become as much a burden as a blessing. For families who have spent years building financial stability or prosperity, the true measure of their success often lies not only in what they accumulate, but in what they are able to impart. Empowering future generations with financial knowledge is perhaps the most valuable legacy a family can offer—one that fosters independence, resilience, and informed decision-making. The transmission of financial literacy is not an automatic consequence of inheritance; it is a deliberate, ongoing process that calls for time, openness, and structured guidance.

One of the greatest misconceptions is that wealth alone guarantees future security. On the contrary, studies have shown that family wealth often dissipates within two or three generations when not underpinned by education and values. This phenomenon—sometimes referred to as "shirtsleeves to shirtsleeves in three generations"—illustrates the danger of treating financial inheritance as a transaction rather than a transformation. If a child or grandchild receives money but lacks the understanding to manage it wisely, that resource may erode through misjudgement, inexperience, or misplaced confidence. The antidote to this pattern is not withholding wealth, but ensuring that the recipients are equipped to handle it with care and responsibility.

Teaching children about money should begin early, and it should evolve alongside their cognitive and emotional development. At a young age, concepts such as saving, spending, and sharing can be introduced through tangible activities like using jars or envelopes. As children grow, these lessons can be deepened through allowances, budgeting exercises, or even guided spending decisions during family outings. The goal is to make money visible and intelligible—not something abstract or taboo. When children are brought into conversations about family goals, priorities, or challenges, they learn that money is not a source of stress or shame, but a resource to be managed thoughtfully.

A family in Sussex, for example, began involving their children in financial decisions by setting a monthly "family budget challenge." Each child was given a small amount to manage for an agreed-upon family activity—such as planning a movie night or shopping for school supplies—within a set budget. The children compared prices, made trade-offs, and experienced firsthand the value of planning. As they matured, they were introduced to online banking tools, savings accounts, and even mock investment portfolios. By the time they reached university age, these young adults were not just financially literate; they were financially confident.

Modelling behaviour is equally powerful. Children and grandchildren learn more from what adults do than from what they say. A parent who discusses investment choices at the dinner table, demonstrates restraint in spending, or contributes regularly to charitable causes sends a stronger message than one who lectures about money without context. Similarly, sharing mistakes—within reason—can be an effective teaching tool. Explaining a poor financial decision and what was learned from it offers authenticity and insight. It shows that financial acumen is not innate, but developed.

For adult children and grandchildren, empowerment involves more nuanced and strategic guidance. Rather than simply offering financial support—such as paying for education, housing, or debt repayment—families can use these opportunities to engage in joint planning. A grandparent who helps with university costs might require their grandchild to research scholarship options or contribute through part-time work. A parent assisting with a home deposit could make the support conditional on attending a financial literacy seminar or meeting with a mortgage advisor. These small requirements reinforce the principle that financial help comes with responsibility.

In some families, more formal structures can support this ethos. Trusts, for instance, can be designed not only to distribute wealth but to educate beneficiaries. Some families establish milestone-based distributions, where funds are released upon the completion of certain goals—graduating from university, starting a business, or reaching a specified age. Others require beneficiaries to take part in family meetings or submit a written proposal before accessing larger sums. While such structures must be designed with care and legal oversight, they reflect a philosophy that sees wealth not as an entitlement but as a stewardship.

Intergenerational conversations about money can be challenging, especially in cultures where discussing finances is considered inappropriate or uncomfortable. Yet breaking this silence is essential if wisdom is to be passed on. These conversations need not begin with numbers. They can start with values. Why does the family prioritise savings? What does financial freedom mean to each member? How have past experiences shaped current attitudes toward money? As these discussions deepen, they can become more specific—covering topics such as estate planning, charitable giving, investment strategy, and succession planning.

A family in Edinburgh tackled this by establishing an annual "family values retreat"—a weekend gathering where parents, children, and even extended relatives came together to discuss not just financial matters, but shared goals and aspirations. Over time, these gatherings led to the formation of a family charter, articulating principles around education, philanthropy, and financial decision-making. While the family's wealth was moderate by conventional standards, the sense of unity and purpose they cultivated was exceptional. More importantly, younger generations felt both trusted and guided—empowered rather than burdened by their future responsibilities.

Technology can be a helpful ally in this process. Financial planning software, budgeting apps, and online courses offer engaging ways for young people to develop their understanding. These tools make abstract concepts—like compound interest, diversification, or tax strategy—more concrete. Families can explore these tools together, perhaps setting up mock investment competitions, reviewing monthly budgets, or analysing spending trends.

Beyond education and structure, perhaps the most powerful way to empower future generations is through encouragement. Many young people today face a financial landscape that is markedly more complex than that of their parents or grandparents. Student debt, gig economy employment, housing affordability, and inflation all create challenges that can feel overwhelming. In this context, reassurance and guidance are invaluable. Young adults benefit from knowing that they do not need to have all the answers immediately, that mistakes are part of learning, and that the wisdom of previous generations is available to them—not as a lecture, but as a partnership.

Equipping children and grandchildren to navigate these complexities involves more than facts and figures. It involves helping them build self-awareness around money—understanding their tendencies, triggers, and motivations. It involves fostering resilience, so that setbacks are met with adaptation rather than despair. And it involves cultivating ethical discernment, so that financial decisions reflect not only personal gain but social impact.

At its best, empowering the next generation is a deeply relational act. It is an investment not just in financial literacy, but in trust, communication, and shared purpose. Families that succeed in this endeavour do more than preserve their wealth. They amplify it—not necessarily in quantity, but in impact. Their children and grandchildren grow into stewards, not just consumers—individuals who view money not as a measure of worth, but as a means to live out their values and contribute meaningfully to the world.

Ultimately, the true power of financial legacy lies not in the assets transferred, but in the wisdom embedded. It is the parent who teaches a child to save, not just to spend. The grandparent who shares how they weathered economic hardship with grace. The family who invites open dialogue about aspirations, obligations, and decisions. These are the legacies that endure—resilient, empowering, and profoundly human. And they are the greatest gift one generation can offer the next.

Final Steps to Financial Freedom

Every worthwhile pursuit reaches a point where contemplation must give way to commitment, where learning transforms into living. Financial freedom is no exception. By now, the foundation has been laid—an understanding of budgeting, saving, investing, planning, and communicating as a family. These concepts, explored thoroughly and thoughtfully, form a robust blueprint for financial independence. Yet the final and perhaps most decisive step is action. Ideas, no matter how powerful, remain inert until they are applied. The challenge now is not to absorb more theory but to move deliberately and with clarity towards implementation.

Taking the first tangible steps towards financial freedom does not require dramatic upheaval or perfect conditions. In fact, the most effective changes are often modest and cumulative. A well-structured family budget, a small monthly investment into a diversified fund, a conversation with children about saving—each of these may appear inconsequential in isolation, yet over time they generate profound outcomes. The misconception that financial freedom demands a grand gesture often prevents individuals and families from beginning at all. What truly matters is momentum—the steady unfolding of intention through action.

A family in Nottingham, for instance, began their financial transformation not with a windfall or a radical shift in lifestyle, but with a simple weekend meeting. They wrote down their financial goals on a whiteboard: pay off credit card debt, start an emergency fund, plan for their daughter's university education. From there, they assigned themselves weekly tasks. One week, they tracked all household expenses. Another, they opened a high-interest savings account. Within three months, they had reduced discretionary spending by 15 per cent and created a budget that reflected their values rather than their impulses. They did not get everything right the first time—few do—but they started. And starting made all the difference.

Procrastination is the most insidious threat to financial health. It disguises itself as prudence, persuading us that we should wait for more information, better timing, or a higher income. But financial freedom is not a destination unlocked by perfection—it is a discipline cultivated by consistency. Waiting often leads to inertia, while imperfect action creates opportunity. The sooner families begin—even if the first steps are small—the more powerful the compounding effect of their efforts will become.

That said, action without reflection can be equally risky. Financial steps must be tailored to context. A family with young children may prioritise insurance and education savings, while an older couple may focus on estate planning and retirement optimisation. Single parents will face different constraints and opportunities compared to dual-income households. Cultural, professional, and personal factors all shape what financial freedom looks like. Therefore, every plan must begin with honest self-assessment. What are the family's current financial obligations? What assets are available? What knowledge gaps remain? These questions, when answered candidly, inform a strategy that is both ambitious and attainable.

Engagement is also key. Financial decision-making must not fall solely on one member of the household. While it is common for one partner to take the lead, shared understanding ensures resilience. If only one person knows the budget, manages the investments, or handles the bills, the family becomes vulnerable to disruption. Transparency fosters not only security but collaboration. Regular finance meetings, open discussions, and documented plans prevent misunderstandings and allow everyone to feel involved and empowered.

The importance of setting goals cannot be overstated. Vague intentions—such as "save more" or "reduce debt"—rarely lead to lasting change. Specific, measurable targets, however, create structure. A family might aim to pay off £10,000 in consumer debt over the next twelve months, build a six-month emergency fund by year-end, or increase pension contributions by 2 per cent within the next quarter. These objectives provide not only a roadmap but a basis for tracking progress. They also bring a sense of achievement when milestones are reached—an essential motivator in any long-term pursuit.

It is also crucial to understand that strategies must evolve. Life does not follow a script. Illness, job loss, market volatility, or unexpected windfalls all necessitate revision. Financial freedom is not a fixed plan but a living process. Families must be willing to adapt without abandoning their principles. A family in Bath, for example, had set aside significant funds for overseas travel in early retirement. When a health diagnosis changed their plans, they reallocated the money toward a home renovation that improved their quality of life. The freedom they had built gave them options—and that is the true value of wealth.

Moreover, financial action must extend beyond the household. In a world where consumerism is relentless and debt is normalised, teaching the next generation is an act of financial protection. Parents and grandparents must engage children not only with allowances and savings accounts, but with conversations about trade-offs, ethical consumption, and long-term thinking. If money is never discussed, or only spoken of in terms of stress or secrecy, children are likely to inherit anxiety rather than aptitude. Empowerment begins with transparency.

Just as important is the cultivation of resilience. No plan, however thorough, will be immune to disruption. What separates families who attain financial freedom from those who do not is not luck, but adaptability. Setbacks—whether in the form of financial loss, unexpected costs, or poor investment decisions—are inevitable.

What matters is the ability to learn, recalibrate, and move forward. Families who meet adversity with resourcefulness and resolve are far better positioned to protect and grow their assets over time.

A valuable exercise in this phase is conducting a "financial simulation"—a hypothetical review of how the family would respond to various scenarios. What if a primary income earner lost their job? What if an unplanned expense required £5,000 immediately? What if investment values declined by 20 per cent? These simulations do not predict the future, but they prepare the mind. They expose vulnerabilities and prompt preventative measures—such as strengthening insurance coverage, diversifying income, or enhancing emergency reserves.

Equally important is recognising when professional support is needed. While many families can implement basic strategies on their own, complex decisions around tax optimisation, investment diversification, estate planning, or pension structuring often benefit from expert input. Engaging a certified financial planner or accountant is not a sign of inadequacy—it is an investment in clarity and confidence. Professionals bring both objectivity and technical knowledge, helping families avoid costly mistakes and identify unseen opportunities.

The final steps to financial freedom are thus not about grand conclusions, but about sustained application. They involve deliberate action, open dialogue, and a commitment to long-term vision. They ask families to not only dream of security and abundance but to work methodically toward it, with realism and resolve.

Financial freedom is rarely an endpoint. More often, it is a threshold—a point at which families have created enough stability, understanding, and flexibility to live on their terms. It is not merely the absence of debt or the presence of wealth, but the ability to make choices free from financial fear. It allows families to support each other, give generously, and pursue aspirations that reflect their true values.

So, the invitation now is clear: begin. Act on what you know. Share what you've learned. Adjust as you grow. And remember that the path to financial freedom is not reserved for the few—it is accessible to every family willing to walk it with purpose, patience, and persistence. In doing so, you not only change your own circumstances. You redefine what is possible for those who follow.

About the Author

Nicolette Sharma is a financial educator, mother of two, and long-time advocate for smart, family-focused money management. With over a decade of experience in personal finance consulting and wealth planning, she brings a compassionate yet strategic lens to the world of household budgeting and investing. Her approach combines practical tools with mindset shifts, empowering everyday families to take control of their financial lives. Nicolette believes that true financial freedom isn't about how much you earn—it's about how intentionally you live. Financial Freedom for Families is her mission in book form: to help parents build stability, security, and generational wealth—without the stress.

www.ingramcontent.com/pod-product-compliance
Lightning Source LLC
Chambersburg PA
CBHW031339230926
51848CB00002B/305
* 9 7 8 9 3 7 1 3 4 3 3 9 8 *